Art à la Cart

Memoir of a Wayfaring Art Teacher

Marianne Bickett

OXFORD SOUTHERN
an imprint of Sunbury Press, Inc.
Mechanicsburg, PA USA

OXFORD SOUTHERN

an imprint of Sunbury Press, Inc.
Mechanicsburg, PA USA

For information about special discounts for bulk purchases, please contact Sunbury Press Orders Dept. at (855) 338-8359 or orders@sunburypress.com.

To request one of our authors for speaking engagements or book signings, please contact Sunbury Press Publicity Dept. at publicity@sunburypress.com.

FIRST OXFORD SOUTHERN EDITION: January 2022

Set in Adobe Garamond Pro | Interior design by Crystal Devine | Cover by Teresa Woodcock | Edited by Jennifer Cappello.

Publisher's Cataloging-in-Publication Data
Names: Bickett, Marianne, author.
Title: Art á la cart : memoir of a wayfaring art teacher / Marianne Bickett.
Description: First trade paperback edition. | Mechanicsburg, PA : Oxford Southern, 2022.
Summary: A grey cart is transformed into a traveling children's art gallery in Marianne Bickett's *Art a la Cart*. This colorful and insightful memoir offers a rare look into what flexibility and creativity it takes to be a teacher, and acts as an inspiration to rethink daunting problems into infinite possibilities.
Identifiers: ISBN : 978-1-62006-436-8 (softcover).
Subjects: ART / Art Study & Teaching | EDUCATION / Arts in Education | BIOGRAPHY & AUTOBIOGRAPHY / Personal Memoirs.

Product of the United States of America
0 1 1 2 3 5 8 13 21 34 55

Continue the Enlightenment!

For Pat, My Forever Sister

Also by Marianne Bickett:

Leonardo and the Magic Art Cart, Art á la Cart Book One

Art Rocks with Ms. Fitt, Art á la Cart Book Two

The Present, Kala's Song, Art á la Cart Book Three

You can find all three books on Amazon.

Contents

Author's Note

This is a memoir, written from my perspective. Great care has been taken to protect the identity of the children and teachers mentioned in this book. However, because it is a true story, I acknowledge there may be those who read this book who may have been at the school and have a different perspective. Please accept my heartfelt gratitude and apologies, if necessary. Everything written did occur, and I have done my best to honor my truth. Creek Side School is the fictional name for a real elementary school where I taught for five years.

Preface

FTER retiring in the spring of 2011, I began the task of organizing my journals I kept during the four years that I taught as a traveling art teacher at Creek Side Elementary School. My fifth and final year at Creek Side, I had my own classroom, but that's another story! What made this period of time different from the rest of my forty-year career as a teacher (special education, mainstream teacher, and art teacher) was the particularly unique challenge of how to teach a quality art program without having a classroom. This memoir focuses on how I learned to go with the flow and create possibilities in seemingly impossible situations.

Regarding labels: Because I needed something to signify which group/class I was working with, I use the terms art students; fourth, fifth, first graders, and so forth; special education students; and ELD (English Language Development) kids. In place of using ELD all the time, however, I have chosen to use kindergarteners, kindergarten, young(er) students, and kinder kids instead. I used ELD when I felt I needed to clearly delineate the program.

I worked with so many children that it would be confusing to not designate which students to whom I was referring. However, it is essential to me (and thanks to my teacher-friend Rose Shank) that I am clear about labeling children. They were all individuals to me. They all mattered. They were far more than their labels. Perhaps it's necessary to have this system of designations. However, there is a danger if we see the label first, then the person. I write this so you understand my use of labels for the purpose of this story.

A note for teachers: At the time of this writing, we are yet in the midst of, and hopefully nearing the end of, the coronavirus pandemic. My husband, Brian Belét, retired just after teaching with Zoom for one semester. It was a huge challenge; I salute all of the teachers currently making the situation work as best they can right now. *Thank you!*

In the spring of 2020, an essay I wrote, "Corona Virus, Instrument of Change: How the Arts Will Usher in a New Era" was included in a collection of essays entitled *After the Pandemic: Visions of Life Post Covid-19* (Sunbury Press). I wrote about the potential of the arts to inspire, educate, heal, and motivate us to rethink and recreate our world. Nearly two years later, as I write this preface, I dearly hold true to the premise that the arts offer us consciousness and a unique avenue to express hope for a future that looks to us to save ourselves and our planet.

Although there are hopeful signs, with vaccinations and thorough precautions, that we may be able to resume some sense of "normalcy," I am skeptical about returning to life as it was before the virus. What have we learned? How might we live more sustainably? Are we reducing our need for fossil fuels and are we finding ways to stop depleting our resources so that there will be food and energy for our children and grandchildren? How might we use this world disaster to make better choices for ourselves and our planet? There is only one Earth. This is our home. May we, together, see the truth of our situation and raise our children with hope for a more sustainable, balanced relationship to our beautiful, precious Earth.

The First Year, 2006:

BEGIN AGAIN

The First Day

It wasn't until after I accepted the position to teach art part-time at Creek Side Elementary School that I was informed the art room had vanished. There were to be renovations to install air-conditioning in every classroom. I was disappointed that I would not have a place to teach. Still, I chose to view the cup as half full rather than half empty, and I realized it was vital for me to make the best of the situation. I was ready and very grateful to be teaching again after a hiatus of a year and a half. Little did I know, at the time, just how much being a traveling art teacher would come to be a positive experience. In the end, it would present me with ideas that would lead to a whole new life.

There were two other teachers with whom I shared a room at the school: a part-time PE teacher, Mrs. Melissa Carson, and a nearly full-time music teacher, Mrs. Ramona Rivers. The PE teacher and I used it only to store our supplies. I had no classroom, but I was given a cart.

On the day before school started, I went to Creek Side to inventory the art supplies. After gathering up materials from various storage areas, I stopped and gazed at the large, homely gray cart before me. I had no idea how I was going to teach from a cart, let alone push it from classroom to classroom in all kinds of weather. The principal gave me a schedule of rooms: I was to teach for fifty minutes and then shove off for my next destination with only five minutes between classes. *OK*, I assured myself, *you can do this*!

Creek Side was a typical California elementary school in a middle-class neighborhood with about six hundred students. Located in Silicon Valley, the school was one-story high, had outdoor hallways, outside picnic tables for lunch, and a gym/auditorium next to the lunchroom that also doubled for lunch when the rains came. It was, in turn, connected to the teachers' workroom, a front office, and the principal's office. The usual portables, added for a growing student population, sat scattered at the end of a row of classrooms. Tucked off to one side, the fenced school garden flourished with teachers' and parents' care and enthusiasm. The lovely campus had a vast, grassy playing field beyond the blacktop playground, with a small forest in the back that I liked to refer to as the wild area. Behind the school meandered its namesake: the beautiful creek and its rich, abundant environment. San Gregorio Creek would play a significant role in my life at the school. My eyes were drawn to the oak trees lining the hidden treasure as I pushed the art cart across the playground to my first class on my first day.

I paused in the center of the blacktop play area to take a deep breath. Scanning the horizon, my eyes beheld the Santa Cruz Mountains, sleepy and blue that morning. A sliver of fog slipped throughout canyons as the sun shimmered on dew that bedecked the playing field behind the school. Everything sparkled, and the world seemed full of hope and joy. The dirt path that led to the creek, bereft of foot traffic coming to school, striped through the shaded grass, the morning sun casting shadows through a few tall pines and ancient oak trees. Now quieted by the dry season, the creek bed was hidden from view behind a wire fence, guarded by oak, buckeye, almond, and elderberry trees. En route to school that morning, I had walked on the short footbridge that leads from the street, just a hop, skip, and a jump from my home. A brave tufted titmouse caught my attention with his exuberant song on the top branch of the elderberry tree. I felt so rich to have a job with such an easy commute of a few blocks!

For a moment, I drew in a deep breath. I was extremely grateful to realize my heart's desire to finally be an art teacher at an elementary school. Doors closed, and new doors opened. It was time to reinvent myself. I was grateful to the grace that opened up new possibilities for me.

Gathering my courage, I continued pushing my cart toward the class, where a group of first graders awaited me. There was no sneaking up on anyone with my clumsy four-wheeled cart. I laughed as the front wheels hit the doorframe and, heaving and pushing it over the threshold, the second set of wheels click-clacked over the hump. I greeted the teacher and saw the more than twenty eager smiles welcoming me. With only a few minutes to unload everything, I wasted no time in getting my materials out. To make the transition, the teacher, Ms. Bell, instructed the children to get ready for art.

"And here is your new art teacher, Ms. Bickett," Ms. Bell announced. She was obviously grateful to be able to leave for her prep period and get some work done, or have a cup of coffee, or both. I liked the teachers at Creek Side, although I felt like an outsider since I didn't know anyone at the school. During the first few months, they were quite courteous and helpful when I had questions but were, expectedly, swamped. The teachers, too, were getting used to a new art teacher and having to deal with me taking over their classrooms for fifty minutes once a week. I did the best I could to not get in their way. After all, I had been a classroom teacher and understood I was on their turf.

It didn't take long to figure out who was more tolerant of noise and mess during art classes, although I never left the rooms messy. Some teachers stayed most of the time during their prep period when I was in the room teaching, and others were quick to leave. It took most of the first year to form relationships with the teachers and to feel like a part of Creek Side School.

Grabbing a poster and a few very large leaves I had collected on my way to school, I left the parked cart in the back of the room. It was ready with papers and pencils to be handed out after my introduction. I always relished the excitement of a new, fresh lesson and accepted the anxiety that accompanied something untested. On this particular day, I was nervous; it had been a year and a half since I'd been in the classroom, and before that, I taught middle school. Prior to arriving at Creek Side, I was confident that elementary students would be easier to manage. At that moment, as I faced the class of first graders, I wasn't so sure.

I stood at the front of the classroom by the whiteboard and gazed at the twenty beaming faces, all looking at me for inspiration. A curly-headed little boy on my left was very animated as he bothered an indignant girl behind him. Right in front of me sat a smiling little girl with long blonde hair who had a cough, and, to my right, a red-headed boy arrived late, making quite a commotion. In an odd moment, the children reminded me of a cup of squirming worms (my father used to fish a lot), unruly as they tried to sit contained in their rigid little seats. I had half a mind to release them, to take them outside to go exploring. However, this was my first day, and I not only needed to get used to them but they, too, needed time to adjust to me. *So, better to stick to my lesson,* I mused. After all, I brought nature to them!

Presenting the large sunflower leaves to the children, I listened to their gasps of awe, as if they'd never seen such a sight. During the summer, we grew many giant sunflowers in our backyard. As I was harvesting the giant flowers, I marveled at the intricate designs that some infinitesimally small bug had left behind on the giant leaves. Delicate spirals in all sizes decorated the verdant leaves, making quite a fascinating pattern. When I noticed these designs, I knew my first lesson would be about lines and patterns. I found some examples by Picasso and Matisse depicting contour lines and a couple of posters with plants painted by Rousseau and Van Gogh. I realized there was not a woman artist in the lot and vowed I would fix that later. Anyway, the children were riveted by the "bug art"!

Lesson: Keep it simple, safe, and fun.

The Birth of "Art á la Cart"

My feet were already tired after two classes, despite having just purchased new, supportive tennis shoes. Foot apparel for me requires comfort first, fashion last. While I pushed the cart noisily across the blacktop, hundreds of kids dashed about; recess was in full swing. I had to use the restroom and go pick up a few more supplies, so I was in a bit of a hurry. I scurried along and tried not to run into kids as they scampered around like little kangaroos.

I noticed a small group of children running toward me as I walked through the busy playground. They seemed very excited; I turned around to see if it was *me* they wanted to see. Stopping the cart, I paused to encounter a little boy and two girls. I guessed they were first graders. There were four first-grade classrooms, and I recognized the boy from the group I just taught. Noticing that one of them was Caucasian, one was African American, and the other child was Asian, I mused on the importance of racial and cultural diversity: It enriches the totality of our learning experiences and helps, I hope, to prevent racism. Children, after all, are not born with prejudices.

"Hey, are you the ice cream lady?" they asked.

A huge smile spread across my face as I tried not to laugh because, much to my surprise, they were serious! Big eyes scrutinized me as they waited for my reply.

"Well now, that's not a bad idea!" I replied. "I should be selling ice cream!"

My answer didn't seem to sink in, so I continued.

"I'm the new art teacher, and this is my art cart."

The freckled-face boy scratched his head while the girls eyed me suspicious-ly. Then, I clarified, "Sorry, no ice cream today!" The little children frowned, not bothering to hide their disappointment.

"Ohhh, shoot!" remarked the boy as he started to turn away. One of the girls paused and said, "Well, if you ever *do* sell ice cream, you need a bell!"

I nodded with a chuckle and agreed. "You know, you're right. But for now, is it OK that I just have art on the cart?"

"Yeah, art is super cool!" I heard as the children cheered, waved goodbye, and bounced away. Later, I would come to know this trio, Mary Jane, Sadie, and Timmy, and we would laugh about our first comic encounter.

Recess was almost over, and I still had some things to take care of that urged me onward. Yet, something about the conversation with the children stopped me in my path. Why not decorate the cart, close up the sides, and put art on it? That's what I said, didn't I? That there would be art *on* the cart! The art cart could be a traveling art gallery! The children could take turns decorating it each month . . .

I laughed as I imagined serving "Art á la Cart" to eager students. All kinds of images came to my mind as I trotted toward the bathroom. An umbrella, a little bell, tiny sculptures on the top, student art on the sides, a poster that I could change every month in the front. After recess was over, I made my way along the hallway to the next class, giggling, my mind filled with ideas.

"This will be more fun than I thought!" I mused. Thus, Art á la Cart was born!

Lesson: Think outside the cart!

An Ordinary Day

Fumbling my keys nervously at the door to Room 5, I opened up the music, art, and physical education room. The classroom appeared oddly vacant and eerily silent, as if waiting for the children to come in and fill the void. Turning on one of the two light switches, I sighed with a bit of envy that this was not my classroom as I saw my prepared gray cart sitting in the far corner of the room. I shook my head and smiled with a hint of sarcasm, "So *that* is my classroom." It was my second week at school, and I learned quickly to have everything ready on the cart for the week ahead.

An involuntary twitch traveled down my body as I squatted to place my soft briefcase in the undercarriage of the cart. Standing back up, I attempted to squiggle my water bottle into the formed cup space by the handle of the carriage. It didn't quite fit, so I wedged it between the tissue box and my lesson plan notebook. I wondered where to put my keys as they dangled from my hand while I began to pull the large, clumsy contraption away from the corner. In a flash, the other light blinked on as the music teacher entered the room. Ramona was an animated woman who was about the same age as me. She created a vibrant music program along with very entertaining music assemblies throughout the year.

Melissa, the PE teacher, entered the room as I was about to leave, and we greeted each other warmly. We had become good friends. She and I developed a mutual camaraderie over the years, sharing frustrations, helping each other with projects, and having lunch or tea when we could. I can still see her, standing out on the blacktop in the early morning chill, setting up her Hula-Hoops or tennis nets. Melissa was a very dedicated teacher who always went the extra mile to create health programs for the children. I always looked forward to her bright smile and cheery disposition, and she made the trials of room sharing much more comfortable to bear.

After a brief discussion about the prep schedule among the three of us, I walked back out the door, with two loud clunk-clunks over the doorframe.

Swiveling the cart around, I noticed how difficult it was to maneuver and reminded myself I needed two hands to steer. So, I tossed my keys on top of the cart and pushed onward.

The four wheels buzzed along the corrugated sidewalk like a giant bumblebee. Children were beginning to line up, and I received curious stares from those in the drop-off line, parents and students alike. Besides the fact that I was new at Creek Side, the art cart was an unknown entity on campus and took some getting used to. I felt a bit self-conscious with all the gawking faces focused on me; it certainly wouldn't be the last time I was a spectacle.

Once inside my first class, the same first-grade class where it all started, I was greeted with cheers. This was a genuinely soothing salve for the ego. With eyes beaming, Timmy ran up to me as I unloaded my supplies.

"Hey, Ms. Bickett, here is a picture I drew for you!"

He handed me a pencil drawing of two little bugs wearing berets, holding paintbrushes and palettes. The title he scribbled at the top read, *Bug Artists.* I was impressed with his creativity and very touched as I looked at his expectant face.

"Timmy, guess what?" I began. "This clever drawing you made will be the first work of art I tape onto the Art á la Cart gallery!" When we were examining the sunflower leaves, we had fun imagining bug artists, and Timmy had taken it to another level.

Timmy was beside himself with pride, and, as I learned in the weeks and months ahead, this was no small thing as he was a sensitive child. I bent over with tape in hand and affixed the drawing to the newly enclosed side panel of the cart. In the front, I had a poster of Paul Klee's self-portrait with "Art á la Cart" printed on it. And now, the children could see their own art on my traveling sideshow.

What could have been a very drab and dreary art supply cart soon became a famous treasure for the children. After class, a few children started what would become a coveted tradition: they volunteered to help push the cart to the next class. I was perplexed with what to do with the cart during recess and lunch. The children vied for the honor of pushing the cart, solving the problem for me. They often got a head start even before I was ready to leave the room. Throughout the next few years, my trusty students delivered the cart quickly and efficiently. Eventually, I had to keep track and had a rotation of two children going with the cart at a time. The art cart seemed to have its own magic and became very popular. I had to be sure everyone had a chance.

Walking to class at the end of lunch that day, a very sophisticated small herd of fourth-grade girls cornered me and asked, "Is it true we each get to take turns pushing the art cart?"

"Sure," I replied, a bit surprised. My, the word had gotten out fast! Without further conversation, they all whooped and gave each other high fives, then bounded off with smiles on their faces. I meant to ask their names, but off they flew before I could say another word. Who knew?

It was a long day, and I was anxious to get on my way home. Stopping off at my mailbox before I left, I found a note from a student crumpled up inside. Opening it, I was gratified to read a sweet message: "I loved the art lesson today!" It was signed by a fifth-grade girl whose name was Aimee. As I walked home, exhausted but satisfied with how things went that day, a fourth-grade boy, who seemed to be very shy, approached me and said, as he shuffled his feet, "I really liked the art lesson today." Two times in one day, I received a special thanks. Wow.

Over the years at Creek Side School, I discovered how grateful the children were and how often they expressed that gratitude, something different from teaching middle and high school. And the hugs—oh my goodness! The very first day I was swarmed by children I didn't even know, and they were hugging me like I was some kind of giant stuffed animal! I didn't mind. My Italian background fit in perfectly with all the hugging. I tried to remember to always let the children initiate any contact as much as possible. Some kids were not comfortable being touched, and I wanted to model respect for other people's personal space. Nonetheless, it was amazing how much they loved you to the point of near worship; well, the lower grades, that is. Once they get to fourth and fifth grades, the innocence starts to fade, at least outwardly.

That next week, I began two new programs: a reading enrichment for first graders and the ELD or English Language Development program for kindergarten students. The addition of these two new classes brought the total number of children I taught every week to over three hundred! I had no idea how I was going to do this, not a clue. I wanted to get to know them and learn their names. When I had my own classroom of thirty-five students as a middle school language arts teacher, there were some students whom I felt I didn't get to know very well. I would try to spend individual time with my charges, but those moments were few and far between. For me, this was always a source of sadness, but we do what we can.

Lesson: Do what you can with what you have.

The Bee Tree

On my walks to and from school, I was often graced with being blessed by the bees. Several carob bean trees lined our neighborhood streets. These trees hummed busily with a multitude of bees in their boughs off and on, spring through autumn. One such tree, an exceptional one that I dubbed the Bee Tree, seemed to have more bees than any other carob tree when the blossoms flowered.

No matter how much I would carefully plan, often unexpected issues would arise each workday morning. Without realizing it, I would rush my short commute to school. Since this was supposed to be only a part-time job, I tried to be efficient with my planning so I had time for other things. It seemed that most of the time, however, I was focused on Creek Side and the children. My thoughts as I trekked to school were about the work ahead of me. On this particular day, though, I was literally stopped by the bees.

I was walking on the sidewalk just across the street from my house, stuffing something into my bag and thinking of the million things I needed to do that morning. My first class would start shortly after the morning bell, and, though I would arrive on campus with forty-five minutes to spare, it never seemed like enough time. There were always unexpected encounters with parents, other teachers, and even students that inevitably slowed me down.

I stopped just under the threshold of the carob bean tree with its twisted bark. This dancing giant, with curvaceous arms reaching toward the sky, appeared frozen in some kind of prayerful incantation. I heard something, something that sounded like a thousand monks chanting in a monastery. Looking up into the boughs of the gentle tree, alive with a multitude of small, white-yellow blossoms, I could not see the throngs of bees yet, but I heard them, and I was spellbound. I am not exaggerating when I say that I felt a shower of love coming from those bees. It was as if they were sending an extraordinary blessing down upon me. Tilting my head back as far back as possible. I finally made out tiny bee bodies hovering about the delicious flowers. I was literally transfixed in another realm. The bees created a bubble of peace all around the tree; surely, anyone walking underneath would be the recipient of this magical ambiance. Anyone who might take notice, that is.

I emerged from the shadows of the carob tree that morning a renewed woman. Taking a deep breath, I felt lighter, more joyful, and at peace. Somehow, all the work ahead of me could wait. The bees reminded me to be present, right where I was. Needless to say, I enjoyed the rest of my walk to school. For many days in the weeks to come, I would stop and humbly receive the gracious blessing of the bees. There seemed to be some kind of forgiveness, too, washing away the past, giving me permission to be a freer person, more loving and compassionate to myself. Believe me, as a teacher, you need all of that you can get. Teachers are a selfless lot. Being able to think of loving things we can do for ourselves is always a gift. I will never forget that first Bee Tree day or all the other days that followed in the years to come when I stood in the grace of the bees and was blessed over and over.

I had been a student of mindfulness meditation for decades, and nature never failed me as my most significant source of inspiration and teachings. Every day offers healing when I am open to receiving the often-hidden—yet often right there in front of me—messages and blessings.

Arriving at school that morning, I felt a wispy breeze caress me as it flowed off of the frosty green field behind the buildings. In my blissful state, I apparently didn't notice a rather large fifth-grade boy huffing and puffing behind me to catch up. We were nearly by the bike racks when he reached out to touch my arm. I turned to greet him and waited for him to catch his breath. I didn't have time to ask the child his name before he started talking.

"Ms. Bickett, I know where YOU live!" he proudly announced.

Snapped out of my reverie, my first reaction was to freeze. I had a bad experience once with a disgruntled seventh-grade girl who found out where I lived years ago. The egg stains on our house never completely disappeared until we finally were able to repaint. Yet as I stood there, unsure of my response, I looked into his big, bright-blue eyes, filled with innocence (yes, even as a fifth grader), and then I felt a wave of relief wash over me. Responding with a grin, I thought of a witty reply.

"Yes, and I know where YOU live!"

I didn't really, but he didn't call my bluff. We both laughed.

"By the way, please forgive me, you know, I am new here, but; what is your name?" I asked him tentatively, hoping he wouldn't mind. I could only use the excuse that I was new for a limited time, so I happily pulled the line out of my proverbial hat.

"My name is Robert, Ms. Bickett. I am in Mr. West's class. Sit right back by the pencil sharpener," he replied heartily. "See you Thursday!"

As he skipped away, I whispered, "Robert, good, I won't forget."

Pausing before moving on farther, I stopped and looked in the direction of the Bee Tree, now a few blocks away, and thanked the bees once again for reminding me to live mindfully. A new day was about to begin.

Lesson: Compassion starts with being kind to yourself!

Wake-Up Call

I was assigned a self-contained special education classroom consisting of ten autistic first and second graders. Special education was no stranger to me; it was the field in which I began my teaching career. Throughout the years, I'd gone back and forth between special education and the mainstream classrooms, so I was reasonably confident I could manage easily. I was to meet with the students once a week after lunch. I had prepared well and thought I was ready. The week before the first class, I had visited the children and their teacher, jotting down notes as I observed them. I asked questions about procedures so I could provide the best experience possible. No problem.

Or so I thought.

The morning was chilly but bright. I needed to shield my eyes with a wide-brimmed hat as I walked to school that day. The night before, I had a migraine, and I was feeling echoes still: a faint headache and light sensitivity. Responding to morning greetings quickly, I made it to the room with little time to spare. (I nearly overslept after finally getting to sleep around three A.M.) Taking a deep breath, I checked the cart to be sure I had all my supplies and hobbled off to start the day. My first few classes slid by smoothly. The children seemed to sense I wasn't feeling well and were quite helpful. After lunch, in a darkened room where my cart was resting, I gathered up my strength to start the first session with my special needs students. Throughout the years, I frequently ate lunch in my room with the lights off to help me relax and rest my weary eyes.

As I approached the room with my cart, the door swung open. A tall blonde girl named May, who I remembered meeting the week before, greeted me.

"Hello, May," I said with sincere welcome. I knew she didn't talk and wouldn't respond; she didn't even look at me. Before I could take another breath, May was all over the cart. I tried to push my traveling dog-and-pony show into the room as she proceeded to stuff anything not bolted down into her mouth. All the while, I was grabbing things away from her as gently as possible. I tried to distract her from her oral explorations of pencils, paper clips, and anything else loose. When we finally made it into the classroom, I was met with nothing short of chaos.

The teacher scurried out without so much as a "How do you do?" In the room, the teacher aides were standing and watching me with expectant smiles. The children were in turmoil as the paraprofessionals then attempted to get them to sit down at the table so I could start the lesson. I wasn't sure what set them off on this particular day. Still, no matter what I did, I was always picking up one child off the floor while trying to keep another from climbing the shelves. One aide kept pulling May away from the tempting cart with all its goodies while the other assistant was putting out fires elsewhere in the room. There I was, the experienced special education teacher, with my jaw unhinged (about as far as it could go) in shock. I was clearly not prepared for this.

The next day I consulted the teacher again, and this time we agreed upon a strategy that did, indeed, serve everyone's needs quite well. We planned everyday activities at the round table for the class to work on with the teacher-aides while I worked with one child at a time on the art activity. This way, we could have lessons on painting or clay, and I could work one-on-one. The plan worked very well, and a bonus was that I got to know each child individually. The strategy also seemed to calm the children down, and everyone was focused and much happier.

And the art cart? From then on, I parked it outside the classroom under the eaves where it was safely out of May's reach.

Note: In my last year at Creek Side, when I had a classroom, the self-contained students were integrated with a group of students near their age, accompanied by teacher-aides.

Lesson: Don't make the same mistake twice.

Crayons, Secret Words, and Germs

Already into our fourth week of school, I began to feel more relaxed. There were many students to remember; I taught over three hundred children that year. I embarked on a mission to greet each child by their first names. (Forget the last names; only in a few instances could I ever recall those!) Realistic? Maybe not, but then again, I used to teach middle school art, where I had five hundred or more students a week. Somehow, I actually managed to know most of their names just in time for the end of the twelve-week art session. Then I'd get a new group to present me with the same challenge all over again. Therefore, I told myself this shouldn't be too difficult.

Seating charts were the key, that is, as long as the children were in the classroom. I asked the teachers to share their seating charts along with class lists, and most of them complied. I received a menagerie of seating charts with names scribbled on them. The dilemma was, of course, the minute I saw a child running up to me at recess, I had to quickly think back to, first, what class he or she might be in (Who's your teacher?) and then where in the class that child was seated. This process would take a few moments, so by the time I finally remembered the eager little student's name, they'd already lost interest and scampered off. Or they would tell me their name after waiting for me to recognize them. I tried not to ask, but sometimes they offered, especially at first, since they realized I was a new teacher. I was continually being hugged during the recess and lunch breaks, and that spurred me to do my best to know who was embracing me.

I've always loved crayons. They are colorful and fun. "You never know when you will have a crayon emergency," I often joked with my family and friends. Always travel with your crayons, and somehow, you can face the world and handle any challenge that comes your way. At least those were my thoughts.

With boxes of crayons in tow, I lured my first and second graders outdoors one absolutely gorgeous fall day. Before venturing out, I presented to them a variety of objects with exciting textures, all of which I had collected over the past couple of weeks. We reviewed what texture meant ("something that tastes good to your hands," one bright-eyed little girl informed me). A natural connection was relating how most surfaces have some kind of pattern, so pattern became another concept that we explored. I showed some examples by famous artists (this time, yes, I had a woman artist, Mary Cassatt, represented).

Before we set out, I demonstrated how to make texture rubbings with crayons. (Most knew how, but there was a trick to it; just try it yourself and see.) It is essential to go either top to bottom or bottom to top, so I had the kids chant "back and forth, back and forth." At the same time, they ran the crayon over the paper with the textured object under the paper. It sounds simple, for sure, but it actually can be a rather challenging task if you haven't done it for a while, let alone never tried this project.

Along with the instruction, I brought out several intriguing examples of items from nature that had textures, delighting in the "oohs" and "ahhs," escaping the mouths of the curious students. They loved the perforated bark filled with woodpecker holes and the rocks I found at the beach that had delicate lines. Monkey tail pinecones that I picked up during a previous visit to Oregon also enthralled them. I brought out oak galls from the wild area behind the school, and the children were ecstatic. How amazing it was to see their enthusiasm for simple things.

I suggested they work in pairs, help each other, and I reminded them before disengaging from the confines of the classroom that names on their work were required. After all, most artists sign their work! I encouraged my students to develop a distinctive signature that expressed who they were and showed their uniqueness.

Once the concepts seemed to be clear, off we flew to the playground. Children were armed with large white drawing papers (selected for their strength yet ability to show rubbings). We were in search of textures within a set parameter of the schoolyard. I learned rather quickly that I needed to be specific about the boundaries of where they could and couldn't wander. Usually, there were a few adventurous souls who might hazard beyond my line of sight.

Apart from occasional pleas for assistance, I was able to stand back a little and watch the children. What a treat. My most successful lessons were the ones that completely engaged the students. Being able to step back and let them discover, albeit with gentle guidance, seemed to be the perfect teaching strategy. And the conversations were truly revealing. Over my many years of teaching, my most precious days were the ones where I could listen in on discussions between students. These conversations could be humorous and insightful and frequently very surprising. Many times, students smelled out something you never would have thought to write into your lesson plan. The whole activity could take on a life of its own, and I learned right along with my children. This particular crayon-rubbing day was no exception!

To my delight, the children discovered (with squeals of excitement), words on the play equipment. I was barraged with jubilant little groups of children scurrying up to me. They held up their papers with pride and showed me words like "start" or "finish" that they rubbed off from under the slides and climbing areas. A fresh, thrilling idea popped into my head: a found object poetry lesson using random words discovered throughout colorful pages of textures . . . wow! But then, the best was yet to come.

Suddenly, a group of very animated little boys, Timmy being one of them, approached me enthusiastically and pulled me aside, warning other kids to back off. "Look, Ms. Bickett, we found a secret word!"

Intrigued, I stepped aside with them, and we huddled together on the blacktop where they revealed, with great pride (like pulling back a curtain at a circus show), the word "sewer." I couldn't help myself; I burst out laughing. There was no use stifling my response. We all laughed together. They cautiously pointed out the cover of the sewer hole right by the playground, something I failed to notice. Before long, their prize word became known to all the children (too soon for my little crew because now their secret was no more), as other students began to locate its whereabouts. Every paper had at least one *sewer* brilliantly engraved onto it. I was beyond impressed.

The next week we created Mexican Quetzalcoatl plumed serpent drawings incorporating textures inspired by our outdoor exploration that day. The variety, colors, and details of their simulated textures informed me that this lesson had sunk in entirely.

The art cart sprang to life with colorful, vibrant, and lively serpent art created by the children. When I entered the classrooms, I was welcomed with cheers as the wee artists recognized the drawings and clapped with enthusiasm. The art cart did, indeed, have a magical spell on the children, and that never faded in the four years I used it.

During my first year at Creek Side, the administration did something that seemed not only inhumane to a teacher but to the students as well. To save money, they combined the younger classes so that ten additional children came in for art. There wasn't enough room, let alone enough tables or chairs. The other ten students created havoc, and there were times when class was over that I left with tears of frustration in my eyes. However, I never allowed my emotions to be seen by the students. They were not to blame for the situation.

Thankfully, a grandmother volunteer, Grandma Jean, was there to help me with my most challenging class, Room 13. I worked diligently on ways to manage the mayhem as well as provide a top-rate art lesson. I did my best to rise to the occasion, and before I knew it, my crying spells on my walks home lessened. Fortunately, my pleading with the principal had happy results. For my remaining years at Creek Side, combining classes wasn't done again until my final year.

After Tuesday with the first-grade students, on Wednesday, I began my enrichment and kindergarten programs. There was a classroom, thank goodness, for the twenty eager first graders who came from all the different first-grade classes for reading enrichment. Without blinking, the principal informed me, however, that I had no classroom for my kindergarteners.

"I'm not worried," Ms. Heart informed me with a sparkle in her blue eyes. "I know how creative you are and how much you love taking the kids outdoors. Plus, there's always the cafeteria when the weather gets bad."

Although that was quite a vote of confidence, I was not expecting this. Granted, I didn't have an art classroom, but I did have places I could use. This new information was both an incredible challenge and a worry. I had the standards I needed to follow and a ready-to-go curriculum. Taking the guidelines, the concepts I needed to cover, I melded them into a completely nature-based, hands-on program. Much to my great joy, it worked like magic.

My little flock of kinder kiddies was adorable. I had two sessions a day, and I collected them from room to room like a mother hen gathering my little chicks. The transition time, in itself, became a part of the lesson. I figured, why not? We spent so much time in transit; I decided to start the lesson en route. Each day, a new child was chosen to be the leader, and he or she had the authority to determine what mode of transportation we would use. I found the imagination of these young minds to be so refreshing. I modeled for them the first few pickups and returns, riding horses or traveling by boat. They caught on without a glitch.

I always had to have my keys with me when I picked up the children. Not feeling comfortable leaving them in my bag in the shared room, my jangling set was often in my pocket, or I carried them in one hand. One morning, Manuel, a precious dark-eyed sweetheart, was the leader, and he decided he wanted to drive a fire truck. He sheepishly asked if he could use my keys. I thought that was a great idea, and so we lined up and proceeded to climb onto the "truck." I warned them to hang on!

We pretended to put on seat belts and hard hats just for fun before Manuel was ready to go. We waited. And waited. I was enjoying the fresh new day and glanced down at Manuel and said, "Well, Manuel, we're ready any time you are! Start your engines!"

Manuel was fumbling with the keys and looked up at me most distressed. I quickly realized something was wrong, and so I stooped down next to him and asked what the matter was.

"Teacher (they didn't call me by my name quite yet). Which one?" Manuel asked hesitantly.

"Which one what?" I asked, not quite getting it yet, though it slowly started to dawn on me what he meant.

"Which key do I use to start the truck?" Manuel clarified.

You know, I had forgotten that whole fantasy/reality issue with small children. They could phase in and out of both worlds and do so often throughout the day. Learning about what's real and not real becomes a lesson later on. I smiled from a profound place in my heart and gave Manuel a hug. He was relieved as I pointed out to him that it was the bigger key with the black-coated cover that would certainly start the fire engine. His earnestness and sincerity, along with the seriousness of the issue, caused me to treat the situation tenderly. After all, not just any key would do! We cheered "hooray" as Manuel started the engine, and we were off to an excellent start.

During each session on Mondays and Wednesdays, we had something amazing to explore outdoors. I used the impressive school garden as much as possible, and we practiced new vocabulary, straight from the curriculum, as we went along. Words and concepts such as under, over, in, out, and between, were a cinch to explore and experience outside.

Unfortunately, in my first month at Creek Side, I began to feel a cold coming on. When I accepted the art position, I informed the school district that I had already made plans to accompany my husband, Brian, on a two-week trip to China that fall. Brian was selected to join colleagues at conferences in Hong Kong and Beijing. I was given the OK to go, and I secured a courageous substitute while I was away. My ELD classes were canceled those weeks, however. Anyway, we had a wonderful trip, but I sat across from a woman on the airplane who was coughing and obviously very sick.

In addition to the everyday germs at school, this added bonus from our trip proved to be too much. My immune system was barely handling the dare to stay well. One thing I was troubled about was the fact that, in the lower grades, fingers go up the nose with complete, unabashed glory. The first time I observed this event, I was in front of the class, going over a lesson. I nearly stopped and tried hard not to audibly gasp, as there he sat, a most exuberant child, at the end of the second row, digging away.

Over the years, I was continually stupefied as to just how unembarrassed kids were at picking their noses, and I wondered if I ever did that. (Yep, actually, I do recall such a thing about my own childhood, so I did my best to shrug it off.) Sometimes, when I could, when the children were working and I was browsing about the room, I would gently offer a student a tissue when caught in the act. No problem. Most kids were utterly unfazed. With all the wiping of noses on sleeves, coughing into hands, and other such germ-enhancing events, little wonder I caught my first of many colds, though this initial one had a little help from our trip. One of those perks of being a teacher!

Lesson: Embrace serendipity!

Seeing the Big Picture

One night in October, full of vim and vigor, I sped over to the school before dark and gathered together as much white chalk as I could. I then spent the next couple of hours preparing for a fifth-grade art lesson. Drawing large shapes on the blacktop seemed like a simple task, but, alas, it was not. First of all, it was not easy, especially with bad knees and a painful lower back, to get down on the ground and draw for any length of time. Secondly, I was attempting to outline giant line drawings so that the students, working in pairs the next day, could go over them with colors and add finishing touches. I hoped they would understand the notion of what a geoglyph was. With the rough surface of the ground, my chalk pieces quickly vanished into dust.

Once Charles Lindbergh had completed his historic flight from St. Louis to France in 1927, pilots began flying farther distances. The discovery of geoglyphs followed, due to the ability to see vast amounts of land from high above the ground. Sometimes geoglyphs are referred to as giant intaglios because they are incised into a material (the earth). Lindbergh was hired to fly over the giant intaglios created by the Mayan people. His wife, Anna, who was a photographer, joined him and took pictures of the geoglyphs. There were many discovered all over the world, including famous ones in the Southwestern United States. It is still a mystery as to how the artists were able to make these images without being able to see them as a whole picture from afar. How did they work out the proportions? What do they mean?

After showing my intrigued students the examples and asking them to come up with their own designs, I invited them to step outside. I assigned them to areas to help finish and embellish our geoglyphs. Having the basic structure in place ahead of time made the lesson manageable in the allotted fifty minutes of the art class.

The students really enjoyed the experience if their loquaciousness was any indication. I was greeted with chalked palms in attempts to give me messy high fives. I obliged a few students who giggled as if they'd pulled something over me. One student, Robert (remember?), approached me and remarked that a helicopter ride above their creations would give an ideal view.

Agreeing with him, I posed a question. "Sure, but how do you think the Native Americans who made the geoglyphs in southern California were able to see their final product? Or . . . did they?"

Robert made a funny face and nodded. "Must have been aliens, then, for sure."

He hopped away as I grimaced.

"Great, I am glad I got through to him," I muttered to myself.

The only mishap during the day was an entanglement between a slightly mischievous boy and a small group of girls. Chester was given to pranks, I later discovered. He drew a goofy picture of one of the girls, Maddie, I believe, and of course, she and her friends quickly retaliated with their own comical drawing of Chester. I found it difficult to have too much sympathy for him. The humorous part was that both parties signed their names. When they tried to claim innocence, all it took was a brief excursion to the scene of the crime. Lo and behold, there was the evidence! The guilty crews wasted no further time cleaning up the pranks, and each admitted to the wrongdoings.

During my tenure at Creek Side, I observed that there was a puerile quality to attempts at sophisticated naughtiness. It was always relatively easy to figure out the events and those involved in such perpetrations. With just a little wiping away of the offending images, all was well.

"They're just kids," I reminded myself. Making a mental note about "give them an inch and they'll take a mile," I understood how children could sometimes push the boundaries, especially during an outdoor lesson. Outdoor excursions were rife with potential rule-breaking, and it did happen occasionally. Fortunately, nothing too serious ever transpired.

That next evening before dark, I arranged with the custodian for me to climb up onto the roof so I could take pictures of our geoglyphs. On top of the school roof, the view was terrific. The geometric, neutral shapes and colors of the tops of the buildings were in stark contrast to the organic, verdant shapes and colors of the trees that lined the nearby creek. The Santa Cruz Mountains in the distance seemed to rise with big, blue-hued shoulders that watched over the playing fields next to the school. I marveled at the pocket of wildness in the belly of a sprawling city. I listened to the plethora of birds singing and breathed in the aroma of the oak and pine trees standing guard in the back of Creek Side. How fun it would be, I considered as I climbed down the long ladder to the ground, to bring students up to the roof for a drawing lesson, a literal bird's eye vantage point.

That next week, I shared the photographs, and my students were really impressed. They marveled at how, as they worked on the images, they couldn't see the big picture and noted how different their perspective on the ground was from the view from above. Robert commented that the aliens would be back, and they would surely appreciate our attempt. During the rest of the year, alien jokes became a sort of touchstone for the two of us, and I enjoyed it very much.

As I listened to the children working that day, I stepped back and thought of all the effort in bringing this activity to life. Teachers really do work hard. And then, at that moment, as I listened to the students happily engaged in drawing, chatting with each other, and laughing, it all seemed so effortless.

Later that week, Brian helped me set up a display in the boardroom at the district office, exhibiting anthropomorphic drawings the fifth graders created in a related lesson about petroglyphs and pictographs. I always loved setting up attractive art displays right where the school board could see them demonstrate the thriving art program in our district.

I nearly forget all those extra hours, the weekends spent at school getting my cart, and eventually my room, ready for the next week. And it wasn't only me doing all the work. There were many times my husband and son pitched in to help move things, carried loads of supplies to school, and collected materials. What stands out the most for me now is the joy of creating something that would be meaningful to children that, I hope with all my hopes, they, too, would remember for years to come.

I remember the thirteen-year-old girl in the YMCA swimming pool who looked up at the passing lifeguards and wished aloud, "I want to do that, be a lifeguard and a swimming teacher." Within a year, with a great deal of hard work and motivation, I had completed all the certification requirements. I became a swimming instructor and a lifeguard. I think of that young adolescent who, in a short time, became a woman and would never stop dreaming and becoming.

Lesson: Take action on your dreams.

Inspiration, Passion, and Frida Kahlo

At Creek Side, one of my favorite artists to portray was Frida Kahlo. Frida Kahlo (1907-1954) was a famous Mexican artist who was married to Diego Rivera, well-known for his large, robust murals. Ms. Kahlo was fun to focus on because she lived such a colorful, vibrant life, filled with tragedy and accomplishment. One day I was looking in the mirror and decided I could pull off becoming Frida for my upcoming *Dia de Los Muertos* (Day of the Dead) theme at school. When I taught special education, I would frequently come to school disguised as Ms. Frizzle, *The Magic School Bus* science teacher, or as a character in a favorite book. Once I even arrived in my snorkeling attire when we were studying the ocean. I was ready to resurrect this tradition at Creek Side.

I went to the drugstore and purchased black hairspray and some eyeliner, and then to Goodwill where I bought a dress and accessories (necklace and earrings included). A beauty shop had just the thing I needed: a clip with fake hair in a bun. Adding a string of ribbons and plastic and paper flowers to the clip in my hair complemented the dress with its large, colorful embroidered flowers. I was almost set. A cheap pair of red shoes (no heels!) and a shawl completed my wardrobe. When I emerged from the bedroom that first Frida Day, my husband nearly fell over. "You look exactly like Frida Kahlo!" He was impressed and horrified!

Fortunately, Brian was available that Friday for an hour to come and take pictures of the event, so off we trotted to school.

I had dressed up the cart the previous day, setting a Frida doll that a friend had given me on the top of the cart with some books about the artist. Her image was on the front of the cart and so as we made our way across campus, we were, indeed, quite the entourage. Smiling at the astonished crowds as we bumped along, I felt like I was in a one-woman parade.

Everyone smiled as I walked by in the hallways that day and all the days that followed when I became either Frida or another woman artist. What a wonderful feeling, to see faces light up and beam with joy when I walked by.

Entering my first classroom, the magic and excitement felt like a room full of bubbles, a joyful beginning to an absolutely fabulous day. No wonder I dressed up as Frida many times in the years to come. She became a trendy guest at school. I thought of all the fuss and bother in getting ready, including rising from sleep an extra hour early. It was all worth it.

The lesson was to engage students, first, in the visual thinking process, talking about various paintings by Frida Kahlo. After the initial startled responses and examination by my students ("So where's Ms. Bickett? How did you get here?" they would wonder aloud), I began speaking in Spanish. The Spanish-speaking children in the room became alert with pride. They knew what I was saying, and the other children didn't! In a few of the classes, Mexican American students helped to translate for the rest of the class. It dawned on me how the Latino children didn't often have opportunities like this to feel proud of their heritage at school. Eventually, though, I transitioned to speaking English with a strong accent. An unexpected bonus of this lesson was that the children learned a few new Spanish words, too.

As we talked about the paintings, I listened to the children express what the images in the artwork meant to them and what feelings came up for them as we explored the art elements in the pictures. Also, I interwove facts about Frida's life for the children, explaining on a side note that Diego Rivera and Frida got divorced. To my great surprise, a student asked what divorce was. Next to her, a confident boy replied with high authority, "It's when two people are married but don't live together!"

In a third-grade class, Brian overheard students discussing whether Frida was really me or not. The students began sketching self-portraits after the presentation, where they started to create a Frida-style painting. They also turned to scrutinize Brian.

"Maybe he's her dad or another teacher, or . . ." Brian didn't care too much for the comment about being my dad, but he did his best to pretend he wasn't listening in on their conversations. On and on, the children debated the issue until a girl corrected the boys and made it very clear that "He's the photographer guy!" My beloved husband finally couldn't contain his laughter at her apparent disdain for her male classmates' ignorance of the truth.

Leaving the classroom, two lively children hopped up to me and immediately began to prod me with inquiring fingers.

"You *feel* like Ms. Bickett!"

They came closer and started sniffing, then said, "You *smell* like Ms. Bickett!"

I laughed and replied to my interrogators. "Well, that's a good thing, right?"

When I finally got home at the end of the day, I was exhausted with a bit of a headache. I didn't wear my glasses on Frida days, and the strain on my eyes was evident. I showered and rinsed the black color from my hair, watching the darkened water swirl down the drain like a mysterious eddy in a stream. I whispered a "thank you" to everyone who touched my life that day.

The next week the kids kept asking me how and where Frida was. Timmy asked why she wasn't with me. I played along with the small crowd now gathering around me at recess time. "Frida had to return to Mexico for a while. She misses her family." Finally, after a persistent girl, Kaly, kept asking me more and more questions, not satisfied with my pat answers, I smiled and admitted, "Yes, it was me, but it was fun to pretend, right?"

My little sleuths grinned in triumph, and Kaly raised her nose into the air and announced loudly so that everyone could hear, "See, I *knew* it was you!" Next to her, Timmy piped up, as if not entirely convinced of anything yet, and said, "The lady who was here last week was ugly!"

"Thanks," I replied, trying not to laugh. "I won't tell her that, though."

Those Frida Days were great fun. I'd like to think that my father, who always wanted to be a teacher, was smiling down at me. I often thought of him and how much he taught me about bravery, integrity, and humor. The irony is that my father, Robert Bickett, never realized what a great teacher he was. Through his actions and courage, I learned how to be strong. My father was a man with a wooden leg, who often used crutches that revealed his amputated right leg. He lost most of his leg in World War II as a tank commander under General George Patton. Yet he hunted, fished, guided us on the Missouri River in a rowboat, and took us on many vacations, to name only a few things. The point is that my father could do anything. He never used his disability as an excuse. I was proud of him. Before he retired as a Veteran's Field Officer, my father became the head of the South Dakota Veteran's administration, with an office in the state capitol building. Yet he bemoaned the fact that he never became a teacher. I always wanted to think that one of the reasons I chose teaching as a career was because of his passion for sharing knowledge and providing rich experiences with his children.

We never know just what our children or our students will remember about us. Children do learn what they live, and though it makes no sense to use this as a guilt inducer, we need to be mindful of how we live, not only of what we say. Our children are always watching and listening, regardless of what it may seem. I'd like to think that my students would never forget the day when Frida

Kahlo came to visit. At least, most certainly, they will remember her name and something of her art.

The days I was at school teaching my sweet kinder children, I moved about freely on campus without the art cart. One morning, as I was passing the bathrooms, a first-grade student from my Tuesday classes darted out in front of me and then screeched to a halt. I stopped and smiled, greeting him, "Hey, Steven!"

Steven scrutinized me as if he didn't know who I was, and then, his face lit up as he said, "Ms. Bickett! At first, I didn't recognize you without your cart!"

I grinned as we parted, little Steven heading back to his classroom, and I on my way to gather my kinder kiddies. The first few times I traversed the campus sans art cart, I admit, I had felt something was missing. I paused to watch Steven close the door as he entered his room and then turned, feeling just a little naked as I walked cartlessly along.

Lesson: Why not have fun?

A Batty Teacher and Georgia O'Keeffe

The art cart was transformed into a flourishing art gallery. In autumn, it was covered with drawings of pumpkins and jack-o-lanterns. The children dubbed it the Great Pumpkin Art Cart, and the name suited it just fine. Halloween was always a great time of year with so many art projects to create.

There was, for example, the Saturday my devoted husband drove me all over San Jose looking for a bat costume. I wanted something special for my first graders and kinder kiddies for Halloween. Finally, we found just the right attire at a Halloween costume shop. I arrived at school wearing my large brown batwings, a headband with little ears (cat ears, but close enough), and a bat tail following me onto the playground. When I was with my kinder kids, little Henry noticed my watch and asked quite earnestly, "Hey, how come you are wearing Ms. Bickett's watch?"

The special education students really enjoyed the costume. I took off the wings and let the children wear them and look at themselves in front of a mirror. Seeing their images, they would laugh with complete abandon. I truly enjoyed being a Batty Teacher.

The following week, Timmy ran up to me and hugged me, something I relished because, as I got to know this sensitive child, it was no small thing for him to hug you.

He looked up at me and said, "You came dressed like a bat lady last week—I *knew* it was you, and I went around telling everyone—so don't say it wasn't you because I KNEW it was!"

It was enjoyable to see Timmy's often-sullen face beam like that, a delicate flower opening and smiling at the world.

As if Frida Kahlo and a bat were not enough, I decided, right after Halloween, to dress up as Georgia O'Keeffe for a drawing and painting lesson. That November morning, I woke up not feeling very well. Still, despite my aching muscles and fatigue, I dressed for the day. I drew wrinkles on my face (adding to the slight ones already there) and put on a long gray wig I found at the Halloween shop. A black Spanish-style hat and a cape with black boots gave my ruse some savvy. I wore white jeans, a tan vest, and a white blouse. Looking in the mirror, I shuddered. I was beginning to feel chills and I wondered if I was getting sick or my chronic fatigue was about to rage.

I gathered up most of my collection of animal skulls and bones and loaded them into my rickety little transport basket. What a hilarious sight I must have been walking to school that day! My plan was to be Georgia, share information about her life, and show some of her artwork. Then I wanted to demonstrate how to draw continuous contour line drawings of the skulls, inspired by her many animal bones and skull paintings.

I was excited as I pulled the little basket on wheels along beside me (it's awkward to manage at best). When I came to the stairway that leads up to the creek bridge, I paused. My joints and muscles really hurt, and even the few steps looked daunting.

Taking in a deep breath, I murmured a little prayer to the goddess of teachers (there is one, right?): "Please help me today. Give me the strength to live my best life today. Help me feel well and help me do a good job. Or at least just give me a boost to make it up these stairs!"

I labored as each step sent aching and searing pain into my legs and hips, but I mustered on. After all, I reminded myself, "I am being paid to do something I love."

On campus I got the art cart set up and realized I needed to check my mailbox near the front office. As I neared the door, the principal stopped me. I was puzzled by her expression, which wasn't welcoming. "Excuse me," she stated briskly. "All visitors need to sign in at the office."

She didn't recognize me! I was flabbergasted! My disguise must have been perfect! I cleared my voice and began to talk, watching her face turn from stern attention to a smile. "I never know if it's you or not!" she admitted to me as we laughed about my costume. Apparently, she didn't recognize me when I came dressed as the bat on Tuesday either!

In the classrooms, Georgia was a big hit. Students pestered me with their usual interrogations, "But where's Ms. Bickett? How did you get here? Aren't you dead?"

I quickly noticed the difference between the innocent second graders and the sophisticated fourth and fifth graders. At the beginning of the lessons, when I appeared as Ms. O'Keeffe, the older students immediately began giggling and shaking their heads, amused but on to me, so to speak. The younger students were often mesmerized with wide eyes and excitement at having an unexpected guest as the teacher for the day. The first and second graders weren't bothered at all that I was pretending to be someone else.

While teaching the fourth and fifth graders, the lesson flowed seamlessly. Though I occasionally winced with pain when I lifted something (and felt like I needed a severe nap by noontime), I was elated. I loved hearing the gasps when I took out the large skulls, especially the horse skull. So many of the students confessed to me they'd never seen nor touched a real skull before.

We used black charcoal on different colored papers to create the contour line drawings of the skulls and bones. I loved the results! Continuous line drawings were (and still are) among my favorite kinds of renderings. They are expressive and free, allowing students to feel less self-conscious.

One thing, however, that dismayed me was that most of the students couldn't seem to handle a little black chalk mess on their hands. They ran to the sink to rinse it off as soon as they could!

I asked them with my Georgia accent, "Have you not ever played in the mud?"

With reassurances that a little charcoal would not harm them, they did seem to really enjoy creating their drawings.

"You were lucky to get your hands dirty today! A world that is too clean is not healthy!" I advised my students. Some of the kids rolled their eyes at me in playful disgust at that thought.

Most of the students were happy with my disguise; however, a few of the children couldn't seem to get past the idea that I was posing as Georgia. They seemed to feel I was tricking them. I finally explained.

"Just imagine you are watching a play. I am portraying someone to help you remember the artist and her work." That seemed to satisfy them. I explained how Georgia O'Keeffe would have sketched images before painting them. Even if you don't go on to paint what you've created, a drawing could be a finished, perfect expression as it is. The results of the lesson produced lively, fluid, and expressive lines. The students created drawings with varying values (lights and darks) and attractive organic (animal, plant, rounded not straight) shapes. Picasso, who created a number of linear, gestural, and expressive drawings, would have been impressed!

The crowning moment was when, right in the middle of my demonstration of how to draw the horse skull, the principal entered the room with the superintendent! I didn't miss a beat and thought to myself, "So what?" I was relaxed and knew I was at my best. Both observers seemed pleased anyway, judging by their bright smiles as they whispered and watched me teach.

Lesson: Go with the flow.

The Invitation

One ordinary day at Creek Side, a small group of fifth-grade girls accompanied me as I pushed the cart across the playground at recess. The sun was shining, although the wind had kicked up. I invited the girls to walk with me to help manage any fleeing objects. I can't recall why there weren't art cart attendants pushing the cart to the next class that day. It was rare for me to be doing the task. These three girls I came to know and cherish. (I loved the individual moments with students when I could get to know them better.) Sarah, Emily, and Maya appeared somber with their silence and lack of usual enthusiasm. I asked them what was on their minds. All three of them began talking very seriously and shared with me about the sorrow in their lives. Each of their parents was going through a divorce.

"I'm so scared. I don't know what is going to happen to me, my family," Sarah confessed.

They agreed that divorce made them very frightened. Everything sure and secure in the girls' lives seemed to be falling apart. Maya confided that she had overheard her father saying, "I wish I were dead," and that really terrified her.

I was saddened by what I heard and wanted to offer them some comfort without being unrealistic by saying, "Everything will be OK." Things were not OK for them, and I wanted to tell them how much they were loved, how much their parents still loved them. Without even really thinking about it, I shared how I went through a divorce and knew how sad I felt during that time.

"No matter what, and you must never forget this, your parents love you very much. They did what they had to do to save themselves; it was never and will never be because of you. When something as important as a marriage ends, it is like someone dying. Everything changes, I know."

The girls lit up, as they seemed encouraged that I, too, understood how they felt, what they were going through.

"In the end, even though the divorce was unfortunate, it actually helped my family to grow, to grow up. We used our loss to transform our lives, and, I guess, now we were stronger for it." I cautiously added that, most unexpectedly, my ex-husband and I recently remarried each other.

I didn't want to give them false hope that the same would happen to their parents.

"Most of the time, that doesn't happen, and even if it does, the new marriage isn't the same. Of course," I added with a grin, "you wouldn't want it to be the same!"

Maya had tears in her eyes. I wanted to comfort her.

"It's OK to feel sad right now," I told her as she moved closer to me.

At that moment, something utterly magical happened. A giant, loving force drew us together. Wrapping our arms around each other, we formed a small circle. Recess was now in full swing, with children running and yelling all around us. We were unseen in the calm eye of the hurricane of newly released children. There we stood in the center of the world, holding each other amid chaos, embracing sadness. We stood together, none of us speaking. We breathed and held the space between us, acknowledging that there was no cure; however, accepting and just being with the pain seemed to give them comfort and peace.

The moment was fleeting. With a sigh, we parted from our circle, the girls each hugging me and then moving off to another place on the playground. Though I needed to get the art cart to the next class and use the restroom, I stood there a minute longer in the center of the world. Maya turned and waved at me with a smile, and I waved back.

I'd like to think that, on that day at Creek Side, something profound occurred. We came together to hold our pain, an inevitable part of life. And perhaps, in some more significant way, we really did stand at the center of everything. That beautiful, all-encompassing hug held sadness so we could let it go. I think of Maya, Sarah, and Emily, and where they might be right now and hope they are OK. I think of my mother and how she never had anyone to talk to about her parents' divorce. At least nowadays there is more support for children, opportunities for them to talk about what they are going through. And that is how it should be. Things should be better for our children. And yet, I wonder . . .

Lesson: Be there. Be present for the kids.

Andy Goldsworthy and Sacred Spaces

A logical artist for me to celebrate was Andy Goldsworthy. In 2001, he created a DVD called *Rivers and Tides* about his intricate, nature-inspired sculptures made from materials such as rocks, leaves, flowers, and even icicles. It seemed only natural that I would engage my students in outdoor sculptures inspired by Mr. Goldsworthy. Every autumn, it was one of my favorite lessons to introduce.

The "oohs" and "ahhs" when I showed the fourth and fifth graders a few scenes from the Goldsworthy DVD were a clear indication of their interest. After we watched the artist in action, I turned the kids loose to work in pairs or small groups, focusing on art concepts. I asked the children to consider what three-dimensional means, and we learned new vocabularies such as found object, symmetry, asymmetry, and radial balance.

They set to work on their preliminary designs with pencils and drawing paper. We brainstormed and made predictions about what kinds of materials they might find out back in the wild area behind the school, where most of the sculptures were to be created. The students incorporated the natural materials (leaves, sticks, pinecones, etc.) into their designs. Reminding them to be sure to write their names on their papers was necessary because of the following week, when we headed out armed with our designs and enthusiasm to get to work.

Somehow, we always lucked out with the weather. October or November was a great month for this project. A few times I was even able to take some of the classes to make their temporary nature sculptures by the creek. We also created the sculptures in the late spring after the rains subsided.

On one day, I headed out with a lively group of fifth graders. Bobby walked along next to me as we moved to the wild area.

"There used to be more trees here by the creek, and I used to sit by these trees where no one else could see me, and it was my sanctuary. I loved to come here; it was my special place. But they cut many of the trees down, and my sanctuary isn't here anymore," he explained. I was impressed with his use of the word sanctuary, and it was not the last time I heard the word used in conversations with students. Another student named Kyle described his sculpture to me as "A sacred place." The funny thing was that I never once prompted them to use the concept of sacredness, not explicitly anyway. Perhaps my reverence for nature was evident.

My faith in this generation was renewed. My heart was touched by how much the students loved being outside and loved the wild place. That was encouraging and hopeful for me. Often when I was outdoors with the children observing them excitedly creating nature sculptures, I heard my name being called. Students would motion to me, shouting, "Ms. Bickett! Ms. Bickett! Over here, come look!" They worked in pairs or small groups gathering up sticks, rocks, leaves, and other loose nature debris. I cautioned them most sternly not to pull up anything or pick anything live or green. Instilling respect for nature was very, very important to me. And still is.

Later that day, I brought out my fourth graders to tour our sculpture garden. They would get their turn the next week, but I wanted them to see firsthand what the older students created. "This is just like Stonehenge!" a student piped up with glee as they came upon the pieces. A week later, a parent stopped me after school.

"My child came home and raved about the outdoor sculptures. It really made an impact on him," she said.

I didn't know who she was or precisely who her child was, but I was very grateful to hear this.

What happened next was predictable. Some of the sculptures got knocked over right away after school when the older middle and high school students walked through the wild area. I warned the children not to get attached to their work (spoken as I waved my handy camera in front of them with a wink).

"How do you think Andy Goldsworthy saves his work?"

"Pictures!" they cheered.

Taking pictures of every single creation helped solve their dismay at the inevitable destruction that would follow. I reminded them about Andy Goldsworthy's work falling apart, melting, floating away. The children seemed content with being able to record their diligent efforts with photographs. With great care, I printed out the pictures, made black and white copies, and then gave each child a copy of their sculpture to color with colored pencils.

We wrote about the experience and attached their poems and thoughts to the photograph on large construction paper.

"You see, then," I told them with pride, "you do have a token, an artifact of your experience."

We agreed that even though the actual creation was gone, it could still be remembered and shared.

What really amazed me, though, was how many of the sculptures actually did survive for a time. Even a week or two later, there were a few remaining structures as a testament to our outdoor work and play. In time, we observed how the wind, rain, and even critters like squirrels helped to dismantle the sculptures. It was a great lesson in valuing the process over the final result. However, that was not to undermine the beautiful, striking pieces the kids created. I was impressed with the lovely designs, the clever use of natural materials, and the overall inventiveness of the students. Little wonder it became one of the most popular lessons, and students pleaded to repeat it later in the year and in the years to follow. (Photographs of some of the creations are at the end of the book following the lesson plans.)

Having a sense of place and a relationship to that space is the key to saving the earth. "We will save what we love" is a paraphrase of something I read once. It was one of my ulterior motives for providing these kinds of experiences for students. In addition to learning essential concepts from the academic standards and having the chance to be expressive and creative, they would also fall in love with nature. It was my profound hope that they would love the trees and the wildflowers and the creek, the lifeblood of the community.

Lesson: Nature is the most excellent teacher.

Clay Pot and Garden Days

School gardens seem so natural, so right for kids. How wonderful to see many schools investing in a garden for the children to enjoy and experience nature. I am gratified to read in newspapers stories of fantastic school projects that transform an empty plot into a vibrant outdoor classroom. Hence, I was drawn to Creek Side's garden instantly. I think of the hours my husband and I spent there on weekends helping Leslie, the Garden Mom, and many days I spent in the garden with my students.

With the help of Grandma Jean, for example, on one lovely autumn day that first year at Creek Side, we had over one hundred and twenty little artists make pinch pots in the garden. The children dubbed them thumb pots because they were quite small. One morning, before this event, I walked into the teachers' workroom, and there sat a large bag of air-dry clay up for grabs. Well, guess who grabbed it? What a gift it was to find the free clay because my art budget was very tight. Off I flew with numerous ideas in my head, mainly how to spread the clay over so many art classes. I decided to use the clay for a lesson with the little kiddies, realizing it would prove a challenge. I always favored doing clay projects and was elated in spite of the problem of not having a classroom! How was I to do this?

As my husband and I gathered acorns the weekend before the clay lesson, I thought about the logistics regarding the clay. Suddenly, I came up with an idea: I could take the children outdoors to create little pots, making the garden into my classroom for the day! I was ecstatic! I could hardly wait! The acorns would be great for creating textures on the little pinch pots, so I happily started making a few examples as soon as I got home.

The children were jubilant about going outside, even though the early morning air was a bit chilly for my first couple of classes. That was a problem easily solved as we slipped on jackets and sweaters while we marched out the door. Once in the garden, we sat in a circle on the lime-green tarp I brought, and I asked the children, "Where does clay come from?"

"The store!" chirped one little boy named Arnold.

"It's mud!" chimed in another student.

"You are both right!" I assured them. "But how is it made before it gets to the store?

"And," I said as I acknowledged the second boy, "what do they do to the mud to make it stick together?"

We talked awhile as my wonderful grandmother volunteer prepared the little balls of clay to give each child. She was a gem, and I was so grateful she would be with me to help most of the day.

I explained how clay was made from the earth, and that sand was added, along with water, and basically, that's clay.

"We were making dirt art today!" the children cheered with delight.

How I loved those little kids! They were free and easily inspired and so appreciative. Demonstrating how to make a pinch pot, I asked the children to pretend they had the clay in their hands as I showed them the process and had them mimic the hand movements. It was great to see the students making their invisible pots first, helping the concept to sink in better. When they each received their little ball of clay from Grandma, they knew just what to do.

We embellished our precious little thumb pots with acorn imprints. The clay pots then were air-dried—no need for a kiln, which was great because the school didn't have one—so we gently wrapped them in damp paper towels. I had no choice but to allow the children to take their pots back to class with them. I gave the teachers a heads-up that the children were to set the pots on their desks, wrapped in the towels, and take them home to dry. Not an ideal way to teach a clay lesson, I know, but I had no place to keep their artwork. I warned the children not to put the pots in the sun to dry and to be sure to allow them to harden in a cool place at home. They were thrilled carrying their little creations back to class with them. I hoped the pots would survive, and, as I heard later, most of them did. Even if they didn't, though, this experience was worth the effort. We learned about clay and how to make a pinch pot. We learned how to use our hands in creating something from the earth that gave us joy. And I even had a few extra little pots that I ended up giving to the children who reported to me later that their pot didn't survive the trip home.

During recess, I had an errand to a kindergarten classroom, and I saw one of my kindergarten students. When Mitchell saw me, his eyes lit up, and he came running over to me, announcing loudly, "I know you, you have magic!"

Remembering the day before when I saw him and his little crew, I recalled telling them about my magic scarf. My sister, Jane, from Oregon, had sent me a colorful, sparkling scarf. As my students and I walked along, I explained that the scarf seemed to have a kind of magic because it glittered in the sunlight, and it made me think of the love I felt for my sister. I let the leader of the day wear the magic scarf. Mitchell hugged me, and I felt a deep sense of joy that he remembered the scarf and the magic it brought to life.

The day making thumb pots in the garden felt like magic. Leslie, the Garden Mom, showed up during my second class, and we discovered a worm (which we realized was a cutworm that was not welcome in a garden!). The children were enthralled by the little critter as Leslie held it for them to see.

The day was warming up. As the children were finishing their pots, I had a moment to stand back and look at the world. The sunlight played on the various green hues of plants in the garden. At the same time, two red-tailed hawks circled above, being chased by a murder of crows (and even though a group of crows is called a murder, I love crows and think they are brilliant). I heard a tree frog in the thicket and felt great peace. Grandma and I helped the children wash their hands using the garden hose. After they dried their little wet fingers, the small artists grabbed clipboards and pencils and wandered through the garden, sketching whatever they wanted. This was a golden time for me to be able to observe my students and listen.

After we cleaned up, some of the children sat under a tree, and I joined them to relax for a few moments. One little girl, Eliza, looked up and said, "The sun is giving us a present of light." How warm the sun felt and how calm the world seemed; everything was encased in a magnificent presence of light.

Another girl next to me, Wanda, sighed, and said, "I want to be an artist when I grow up!" I leaned over and told her, "You already are an artist!" She beamed, and her smile was still there as all returned to the classroom with happy hearts, carrying the little clay pots they had made.

Lesson: SEE your students!

Getting Unstuck

Because it was still autumn, I planned to use the school garden and outdoors as much as possible. Soon the winter rains would make this opportunity difficult. On this day, I wanted to take my first graders out into the garden to draw. Emboldened by the success of the clay pots, I created a fun drawing lesson that the children would paint during the next art class indoors.

Once again, it was a chilly fall morning, but already the glaze of frosty dew was hissing its misty breath out on the playing field. As I pushed the cart toward the garden gate, I paused to appreciate the subtle beauty of the area as the mist looked like sleeping spirits rising to dance in the sunlight. Yet, I was a little anxious. A parent stopped me in the hallway to talk, and I did not have much time to get things set up before I was to collect my students.

After I unlocked the gate, I saw with dismay that the ground was still muddy from yesterday's watering. *Something I had not anticipated,* I mused to myself as I pushed the cart onto the water-saturated path. Underestimating the degree of muddiness, I pushed the cart harder and harder until it was stuck! No matter what I did, the big lug of a cart sank deeper and deeper as I realized time was running out. My heart nearly burst. It was beating so hard; I had to get things ready, and the bell would ring soon! The image of the Titanic seemed appropriate to me at that moment, the monstrous beast sinking with my despairing moans. Panic grabbed me like a thief, and I felt everything swirling around me in a warp of terror. I could never be late! Suddenly, I stopped and looked around me.

There I was, stuck in my pattern again. I was stuck! Anxiety has been my unwelcome companion most of my life, and it seems a default that I jumped to time after time. What was the big deal? Why was the thought that I might be a few minutes late be upsetting? Without warning, a wave of joy rose up through me as I started laughing out loud. I raised my fists into the air, saying with high authority, "I am doing the best I can!"

As a recovering perfectionist, I obviously still had a way to go. I wanted everything to be perfect that morning, and it was not going that way.

Breathing calmly, I moved as my flustered heart began to beat more regularly. I unpacked what needed to be ready before the children arrived and left the cart where it was. Then, I smiled as I noticed the shift in energy as I gathered my first group of kiddies. What seemed to be so stressful had become light and free.

The lesson went wonderfully that day. The children were intrigued by the stuck cart and offered countless suggestions as to how I could get it out of the mud. Not to worry, I assured them, it would be fine, though I was not sure myself how I would accomplish the feat. The children were drawing the giant sunflowers that were nodding their weighted heads toward them as if looking down at the little artists and watching them. Soon the flowers would be dry and cut down, the birds already enjoying feasting on the delicious sunflower seeds.

Little Timmy came up to me as the children were happily drawing.

"Do you want to hear a fart?" he asked.

I laughed and responded, "Well, no, but it looks like I am going to hear one anyway!"

He proudly put his hand under his armpit and produced a fart-like sound with a satisfied smile. "Wow," I said with a nod and grin. "You really have talent!"

"Don't you just love sunflowers?" I asked the children as I mingled, admiring their lovely contour line drawings. I showed them examples of giant flowers by Georgia O'Keeffe, along with a few of my own drawings. Encouraging the children to work large, we practiced first on some newsprint. We then transferred the images to huge watercolor paper.

"We'll paint them next week with watercolor paints," I explained as the children smiled happily.

Stepping back, I watched my students draw with sincerity and focus. The scene was precious: little children gathered around giant sunflowers that seem to gaze at them intently, almost protectively. Like stoic guardians watching over the little innocents.

Sarah, a perky little blonde, stopped and looked at me, saying, "The sunflower I'm drawing is looking at me!"

I nodded and smiled; I was thinking the same thing. The day was magic again, despite the challenges of taking five classes of youngsters outdoors. I was satisfied.

I am happy to report that at the end of the last class that day, my darling little children helped me roll the cart out of the mud with organized effort. Some pushed from behind with me as others pulled from the front. What a hilarious scene that must have been! The students were so proud of themselves. The entire class was involved in directing and pushing the cart out of the garden, muddy wheels, and all. We cheered across the campus to their classroom. What a sight! Students helped clean the art cart, and it was ready to go again. The funny thing was that getting unstuck was one of the easiest things I had to do that day.

Lesson: Lighten up!

Critters and Talking Turkey

When I was a Resource Specialist at a middle school, I had my own classroom where I met with small groups of learning-disabled students. They came to me for assistance in math, English, and other areas of need. This was in addition to my travels to various classrooms to aid teachers as well. Anyway, somehow or another, a very hairy little hamster the students dubbed Bear arrived at my doorstep one day. This was the beginning of both an amusing and distressing relationship.

We kept Bear in a rather large aquarium a parent had donated; however, it lacked a top cover. So, as any good classroom of students and teachers would do, we improvised with some wire netting and boards to create a makeshift top. By the next day or two, we realized Bear had a disturbing skill: he could chew through just about anything. Most of the time, he escaped during class, and we would go back to the drawing board and create what we were sure would be the perfect escape-proof top. But Bear was one to never say die!

One morning, arriving at school, I discovered Bear had chewed through a thick new piece of plywood we had set on top of the aquarium with old phone books as weights. He was nowhere to be seen. Despite our efforts to locate Bear, two weeks passed to no avail; our little varmint had flown the coop. I borrowed a trap—a contraption that had a small maze, leading to food, that would trap a little critter without harm—and set it out, even going to the school late at night to check it from time to time. Inside, we placed lettuce and carrot sticks, foods we were sure hamsters loved, only to find the food gone sans any trace of Bear. What a talented little guy he was!

From time to time, as we went about our work in the classroom, we would hear scratching sounds from inside the walls. I was quite sure Bear found residence in the spaces between classrooms and figured someday he was bound to come out. Sure enough, that day finally came.

The sink in the back of the room was dripping, and I had placed an order for its repair. A workman showed up one afternoon to fix the plumbing as we went about our business. Suddenly, the terrified man jumped up and screamed.

"A rat! A rat!" he yelled.

We turned to see the commotion as he stood pointing to a very bedraggled and thin little hamster emerging from under the sink. "Bear!" we cried as a student ran to pick him up. Everyone huddled around the girl who held the now very tiny-looking creature in her hands. It was Bear all right, a little worse for wear, but OK; that is until someone noticed his nearly bursting jowls.

One of the students was very familiar with the habits of hamsters, so she pointed out that they keep food stored in pouches by their mouths. I wasn't about to stick my fingers near those razor-sharp teeth. Still, somehow, this budding biologist managed to gently coax out the contents of Bear's pouches. Lo and behold, little nuts and bolts tumbled out! Without further ado, I am happy to say Bear chomped down his food quite eagerly that day and seemed content to stay close to home.

I was beaten, though, and decided our precious little darling Bear needed a decent home with a family who could outsmart his escaping ways. Thank goodness the very same animal-wise girl was delighted to bring her parents to me the next day. They promised they could handle his wiles and happily adopted Bear. Bear became quite the yarn in our classroom; we produced stories and pictures about him in our monthly newsletter and never forgot his persistence.

Over the years, I had many classroom pets of all kinds so. Naturally, I wanted to find a way to include animals in my art curriculum at Creek Side. During my fallow time away from teaching before coming to Creek Side School, I volunteered at a friend's small horse ranch. I took care of an old Arabian mare named Annie. The point is that I developed a friendship with the two women who ran the ranch, Amy and Heather. When I went back to teaching, I asked if they might be interested in bringing some of their animals to school from time to time. On Amy's property, she also had a turkey and some chickens, so we agreed on a few visits. I was able to procure funds from the PTA to pay Amy and Heather. Our adventures were about to begin.

It was before Thanksgiving that first fall at Creek Side, and who better to bring to meet the children than a rather large, outspoken male turkey? He would arrive with a full, gorgeous array of feathers and plenty of gobbling. My students and I were very excited!

The school garden was a perfect enclosure for the turkey's visit, so the day before, I prepared the area for the special guest. Parents and teachers had been notified (along with the principal's approval). To my great delight, I had parent volunteers lined up the entire day. Although I taught Mondays through Thursdays only, I had arranged for this to take place on a Friday, volunteering my own time as well. One mom came up to me with a huge smile and confessed she just couldn't stay away that day because "my daughter talked nonstop all week about the turkey coming on Friday!" Everyone was excited, and the weather supported our adventure with some morning clouds that gave way to a mild and pleasant November afternoon.

When I first informed my classes I would be bringing a turkey to visit the next week, little Timmy raised his hand most seriously and inquired, "You mean a LIVE one?" Later I discovered, much to my great amusement and surprise, that almost all the children thought I was going to bring a *cooked* turkey to school! Apparently, many of the students had never seen a *live* turkey before, let alone been able to touch or converse with one.

Heather and Amy drove up with our turkey and a few chickens accompanied by a topknot duck, which later became known as Hairy. The children all emphatically dubbed the turkey Tom (what else?), who arrived in a large dog crate. My husband also managed to come to the school to help, though he was not able to stay the entire day. I had the art cart parked in the garden with colorful construction papers and bright chalk pieces for students to draw the turkey and make turkey feathers. Pencils, clipboards, and papers were also available for the children to draw Tom throughout the day. I decided to give the children free rein as to how they wanted to artistically interpret our guests. Later, we would write and paint pictures about our experiences with Tom and his feathered entourage. A local newspaper even featured an article about the event with a photo of a student with Tom.

As I brought each class out to the garden, we tiptoed quietly to not startle the birds. I prepared each class by talking about respecting animals and how to approach Tom and the others slowly and gently. The children had many questions ahead of time, and I answered most of them but decided they should also ask our guests, Amy and Heather. Some children remembered to bring the questions they had written down with them to the garden. With my camera in hand (Brian and other parents were also taking photos), it was incredibly enjoyable to observe the children interacting with this large, gentle bird.

Tom was very kid-friendly, having entertained many groups of children at the ranch during summer camps before his debut at Creek Side. The children made a fantastic discovery: When he became agitated, his bald head turned bright red, and, when he was calm, his head turned blue! Emily, a fourth grader, approached me and said, "When you said you were bringing a turkey today, I thought you were going to come to school leading the turkey on a leash!"

Throughout the day, we composed poems about Tom as we explored how he might be feeling (head colors, body language, movements). Tom was very gracious, he allowed the children to touch him, and he liked to follow the children around, examining the garden and enjoying his treats and water.

Something magical happened as I noticed little preschoolers from the enclosed playground next to the garden hanging onto the fence and watching us most intently. There were a few students who were frightened at first not only of Tom but also the other birds. With some coaxing by Heather and Amy, the anxious children warmed up to the critters. Before I realized what was happening, I saw these same formerly fearful students gently pick up a chicken and the duck. Then they walked carefully over to the fence where the preschoolers were looking on.

Listening in on the children's discussion, I heard these now courageous students explaining to the little preschoolers not to be afraid. They shared facts about the birds they had just learned, such as how to hold them and what their names were. What a delight to observe them instructing the little guys! The younger students were mesmerized as they reached through the fence to pet the feathered visitors. I didn't envision this sweet scenario happening ahead of time, but I was grateful for the serendipitous magic! There was a great deal of learning going on that day on many levels.

Chances are, these children might never encounter a live turkey ever again. The following week, we had philosophical conversations about becoming vegetarians (or not). The children began to make the connection between the live animal and what they usually encountered, which was processed, plastic-wrapped meat that was called 'turkey.' I needed to tread carefully regarding the topic, as most children eat what their parents eat and don't have a choice about protein sources until they are young adults, at the earliest. My job was to remain neutral on the subject while guiding my students to become more compassionate toward animals.

We all learned to say, "gobble, gobble." Throughout that day, and in the days beyond, as I pushed the art cart around the campus, I occasionally heard echoes of little turkey voices emanating from classrooms. Tom touched many lives that day! I leaned on my cart on the playground and listened to the gobbling from the rooms. All the work of writing up the proposal, presenting the idea to the PTA for funds to pay for Tom's visit, and the efforts of the parents really made a difference.

I'm not sure how much later it was but I was very saddened to hear the news from Heather and Amy that a coyote had broken into Tom's enclosure where he and his feather-mates met their end. I never shared this with the children, but they did ask about him from time to time. Even into the next year, I was asked if Tom could return. Not wanting to disappoint anyone, a turkey did appear again, at least for the next two years. Who would I recruit to appear as a turkey?

Brian looked great in the turkey costume I had ordered online. In spite of all his efforts, though, it was tough to replace Tom. Hence, I eventually abandoned the attempt, realizing the experience with a real turkey could never be duplicated. The day when Tom came was a great gift. Yet, I feel nothing but compassion for the hungry coyote who couldn't resist a plump and tasty meal.

When I think back to that day in November, as the children got to know Tom and the other birds, I had a profound prayer. That the memory of this experience would live through choices the students would make throughout their lives. Thanks to Tom and company, of course.

Lesson: Teach compassion for animals.

"Mother Nature has good thoughts."
—Elizabeth

The rains were returning, and soon it would be winter break. We were out spreading wildflower seeds before the arrival of a storm. As we were happily chatting and scattering, I admitted to the students that I often talked to trees. My colleague, another teacher who was out with me that day, teased me, and a few children laughed with her. I gave them a grin back and shrugged off their amusement. On the walk back to the classroom, little Ruthie ran up to me and tugged my arm.

"Don't worry, Ms. Bickett, I talk to trees, too," she said. We walked together in silence, smiling at our shared secret.

I finally got the creek adoption papers signed. I did not even wait until after the holiday season before I started bringing kids to experience the wonders of the beloved creek environment. This was no easy task. First, I needed to create a specific permission form that clearly outlined my objectives, provided information for parents, and solicited parent volunteers for creek walks. No child could be taken off-campus without his or her parent's signature on the creek form. Keeping track of each class—over ten of them—calling the volunteers, and making sure everyone was prepared was time-consuming. After all the effort, there were only two classes I was able to take to the creek before January because they were the only ones who had all the forms returned on time. So, off we went, one at a time.

The first class walked down the pebbled dirt road along the creek, and the children were ecstatic. I pointed out vegetation, and we stopped to listen to birdcalls. We savored the beauty of winter in this special place. Toyon berries brightened up the path as we headed to a dry creek bed to simply listen and practice being still. Sweet Ruthie remarked, "I can breathe easier down here."

This statement seemed to ring true for all of us that day, as we all breathed a deep collective sigh and felt our muscles relax, our hearts open up. The day unfolded with splendor before us.

Both classes composed creek poems. This phrase from a poem written by a third-grader, Elizabeth, stays with me to this day: "Mother Nature has good thoughts." Already I saw how the creek was going to change my art program and expand our little world. The stream was now ours to explore and appreciate. Later, in May, the entire school and surrounding community would be invited to join us for our first (of many) bi-annual creek cleanup days. With the help of my husband, a neighbor and her daughter, Carrie (a colleague from school), and other parent volunteers, we managed to do our part in keeping our lovely creek area free of trash. It was and still is, however, a never-ending battle.

Every year I planned art lessons relating to Kwanzaa as part of the gift-giving spirit and to celebrate the African American cultural event. One day, just before winter break, we prepared to create a collage representing the holiday. As the children were working joyfully on their projects, Phil, a fourth-grade boy with a tousle of blond hair, came up to me as I was wandering about the room talking with the students. He pulled on my sleeve and motioned for me to follow him to his desk. With great curiosity, I went. Phil seemed very enthused about something! When we arrived at his desk, Phil wrote out his last name and then proceeded to "show me some magic," as he put it. Carefully erasing several selected letters, Phil stood back, beaming as he presented to me his "magic." The ensuing word that remained, sans the letters he deleted, was "s–h–i–t." Another student walked by, and Phil scurried to cover the word and whispered to me that it was his coveted secret.

"There's a bad word in my last name!" he whispered.

I laughed and assured him his secret was safe with me. Once again, I was amused and amazed at what these young minds came up with!

One thing that always touched my heart was the generosity of my students, and Creek Side was no exception. Over the years, I used to have my middle school students make cards for the local hospitals and nursing homes to give to patients. I decided it was a good tradition to continue. The children were very thoughtful and caring in their sentiments, and there was a plethora of cheery artwork. I brought a bag full of colorful, sincerely created cards to the front desk of our local hospital. I informed the attendant this "Santa bag of cards" was from the children of Creek Side School. It became an honored tradition during my time at Creek Side, with the children reminding me when the time arose that giving always gives back.

Lesson: Model generosity.

Serendipity

I took my first group of fifth graders, Mr. Willow's class, to the creek in January. The weather, misty and damp, was almost daring us to cancel our plans. Regardless of the forecast, the kids were set to go. The parent volunteers all showed up, so off we headed. I was very excited with ideas about what I wanted to achieve on the walk. However, being the first excursion for these students, I just hoped the children would have some time to get to know the area and a few of the landmark trees. It was my intention that we would be open to whatever presented itself to us that day. As it turned out, we were not to be disappointed.

I brought the students on the main path, the wide, pebbled road, because the muddy trail was out of the question today. The Toyon bushes were alight with bright-red berries, the Christmas berries still speckling with greenery like decorations on a holiday tree. I wanted them to get to know the Toyon and to learn that the birds enjoyed eating the berries and that you could make Toyon berry jam (they should never be eaten raw). The indigenous people of California made, and probably still do make, a sweet Toyon berry concoction. I cooked some up myself once. It was a bit bitter but passable.

The small rosy berries had rather large seeds inside of them, so it took a great deal of work to cook the berries and stew them around in a colander to get the seeds out. Then, they required a great deal of sugar, as they are very tart! I shared this information with the kids, along with other facts, as we walked along in the mist. The heavy fog hushed everything. Even the enthused students seemed quieter, more alert as we moved cautiously together. We listened for birds, heard a few chickadees and towhees rustling about, but the silence was magical. I asked the children to try to walk in stillness, see what they could grasp with their senses, and take it all in. By the end of the walk, everyone was mesmerized. The peace and calm were palpable.

Our fifty minutes seemed to fly by; it was soon time to return to school. The introductory walk was a paradox: it was timeless, and yet, over all too soon.

I mentioned that our school mascot, the peregrine falcon, could be spotted by the creek from time to time. I shared how I had seen one dart overhead and watched it fly high into a tree branch one time. Suddenly, we all stopped at once. Above us soared a peregrine falcon with a baby crow in its beak, dramatically followed by two frantic crow parents cawing desperately as they chased the falcon. We watched in awe, literally with our jaws dropped open, our eyes fixed on the scene unfolding before us in the sky. Before long, the birds flew out of view into the trees along the creek. There was an eerie silence, some rustling noises, and then, the two crows emerged, sans their crow chick, and flew back slowly in the direction from whence they came. There seemed to be heaviness and sorrow in their wings as the parents retreated. This prompted a very poignant discussion about the cycle of life and death in nature.

Robert piped up "That's so cruel!" with the rest of the class agreeing that they felt sorry for the crows. I wanted to respond in a way that validated the students' feelings but, at the same time, brought the event into a more objective perspective.

I asked the students, "Where do you think the crows get their food?"

We talked about how crows were scavengers but how they also were known to grab a baby bird or two from the nests of other birds.

"We must be careful," I warned them, "about putting our human notion of 'good and evil' onto nature. We often project human concepts onto animals that are most unfair to the creatures of the wild world. They do what they do without bad intentions. They need to survive, too!"

We needed to get moving because our time was indeed running out. We walked back quietly and quickly to the classroom, where we would pick up the discussion as I packed up in a hurry to leave for the next class.

"Think about it," I began as I had literally one minute to wrap up our conversation once back in the classroom. "What if you had to kill to eat and feed your babies? Where do you get your food?"

An eager girl in front of me jumped up, waving her hands wildly, so I called on her to save time.

"Wrapped up in Styrofoam trays from Nob Hill!"

"Correct!" I chimed back and looked at everyone. "We've lost our connection about where our food comes from. Now, do you think the falcon was cruel? What about *their* babies who wait hungrily for *their* parents to return to the nest?"

Two cart-pushing recruits helped me get my noisy vehicle out the door as I called out to the kids, "We'll continue this discussion next time. In the meantime, yes, I am sad for the two crows today. I bet they were sad, too. But they will move on, have more babies; life goes on . . ."

I mentioned to the teacher that perhaps the students could write or draw about their creek experience if there was time. Regardless, the following week in our art journals, I gave my students some time to remember the "Day of the Peregrine and Crows."

As my two art helpers pushed the art cart with me to my next class, we walked in silence, quietly, reflectively, as the clouds kept a gray vigilance over the world. We seemed to disappear into the dense mist, wrapped in the mysteries of this life, and the awareness of the constant drama that happens all the time, just a breath away.

We had just finished wrapping up our lesson a couple of weeks later when Mr. Willow asked me to wait. At first, I thought I was in trouble, and my mind raced with what could have possibly happened. A few students stood up and explained they'd collected money because they wanted me to buy a camera. Mr. Willow said, "You bring art to a new level!"

During our maiden voyage to the creek, I must have said something off-handedly about not having a digital camera. Up until that time, I used my old camera to take pictures at school. I often thought of how useful a digital camera would be for documenting the creek walks and organizing and saving the numerous photos on my computer. I had no recollection of saying anything. To my great surprise, Mr. Willow and his students handed me two hundred and thirty-five dollars in cash that they had collected for me to buy a camera! I was beyond speechless, stunned by their generosity. I said, *"Thank you,"* wiping my eyes and nose with a tissue handily in reach on the art cart, and stumbled on my way to my next class. Those are moments I will never forget.

With Brian's help, we found the perfect camera online and purchased it promptly. From then on, I was able to take hundreds of photos over the five years at Creek Side, especially of kids at the creek. I regret that when I retired, I didn't think I would have much use for all those photographs, so in the spirit of moving on, I deleted the majority of them. How I wish I'd stayed my determined hand so I could have them now to share in this book! Yet, it was the experiences, the moments that I keep ever tucked in my heart.

Lesson: Make meaningful connections.

Vincent Van Gogh and Compassion

I often designed art lessons to revolve around nature, and that includes the sky, especially the night sky. Vincent Van Gogh's *Starry Night* painting was always a big hit with the children. It lends itself so well to storytelling and emotions, as well as learning the principles of textures and colors. Now that it was January, my favorite time to focus on the night sky, I planned a particular painting lesson for the first-grade classes. Van Gogh's painting was very engaging, as the children were captivated by the colors and textures. I'd like to think Vincent Van Gogh would be touched by the responses of the children and how his painting is still very much alive today.

The painting mesmerized one little boy, Patrick. He was in the special education class comprised of autistic students. Up until that point, he had never spoken a word to me. Turning to look right at me after he examined the painting thoroughly with his bright-blue eyes and his inquisitive hands, Patrick peered directly into my eyes. He said proudly, "Van Gogh!" That was a moment I will never forget. I chuckled when he continued to say "Van Gogh" for weeks to follow. It became a tender kind of connection between us, bringing us closer as a teacher and a student. This event was pivotal for Patrick. He began to open up his world to me a little at a time, all because of Van Gogh's haunting and beautiful work.

In another class, we engaged in discussions about *Starry Night* that led us into, serendipitously, a discourse about where the stars go during the day. I read a lovely book written and illustrated by my friend Jan Pitcher, entitled, *Where Do the Stars Go,* when we were finished with the lesson. Little Molly, a first grader, raised her hand. I called on her as I started to gather up my things to move on.

"The sun melts the stars away in the morning, so that's why we don't see the stars during the day!" she announced.

I had tried to explain how the sun's rays outshine the stars during the day, and so her explanation seemed entirely in line with our conversation. One thing

I love about children this age (about seven) is that magic is always a plausible cause for just about anything.

Timmy, however, was in one of his off moods. Sometimes the most innocent thing could set him off. As I was about to leave class, he exploded while having a discussion with a classmate. Timmy stood up and crumbled his paper into a tight ball, tossed it at the garbage can, and hid under a table. I looked at the other boy questioningly, but he merely shrugged his shoulders and said, "I didn't say anything, Ms. Bickett! All I said was that his sun wasn't big enough!" Timmy was very sensitive, and I knew I had to do something. Looking at the clock, I sighed. I didn't have time for this, and I felt a headache coming on.

Instructing the two cart pushers to go on their way ahead of me, I found Timmy under the table, got down on my knees, and whispered to him.

"Look, Timmy, everyone's a critic. Do you know how many times I've heard remarks about my art? William didn't mean to upset you. He was just trying to help you." Timmy stared in silence and didn't respond. I sighed again and tapped him on his arm, "Timmy, I need to go now. Look, Mrs. S. is back. You need to let this go."

Timmy was wringing his hands together and then spoke up. "I was making the picture for you. William is always butting into my business, so I just told him to stop!"

I assured him that next week I would have a discussion with William. Then, an idea hit me. "Timmy, will you walk with me to keep me company?" He turned and looked at me, considering my request.

"Let's go!" Timmy said as he quickly crawled out from under the table. We walked together to my next class, and then I asked him to draw me a new picture.

"You can make the sun any size you want," I assured him.

Timmy grinned and scampered off. I felt a close bond with Timmy, and I was not sure why. Perhaps I understood him, saw a little of myself in him.

Another Tuesday with my first graders presented us with a stormy day. I planned to take my little artists on a creek walk in connection with a lesson about the winter landscape. The rain was really pouring down, terribly so. Pushing the art cart across the wide blacktop was most trying, not to mention soaking everything despite my efforts to cover the cart with a tarp. The wind was mighty as it lifted the tarp under the rocks that I had found to weigh it down. *Next time,* I reminded myself, *use bungee cords!*

I walked into one room looking like the proverbial drowned rat, feeling rather tired already, although it was morning and this was only my second class. I came armed, though, with a *Wallace and Grommet* cartoon DVD and an ingenious plan for the children to draw a moonscape of their own after we viewed the twenty-minute presentation. I was amazed at how all the children jumped for joy when I mentioned the DVD. I had no idea how popular the characters of this show were to them. In this episode, Wallace and Grommet created a rocket ship and went to the moon for a cheese holiday. After the animated program, I explained the lesson, and the children were very excitedly on their way to creating imaginary moon scenes.

I was intrigued and amused by their discussions about the moon. We discussed how sometimes the moon does look like it is made of cheese. To my amazement, some of the children were actually wondering if the moon *really was* made of cheese. (I had to remind myself these were little first graders, after all, and they yet hover in that nebulous zone between fantasy and reality!)

As I walked around the room, checking on their work, I overheard a conversation between a sophisticated little girl and an adamant little boy.

"The moon is made of cheese!" he said stoutly.

She replied firmly and with high authority, glaring fiercely into his sparkling eyes, "No, it isn't! It's the sun!"

I had to keep from bursting out with laughter as I made my way back to the cart. Time flew by all too fast. It always did. There were so many times I wished I could have taught longer but fewer art classes each day.

I moaned aloud as I reluctantly started to pack up supplies to leave. My two cart assistants for the day eagerly helped me collect the artwork that the children would finish later on. The room began to bustle with the energy of transition. I warned the two cart helpers that they were not allowed to actually push the cart to the next class that day. It was too wet and windy. They agreed to wait for their turn next week.

I glanced out the window as I struggled with my heavy raincoat and gasped at the nearly horizontal rain. I began thinking about the trip back across the playground and three more classes I had to teach that day. A tinge of resentment at not having my own classroom bubbled to the surface. On a day like this one, I did not relish being a traveling teacher.

"What's the matter?" asked an astute boy who was watching me.

Without too much filtering, "Some days it's difficult to push around my classroom."

Not realizing other children overheard this conversation, I heard some laughter from the rest of the class. One boy, though, who happened to be standing by me at the sink, took a few curious steps toward the cart and stooped to peer inside just to check. It was an amusing gesture on his part, and I smiled at him as he stood back up.

"You don't have much room in there, Ms. Bickett," he said with concern. "Where do you sleep?"

His comment brought me back to my early elementary days when I thought all teachers lived at school.

I gave him a hug and assured him not to worry.

"It's OK, really. It's just that stormy days like this make pushing the art cart between classrooms more challenging," I attempted to explain to him as I left. As I headed out into the blustering weather, I heard his voice trailing behind me, "You could come live in our room. I am sure our teacher won't mind!"

Battling the wind and rain, I heard my name being called faintly from a distance. I turned around and saw one of my fifth-grade students running up to me. It was now recess time, and everyone was snug in their classrooms, playing games and being excused in small groups to use the restroom. Maggie caught up to me, covering her head with her hood and grabbing onto the cart handle, assisting me to push it along a bit faster. This was helpful as I was using one hand to steer and the other to hold down the tarp.

She beamed at me as we scurried along.

"I was at my grandfather's ranch this weekend, and we found a cow skull! It made me think of you!" she said, shouting so I could hear her voice above the wind and rain.

A huge grin covered my face, and I started to laugh. Maggie was referring to the skull lesson I did with my upper grades in October, the day I was Georgia O'Keeffe. A more delightful compliment could not be found to be remembered like that.

I thanked her profusely for the push and for the uplifting comment. Maggie smiled broadly, waved, and then scampered on to her classroom. I made my way to the class, where I was to begin teaching in a few minutes. The wind seemed to be funneling down the corridor, so I was eager to get out of the stormy weather. I knocked once, waited, knocked again, waited again. Finally, I had to pound before a timid little face peeped out as the heavy door of the classroom opened cautiously. I pushed the art cart into the classroom, and, with only a few minutes to spare, I rushed down the hallway to use the bathroom. When I returned, I gulped down water out of my canteen and then began the lesson right on time. All in a day's work.

Lesson: It's all good.

"The first thing you need for art is one sharp pencil." —Maddie

January and February of my first year at Creek Side were hectic months. When I taught middle school, I had my students participate in a waterfowl art contest, so I tried it with my fifth graders. I brought in all kinds of photos of ducks and geese for the students to use. As I always did with my art lessons, I included interesting facts about the subject we were studying that connected art to science, math, and the environment. I gave the children resources so they could follow up with further research. It was gratifying that during the weeks we studied the birds, many students brought in books they had checked out from the library about waterfowl.

We proceeded to create sketches, focusing on composition first. Then, I offered the students their choice of media to complete their final piece. They could choose watercolors, pencils, color pencils, oil pastels, or any combination. Their artwork was genuinely astonishing, and I sent in as many masterpieces as I could just before the deadline in early February. We waited to hear the results of the contest for a month or so.

I wanted to expand the experience of drawing birds to both my fourth and fifth graders, this time using subjects more realistic than just photographs.

I borrowed some stuffed waterfowl from the Youth Science Institute, where I once taught during my early years in California. I felt it was important to see real birds up close to draw. We were sketching the birds to prepare for a scratch art project (where the results look like etchings). On creek walks, I pointed out some of the many birds who live in the riparian environment. There were chickadees, towhees, scrub jays, crows, sparrows, Cooper's hawks, red-tailed hawks, and rarely seen peregrines. We couldn't make it to the perc ponds (large ponds in the Bay Area used to replenish groundwater) to draw our annual visiting ducks. I figured it was an excellent opportunity for the students to draw real birds, albeit dead ones. With Audubon examples to show my students, along with other bird drawings and paintings from masters such as Da Vinci, I felt they were prepared for the real McCoy, so to speak.

What I was not prepared for was the reaction of the students. Many of them couldn't seem to get past the notion that they were stuffed, once-alive birds. The thought never occurred to me that this might be disturbing to some of the children! I assured them that the birds were sanitary and that they were killed humanely (I hoped). Explaining further, I said that in the early days of biology, many animals were shot and stuffed so people could learn about them. The specimens I brought on that day were older ones. A few were even beginning to fall apart as I placed them on each table for small groups of young artists to draw.

After demonstrating how to draw a quick gesture sketch of the bird and then a more extended contour line drawing, I enjoyed wandering around and watching the (amazing) results created by the kids. I also shared how to render values with pencil, going over hatching and cross-hatching marks that would serve them during their scratchboard project the following week. The gesture sketching involved using black chalk pastels. I wanted the children to be loose and free at first, capturing the essence of the shape and relaxing before focusing more on more delicate pencil details in subsequent attempts.

As I walked along the hallway during lunch, a fourth-grade girl ran up to me with huge, happy eyes and said she heard we were going to "get dirty and draw dead things in art class today." I laughed as I recalled how the students had a tough time getting their hands a little messy from the black chalk, so I assumed that was the dirty part! Funny how word got around!

At the end of the day, I had the birds all gathered into a large box. I was leaving campus via the front of the school, where my car was parked. I wanted to return the birds as soon as I could at the end of the day. A significant number of children seemed to come out of nowhere, drawn by my box that had bird eyes peeping out through the opened top along with stick-like legs protruding haphazardly. It must have looked pretty curious!

We inadvertently created a commotion in the hallway by the front office. I set the box down so the children could see the birds and explained to them, "No, they are not alive, but yes, they are real."

I was interested in the confusion and fascination the children displayed. As I gathered up the box, with its bird heads and feet poking out, the principal was walking by with a guest. The guest stopped and stared at me, somewhat horrified. My confident principal smiled at her and explained happily, "Oh, that's just Ms. Bickett!"

My immense gratitude goes to the YSI, particularly to my friend Bonnie LeMat, who loaned me the birds that day. I heard over and over all day how "I've never touched a live, err, ah, dead, real bird before!" The drawings turned out fabulous, and next lesson, the students produced finely detailed etchings of birds that we displayed proudly in the front office. I can't help but think that going to all the trouble to bring in the stuffed feathered friends made a difference. Surely, photographs would have worked well. However, it always seemed a good rule of thumb to go for the real thing.

The stuffed-bird experience reminds me of a day when I had my little kindergarteners outdoors exploring the concept of living/nonliving. Late February had brought heavy winds and rain, so we had to take advantage of a breezy but sunny day to wander outdoors. I asked them as we watched crows and seagulls fly overhead, "Are birds alive?"

"Oh no!" they replied emphatically.

Their answer completely mystified me! I assumed I had covered the concepts pretty well with the story from the ELD curriculum book I read before we headed out.

So, I backed up, and we went over again what 'alive' meant. In a case like this one, practical, real-life application seems critical for the children to transfer the concept from the story and discussion. They didn't even seem to know that plants were alive! When we found a stopping place, I brought out a couple of stethoscopes I had for the day, and we listened to our heartbeats. We talked about how the crows had heartbeats, too. The children were astounded. But then, it seemed to confuse them that plants were alive but don't have heartbeats. That encouraged me to be sure to include a "heartbeat of a tree" lesson soon. It was one that I had done many times before at other schools.

The following week, I brought my faithful dog, Lizzie, and they listened to her heartbeat, too. I needed to clarify that just because we can't hear the heartbeat of an ant, for example, it doesn't mean it was not alive. This lesson flowed seamlessly through the Valentine season. I was confident they grasped the concepts upon which we could build in subsequent weeks.

One beautiful March day, as we were heading back to their classrooms, little Eddy tugged at my sleeve. He had a very pensive expression and said, "Even angels are alive."

I wasn't quite prepared for that one. I realized the word alive did, indeed, have other applications, such as "bringing something alive" means making it real, giving it "life." All I could do was smile at Eddy and hug him.

"You know, angels can be very real to some people, and they seem alive," I replied.

That seemed to satisfy him, but it gave me something to ruminate on. I considered that the notion of alive/not-alive is not quite as simple a concept as I had first thought. It was yet another example of how I learned so much from my students.

I discovered the next day that our third-grade group art project *Otters in the Water* earned first prize in the Long Marine Lab's art contest. I had entered our project before the winter break. We were elated, and I attended the ceremony with a few parents and students. It was a long drive over the mountains to the facility located just at the north end of Santa Cruz. For years as a middle school art teacher, I would make the long trek back and forth and always had winners from my school. For the next couple of years at Creek Side, I entered the contest with winning results every time. I was proud of my students and their heartfelt creations as we learned about sea otters, sea lions, whales, and many other ocean treasures. The following year, our *See Lines on the Sea Lions* won first place, too.

One of my fifth-grade students, Anna, won a special prize of recognition in the waterfowl art contest. We were told her art would appear in their calendar, but, unfortunately, we never saw it. She received a ribbon and her photo with a copy of her artwork in the local newspaper. We were all proud of her, especially because this was such a highly competitive contest, and the winners were mostly high school students. It was a priceless moment for Anna and all of us.

Lesson: Go for the real thing!

Art is long. Life is short.

In April, a fourth-grade girl lured me into talking about my appearance as Georgia earlier in the fall. I was in the middle of a new lesson when she raised her hand.

"Georgia O'Keeffe," she began with great authority after I called upon her to speak. We were starting a lesson about color, and I referred to Ms. O'Keeffe's use of color, bringing out a couple of posters that the children had seen before. Earlier in the fall, my focus was on composition, subject matter, and lines. This time, we were embarking on creating large-scale flowers inspired by O'Keeffe's flower paintings. The class of attentive students stopped their work and looked up as Sadie stood to emphasize what she was about to say. "Georgia O'Keeffe," she repeated the name emphatically again, "is really dead."

The students stared at her and then at me, waiting for my response. I smiled and thought of a quote in Latin, "*Ars longa, vita Brevis*," which means "art is long, life is short." I said the phrase as I wrote it on the board. Puzzled, Sadie, with her hands on her hips, squinted her eyes and pouted a little before saying, "Yeah, so how was it possible that she came in October?"

Uncertain about how to proceed, I paused and then answered.

"Well, her art is still very much alive, which is what the quote means," I said, pointing to the whiteboard. Sadie, still standing as the class was still listening, pointed her finger at me and announced accusingly, "Well, so you admit she is dead then!"

"Well, yes, in fact, Georgia O'Keeffe died in 1984 at the age of ninety-eight," I confessed.

Raising her hands and clapping them together, Sadie then shouted, "So, it *was* you after all!"

I had given the children many essential facts about Georgia O'Keeffe in the fall. I had even written down her birth/death dates on the board. Goes to show you that you can never be sure of the impression you make! I acknowledged I was merely acting out a part, like being in a play. It had not been my intention to trick them, though, it seems, some students interpreted the event that way. Regardless, I hoped that Sadie and the others would remember Georgia O'Keeffe better for my having dressed up as the artist.

It was springtime at Creek Side, and after spring break, the days seem to tumble rapidly by like bubbling water in the creek. Arriving at school one day dressed once again as Frida Kahlo, I happily pushed the cart around. I enjoyed all the smiles and stares and pointing fingers ("It's *her* again!"). With my little kiddies, we were decorating paper plates with Mexican sun designs in preparation for Cinco de Mayo, coming up soon in the first week of May. I took their finished products to a nearby taqueria to display for a week. There were reports of how fun it was for parents and children to visit the local business and enjoy great tacos while they saw their artwork in the windows.

As I headed into a first-grade classroom, little Timmy eyed me suspiciously. "Did you come back to life again?" he asked.

Another student, rambunctious Amy, jumped up with her red hair flying. "Hey, that's the ART teacher!" she yelled.

I began the lesson with pictures of the sun. "What does the sun do for us?" I asked.

Timmy blurted out, "It melts our ice cream!"

I attempted to interweave learning a little about our sun, exploring Mexican culture, and creating their colorful sun designs all into one lesson. Being dressed up as Frida again was an excellent opportunity to find out what they remembered about her from earlier in the year. Angie piped up, "You were married to that big fat guy!" In addition to Angie's recollection of Diego Rivera, the children recalled things like, "she liked monkeys," "she had one eyebrow," and "she had a toilet in one painting." I loved their honest answers, and, of course, the sun plates turned out fabulous.

Angie sauntered up to me and asked me to autograph a piece of paper for her; I did so quickly without too much effort. Out of the corner of my eye, I noticed she and a few other children were snickering and winking at each other. I shrugged it off as we started to clean up for the day. It wasn't until the following week I discovered their motive.

With great care and attention, I hung the Mexican sun designs in the windows of the taqueria, and they fit perfectly with all the authentic décor in the place. Stepping back as I drank my carrot juice, I pondered to myself, *It's worth it, the extra work.* Besides, I got to enjoy some great food while I was working.

Oh, and the motive for my autograph? My little detective students greeted me the week after the Frida visit with triumphant, satisfied expressions as I entered the classroom appearing as myself again. Angie quickly jumped up and asked me to sign my name. I was in a bit of a rush to get going, and so I complied without too much thought. We were working on painting flowers, using real ones I bought from the local nursery, and the children were lively and contentedly working away. Halfway through the class, Angie marched up to me, producing two pieces of paper: one with Frida Kahlo's 'signature' and the other with my signature. This bright-eyed little girl smiled broadly at me.

"You see, it was you! The handwriting is exactly the same! We *knew* it was you!" she said triumphantly.

I shrugged my shoulders.

"Who knew?" I asked with a laugh.

I was impressed with her bright idea, though, and nodded approvingly at her as she beamed in all her glory. Well done, sleuth girl!

The first year drew to a close very fast. I was exhausted but thrilled to be teaching art at Creek Side and was happy to learn I'd be back the following year. I was offered a forty percent position and accepted it. However, I was offered a full-time art position again at the middle school where I once taught. We needed the money, no doubt, but there was no question in either my husband's mind or mine as to what my choice would be.

There was something I still wanted to do before the school year ended, so I woke up one morning during the last week of school and asked myself, *Should I?* Then, the answer came quite clearly: *Why not?*

I found a dark dress, a somber shawl, and looked most serenely bland as I emerged as the *Mona Lisa.* We spent a lot of time during the year talking about Leonardo da Vinci and looking at the Mona Lisa. The children kept nature notebooks and sketches in the spirit of Da Vinci. These contained drawings of plants, animals, and other sketches the children created when inspired. So, I figured, "Mona Lisa" needed to make an appearance.

As I walked about during the day, it was absolutely hilarious. Kids kept pointing at my shoes and saying, "Why are you wearing Ms. Bickett's shoes?" Everyone had to guess who I was trying to portray, with very few hitting it right. One teacher even asked me if I was supposed to be Mother Theresa!

But the best comment of all came at the end of the day. I was getting ready to leave when Timmy came to me. I had just parked the art cart and was heading toward the school gate.

"Ms. Bickett, how could you be so old when you look so young?" he asked.

I couldn't help but laugh.

"Timmy, I love you!" I said as he hugged me and then trotted off happily in another direction. I wandered home with a full heart, stopping under a tall pine and listening to the wind sail through the needles, sounding like a mountainside of pines, far away in the forest. But then, I reminded myself, *This is a forest, right here.*

Lesson: Congratulate yourself!

The End of the First Year

I always tried to make learning more fun and memorable. We were learning about line, shape, color, texture, form, value, and space, the so-called Art Elements. When I taught middle school, one day, I was talking too fast, and I slipped and said Art "Elephants" instead of Art "Elements." It became a kind of joke. However, my middle school students and I discovered that it was a smart way of remembering the Art Elements. So, at Creek Side, I drew an elephant and labeled parts of the elephant with a corresponding art element depicted clearly.

The second graders made their Art Elephants, and we kept them in the portfolios to use as needed during the year. For my first-grade enrichment class, I had an idea. My sister Jane had told me about an elephant sanctuary in Tennessee (see the website in the **Resources** section at the back of this book). She had sent me a book about the elephants there. I read the story to the children, and we decided to draw elephants and write poems to send them. It was a great project, and I donated money to the sanctuary on behalf of the kids; they always asked how the elephants were during the year.

At the end of the year, a fifth grader raised his hand in class.

"Art Elephants really help me when I need to remember the Art Elements. I explained what they were to my grandmother."

It was always great to hear things like that.

It felt like a literal blink of an eye since April break; the last six weeks of school were a blur. Heather and Amy brought baby chicks for my kindergarten students. We brought them into the garden where we'd met Tom and the others back in November. Something I was not expecting was that the little children were afraid of the chicks at first! We watched the chicks and listened to them and held the little chicks for the children to touch. Before you knew it, the kinder kids were holding them timidly in their laps. I made a booklet of photos with the children holding the chicks, and we talked about our experience the following week. These children, who barely spoke at all in autumn when we first met, now chattered with great enthusiasm about the baby chicks. They created drawings and collage art of the birds and pretended to be chicks. I was grateful for my friends who brought this opportunity and grateful it seemed to have made a lasting impression.

The field behind Creek Side was an expansive, grassy play area. On the last day of school, I was returning from lunch and met up with a group of fourth-grade boys, all excitedly motioning for me to join them and pointing at the sky. I ran to join them and tilted my head upward.

We had a resident red-tailed hawk that often soared about over the creek behind school. There he was, handsome with sunlit tail feathers, being chased by a couple of frantic crows. Watching the captivating drama, we were all nearly late for class. The bell rang as we were oblivious to the rest of the world.

Often children brought me bugs and other critters from the playing field, dead or alive. One day, it was a gaggle of little girls who came running to me with a ladybug in tow. I enjoyed their awe and excitement over such a find but, ultimately, urged them to set her free. We stood back and wished the little spotted lady well as she fluttered away and disappeared like magic into thin air.

I was walking along, going over my mental checklist of all the things I needed to do before school officially closed for the summer. Just then, a favorite teacher of mine, Ms. Haines, approached me, her eyes beaming, a broad smile on her face.

"Are your ears burning?" she asked.

I shook my head in confusion. I didn't understand what she meant. Ms. Haines explained that at the staff meeting yesterday, many of the teachers were singing praises about my programs at the school. As a part-time teacher, I was not required to attend staff meetings, but I often did. I wasn't able to make it to the meeting the previous day.

Blinking my eyes in near disbelief, I warmly thanked her for the information. Admittedly, I felt my efforts were appreciated, but I never imagined I'd be a topic at a staff meeting! The happy faces of my students were usually all the feedback I needed to know I was on track. But it was good to know my colleagues saw and understood what I was doing and supported the programs I taught. Art and enrichment are not fluff. They really do make a huge difference. Little wonder Creek Side School students always had outstanding test scores. I believe it was because the children were happy, loved learning, and had rich ancillary experiences that complemented their academic studies.

As I had done for many years, I gave each child a certificate at the close of the year. I smiled as the students beamed at the "Artistic Licenses" I had created for them. It reminded me of an experience I had that spring when Lizzie and I were enjoying one of our daily excursions.

The late-afternoon sun warmed our spirits as we merrily made our way past the school. We were on the stairs by the footbridge over the creek when two hefty high school boys walked past us. Suddenly I heard my name. Turning to face these young men, I recognized them from the middle school where I taught.

"Do you remember us?" they asked.

"Of course I do!" I replied, now recalling them very clearly.

One of the boys said to me, "I still have that Artistic License you gave us at the end of the year. It's hanging on the wall in my bedroom. It was very cool that you gave those to us!"

The other boy agreed. We talked for a few moments, including how things were going for them. The certificates resembled a driver's license entitling them to total freedom and authority to create what they wanted. If anyone questioned their art (I did have to be clear I did not condone defacing property), they could show them they earned their artistic license!

As Lizzie and I walked on, my heart swelled with love and joy. You just never know how you impact your students, what stays with them, and how even little things can make a difference. The "bad" days fade away (though I don't believe any day is completely bad), outshined by the positive and gracious experiences.

Except for my kindergarten students, I took every class to the creek at least twice during the spring. During these excursions, we had all kinds of wondrous adventures that were exquisitely matched to state and national standards for art, literature, and science. Most of all, we had the opportunity to learn and have fun! Suddenly, everyone was asking if they could go to the creek with me. I usually got home from school wholly wasted, my feet throbbing, my energy spent, yet, I wouldn't trade all those creek walks for anything.

I also brought Lizzie to Ms. Carrie's preschool special education class once a week as a volunteer. Often, we went on creek walks with Carrie and her delighted students and parent volunteers. (Photos are at the conclusion of the book chapters.)

As a way to further the connection to the beautiful stream that ran behind the school, we hosted our first of many official River Day cleanups on a Saturday morning that spring. Carrie was there to assist me with the required registration forms and other paperwork. Creek Side School was about to begin the bi-annual tradition of collecting trash along the creek.

Many parents arrived with their eager children to don gloves to pick up plastic candy wrappers, soda and beer cans, and even a few lost school balls along the creek trail. We used two types of bags, one for recyclable objects, the other for trash. I was proud of the new sign the Water District constructed at the end of the road at the street entrance gate: "Creek Adoption by Creek Side School." By the end of the morning, our creek was, indeed, pristine again. Whenever I walk by that sign now, I feel my heart grow just a little bigger. The river belongs to all of us.

In the springtime, I usually wrote a poem to commemorate the year. Funny thing, I can't seem to find the poem I wrote for the first year. But I'll never forget the last day.

I was walking home, it was late, and I had just spent hours putting supplies away and cleaning the art cart. Several boys, Timmy included, joined me for a car wash as they sprayed the old gray cart with a hose. After wiping it dry, I parked the clunky four-wheeled cart in the corner and turned off the light, pausing and looking back at the cart, the room, everything. I already looked forward to redecorating the art cart for a new year in the fall. The magical art cart traveled many miles, and it deserved rest over the summer. It was as if this whole first year was there, waving goodbye. For the most part, it'd been a great year.

Natalie, one of my first graders, won first prize in a county office art contest. One of the many articles I'd written about art was published in *School Arts* magazine. I received a grant for my fifth graders to paint small murals on two panels and brought in guest animals. I adopted the creek to start a vibrant creek program, and I began two new programs at the school for English Language Development and first-grade reading enrichment . . . whew! An image of a hammock came to my mind. Before I knew it, my husband went out and bought just that: a huge hammock that he set up in the backyard for me to rest and recuperate over the vacation. I felt satisfied and yet unfinished. Somehow, though, I knew I hadn't learned what I needed to from this job. The children seemed to unveil aspects of myself that I often preferred not to see. Most of all, they showed me how to stay close to my truth. Those were my thoughts, complete and unsettled at the same time. I took in a deep breath, closed the door, and headed toward home.

It was a brilliant day. The sun was gorgeous as it angled toward the horizon, casting summer shadows along as I made my way across the playing field. I was relieved to be done, and I was looking forward to a summer's rest. As I dragged my feet, suddenly, I turned because I sensed something. A tiny blonde-haired girl was bobbing along toward me from the after-school care room. Parents were starting to arrive to claim their children, and there was a mop of kids hovering in the distance. But there was something unusual about this child running toward me, her golden hair on fire in the light of day's passing, so I stopped, curious to know who she was. I didn't recognize her. After all, even though it seemed I taught nearly everyone on campus that year, I surely didn't know everyone. I remember she was wearing pink shorts and a pink short-sleeved top.

This tiny child finally reached me, huffing and puffing.

"I know you!" she exclaimed.

She pointed a sure finger at me with a huge grin, pivoted on her heels, and then took off back toward the classroom she had come from.

I stood there for a moment, taking in the vision, her little head bobbing again in the light, triumphantly running with her arms out wide. It was the kind of picture you imagine when you think of the innocence of childhood.

Funny thing is, though, I had never met this child. I didn't know her name or anything about her. In the years to come, I never saw this child again. It was as if she appeared and returned from nowhere, like an angel with little pink wings, waving as she flew away.

Lesson: Each day is a gift.

The Second Year, 2007:

ROUND TWO

Something New

That summer, after my first year at Creek Side, I visited my mother in Rapid City, South Dakota. Rosemary, my mother's name, was a gifted musician and had a beautiful voice.

I can still hear my mother's voice as she sang lullabies to us at night. All my life, I've made up songs, like she did. It was no surprise when I found myself teaching "We Love the Creek" to my first graders later in the year. I composed the short tune for a play the children had written about going to the creek and all the beautiful life they found there. (You can find the words and music following the lesson plans at the back of the book.)

My tradition was to process my summer travels and infuse my learning into the new year. I spent the rest of the summer before my second year at Creek Side conjuring up new and exciting curriculums. My friend Rose and I visited the San Juan Islands in Washington State, and Brian and I managed a short but wonderful trip to England. We experienced Stonehenge in the pouring rain, our great fortune because there were barely any other visitors at the monument that day. Later, as we took the train past giant chalk horses, I dreamed of several invigorating art lessons, thinking of crop circles and other forms of earth art. I returned from that trip refreshed and motivated to create an even better year for the students at Creek Side. It had always been my policy to never repeat precisely what I'd done year after year. If I was bored, then, of course, how could my students get excited and learn? I discovered new things and became enlivened to share these experiences with my students. That was at the very core of my passion and love for being a teacher.

Hence, in August, I returned to Room 5, armed with new lessons. I marveled at how wonderful the beginning of a fresh, new year felt: like an unwrapped gift sitting in front of me, waiting to be opened. After about a month into the new year, a teacher could be in danger of losing that initial impetus. I planned particularly exciting lessons over the year, so I had something to look forward to, along with my students.

Ramona created the art prep schedule again. I was grateful I didn't have that task. Thankfully, there would be no combination classes this year, and I noticed the difference immediately. I showered Ms. Heart with overflowing gratitude until she begged me to stop.

When I turned on the lights of Room 5, the art cart looked lonely in the corner, empty and dull gray. The cart seemed more like a clumsy old truck, of great utility and endurance but lacking in any creativity until it was transformed with art. One of my first enjoyable tasks was to close up the sides of the cart with large pieces of cardboard and affix the Art á la Cart poster on the front. I rotated posters every month, and the poster I used at the beginning of every year was a Paul Klee self-portrait, to which I added the words "'Art á la Cart' with Ms. Bickett." I deliberately left the sides blank, waiting for art from the children. I placed my supply order, made my trip to the RAFT—Resource Area for Teachers—supply store (they collect all kinds of used, recycled, and donated items for teachers to rummage through), and took a deep breath. Melissa, Ramona, and I attended the first staff meeting, which lasted a full day. We vowed to make a concerted effort to be more a part of the staff. I always loved seeing my colleagues after a summer's absence, as we enjoyed sharing what we did over the summer, like a classroom full of kids. The energy was tangible, everyone eager to begin again.

Unlike the previous year, many students recognized me, and I was assailed with all kinds of hugs. Children waved and yelled hello from the distance as I made my way across campus. I felt like I was returning home from a long voyage, welcomed back this time, a part of the school instead of an awkward newcomer. I realized how challenging my first year was, breaking the ice with some of the teachers, getting to know the children, and having to start a new art program from scratch.

One day a teacher gesticulated wildly, complaining about "those special ed kids," and I decided I had had it. During the first year, I listened to her ranting and raving about how much trouble they caused, and I did my best to just listen and to be sympathetic. This day, I did my best to try to stay calm. As I set down the papers I was loading onto the cart, I turned to face her.

"Stop," I said clearly. "It really bothers me when you talk like that about special education kids. *I* used to teach special education!"

I pointed out that, as difficult as it can be, "They are *all* our kids."

We came close to a full-fledged argument, but I did my best to express how I felt and go on my way. I was tired of hearing her negative comments over and over. Hence, as I left the room, I requested, "You can feel how you want, but please, from now on, don't bad-mouth special education children when I'm around. I don't ever want to hear about it from you again."

I fussed and fidgeted all day, as it was not easy to confront a colleague; she was not an easy person to disagree with. To keep the peace, I apologized after school for any misunderstanding. Still, I made it clear, again, I would not tolerate further discourse about "those special ed kids." After mulling over our discussion during the day, I realized this teacher needed to be heard, so I tried to empathize with her. I understood it was a challenge when special needs children were integrated into mainstream classes. I encouraged her to ask for help and advice when she hit a wall. I did my best to be considerate of her feelings but defended my own opinions and the kids, who belonged with her as well. As the years tumbled by, however, her complaints rose and fell. So far, this year was off to a bumpy start.

There was an excellent special education teacher, Francisco, who approached me about having art with his severely handicapped class, third through fifth graders. I asked Ms. Heart about any funds to add his class, and there were none, so we struggled to find a class where he could mainstream his students into art, which was what should occur anyway. The only time that seemed to work for him was during a third-grade class of thirty students. He could bring in about five to six kids, and despite the large class size, I agreed wholeheartedly.

I shared this with the regular teacher, and for some reason I will never understand, she and another teacher stomped off to the principal to complain. They were upset that this could cause a problem, having those few extra kids in the room while I taught art. Where were the teachers last year when I was over-whelmed with ten more students, without extra support? I was baffled because I did not understand why this concerned them in the least; I simply informed the teachers as a courtesy. We ended up working out a deal for Francisco to bring his students another time, but he had to switch his lunch schedule around to make this happen. I appreciated Francisco because when he brought his students for art, he always stayed. However, he should have been able to have a prep period. We enjoyed a very successful art program together that year, and it was clear having 'those kids' in the room was suitable for everyone. I witnessed, as I've seen so many times before, students learning about compassion. Before long, students from both classes formed friendships with each other.

I never heard from either of the teachers who complained. Still, I suppose, in the end, this arrangement worked out for everyone anyway.

One of my favorite lessons was introducing Wassily Kandinsky and Arnold Schoenberg. The artist and composer worked together during the early twentieth century in Europe. Kandinsky was quoted saying, "I paint sounds." I loved to show examples of his work and play a little Schoenberg for the children, along with other music I selected for the day. There were many ways you could teach this lesson. This time I had the children first draw and paint in the air as they listened to music, just to get the idea of responding to the sounds and not worrying about the marks they made. Next, we used paper and watercolor brushes with black ink as we experienced the sounds. Sometimes I turned off the lights during this step. We weren't concerned with what the marks looked like. The children could embellish their black lines with other colors as we continued listening to music. The students said to me, "This was the funniest art we've ever done!"

How refreshing it was to recognize students from the previous year! How amazing it was to see the changes that had occurred over the summer. I marveled at how fast they grew in elementary school. Year-to-year, there were noticeable differences. Thank goodness we stop growing at some point! Maya was gone, along with her cluster of friends, and I realized how much I missed them. Timmy ran up to me wildly, flailing his arms about with a broad smile and embracing me so tightly I had to gasp for breath.

"I missed you, Ms. Bickett!" he chimed, and I conveyed the same sentiment.

"Timmy, this year, will you help me keep track of who pushes the art cart for your art class?" I came up with the idea to have students manage the bookkeeping involved in art cart duty as it became too much for me. Delighted, he scampered off, waving. Natalie found me, flashing her big grin, her eyes sparkling as we nodded at each other. It was great to be back.

I scattered the year's fresh new art all around the district office, as I did all during the previous year (and in years prior when I taught middle school). The extra effort involved was noted though. A very kind secretary (a parent of a former student I had in middle school) thanked me for the lovely art and assured me it brightened everyone's day. The human resources director passed me in the hallway and also thanked me. In all the years I'd been hanging art at the district office, this was the first time I'd been acknowledged, and it felt good.

As most teachers will tell you, we didn't depend on hearing positive feedback. It was often the negative things we heard if we heard anything at all. My greatest reward was the smile on a child's face, laughter, and engagement in a lesson. And, of course, the sincere hugs and words of gratitude I heard from my students every day.

Lesson: Acknowledge others.

"Hey, it's turning green!"

Every Autumn I was inspired by the changing colors of the leaves. I would gather newly fallen leaves as examples to show my students. I collected leaves of all kinds, the large-handed sycamore, the lacey maple, and the toothed birches. There were so many to choose from. I was like a child in a candy store, scampering about with my bag, and picking up leaves as Lizzie waited patiently for me on our walks.

For each grade level, I created a different color wheel. Obviously, the wheels became more complicated when making them with the older children. The little kiddies had a wheel with the spaces for the three primary colors (blue, red, yellow) and secondary colors (orange, purple, green) in the shapes of leaves. Since I did not have an art room, and there was no place for the color wheels to be displayed, it was only feasible for them to create this assignment with crayons. It nonetheless instilled the concepts, and we could save the results for later reference.

Crayons are wondrous, though—they mix pretty well—and it gave the kids the idea of blending colors. I presented leaves that showed nearly every aspect of the color wheel, except for blue. Timmy chimed that the leaves couldn't possibly be blue because the sky was already blue.

"It won't work for the leaves to be the color of the sky because then you wouldn't see them as well!" he said with authority. Smart kid!

Thus ensued an animated discussion about sky colors. I ended up suggesting to the class that they should watch the sunset that night and use crayons or watercolors at home to show what colors they see. The following week, little Sandy came up to me and said, "The sky already looked like a painting, so I didn't paint it."

I stood back after my colorful leaf presentation to listen to the children as they squealed in delight, "Hey, it's turning green!" and "I made mud!" I challenged them when they finished with the elemental wheel to mix all the primaries together in the center. They took great pride in making a brown mud color. On another day, I got the notion to take my second graders out to the garden to make mud pies. It seemed like a logical connection anyway.

I was assigned second, fourth, and fifth-grade art in addition to my two other enrichment programs, the English Language Development kindergarten children and the first-grade reading class. So, I followed the first graders I had the previous year into the second grade and was relieved to know most of the children quite well. As soon as I could, I sent home the hundreds of creek permission forms. That way, I could begin taking classes on creek walks to enjoy the autumn weather, colors, and all the changes going on in the riparian environment. This was a huge chore, and I was very thankful for a few parent volunteers who helped me get forms collected. It was the students, however, who did the most work. Quite by accident, I discovered how eager they were to help. Without a parent in one class, a student volunteered to check off names and put the parent-signed forms in an envelope for me. Even the younger ones wanted to take on responsibility; it was truly amazing.

My friend Chris Carson-Seals, a park interpreter for the Santa Clara County Parks, came to give presentations on petroglyphs and pictographs. I had worked as a volunteer with Chris and an archeologist to create a Rock Art Program for the county parks. She was the interpreter at a place called Chictactac, or Place of Dancing (Ohlone), near Morgan Hill. Chris came the previous spring, and we agreed the lesson was a great success, so every year at Creek Side, my friend presented to the fourth- and fifth-grade classes.

After just two classes, she was exhausted and marveled, "I could never have a job like yours!" Sometimes *I* felt I couldn't do a job like mine.

The students enjoyed incising with toothpicks designs into flattened clay pieces, making their own petroglyph necklaces. The following week, they created foam board prints of their images. The concept of subtractive work to make petroglyphs, as opposed to the painting of pictographs, was reinforced with the lesson sequencing. As Chris and I made our way back to Room 5 to eat our lunch, we were bombarded with children carrying their creations around with them. If they weren't fourth or fifth graders, they asked when they would get to make clay necklaces, too. The word always got out fast!

I wanted my second graders to start keeping art portfolios like I did with the older kids. The apparent problem was that I didn't have a classroom, so I had to ask the teachers for a bare spot to keep the student's work. Most of the teachers were great, giving me a shelf, drawer, or even a cubby. Only one teacher looked down her long nose at me, being she was much taller than me, and refused my request. I was hurt at first and confused about why it was a problem for her; but, eventually, she retracted her initial decision. Not all their art went into portfolios. After being displayed, most of it either went home, or some teachers kept some of the pieces for a yearlong memory book.

Many parents told me how they put this or that project up on their walls at home. It was always my policy to let kids take home their art as often as possible for their great Refrigerator Art Galleries. I forever treasured my son's artwork and never tired of hanging it up around our home.

The autumn of my second year at Creek Side seemed to be a bit of a blur, but there were moments, snapshots that I remember now, years later. Although most were insignificant events, ones that we tend to overlook, somehow, because things happened with children, it seems more magical, more precious to me. Like the day when I was drained and discouraged as I packed up my bag to go home. It had been a long day, and I was worn out, achy, longing to just plop on my bed and nap.

I was walking down the hallway, the school had been let out over a half-hour earlier, and there was a buzz of children outside playing as part of the after-school program. I could hardly keep my eyes open, but I smiled at them and acknowledged their hellos. Suddenly, I was grabbed from behind! Little Amy literally spun me around (I was like a rag doll at this point) and said to me, "I loved the art lesson today. It was fun!"

Her sweet energy nourished me. I was struck with just how powerful gratitude was, how important it was to say thank you to people when we feel we've been gifted with something. I hugged Amy back and thanked her for telling me. She nodded as she skipped away. The funny thing was, I survived the trek home and even managed to take Lizzie for a walk before I rested. Gratitude does change everything.

A little ring-necked snake presented itself to me one day while I was picking up trash at the creek with my husband and neighbors, and so I decided to care for it just long enough to show my kinder kids. I had new kindergarten students who were bursting with imagination. We were off to a great start. I did have use of a new classroom, where I also taught the first-grade reading class, so that was reassuring in times of inclement weather.

I brought the little snake to show the kindergarteners, and I was amazed at how afraid a few of them were of such a tiny, tiny snake! It was around the size of a pencil, half as thick and just barely longer. Eventually, they not only got used to the snake but became really excited and held him very tenderly. They fired off questions: "Where are his legs, what does he eat, and where are his parents?" I assured the children I would let him go at the end of the day, placing him back where I found him. The children were very concerned about getting a disease from the snake. I assured them that would not happen, especially because we were all washing our hands carefully after touching him.

The children thanked little Stripey (the name they gave him) and said their goodbyes. Stripey was happy to return to his home later that day.

Lesson: Gratitude changes everything!

"I want to paint like the moon sings!"
—Sally

Monet has always been a favorite artist of mine, especially when teaching younger children. There's such loving energy, color, and peace about his work and no inappropriate images. We looked at one of his water lily paintings, and I quoted Monet, "I want to paint like the birds sing." The children were engaged with tempera paints, creating large textured flowers using combs and other tools to brush through their work to emphasize texture. We thought aloud about the primary colors and how we could mix secondary colors.

It was a challenging lesson because we had no place to set the paintings to dry, so we did our best to spread them around the room for the day. The teachers were pretty good about tolerating the situation throughout the year, letting me use their classrooms if the students' pieces weren't quite dry by the time the lesson was over. I eventually wrote a grant and was able to purchase a large drying rack, only to find it was useless. Dragging the clumsy thing from room to room was a logistical nightmare, so I ended up donating it to a middle school art program.

As the children were happily painting, I played a tape with birds singing and, during all the chaos (spills, cleanups, and refilling water), there was a gentle calm. I could feel Monet's presence. I imagined his big burly form smiling broadly as he watched the children, who were inspired by his work, creating lively and colorful flower scenes. I encouraged them to zoom in and see the flowers magnified. We pretended we were looking over a bridge and seeing the flowers in a lovely imaginary pond. The results were simply gorgeous.

Timmy was hard at work. I was glad that he was having a happy day; some days he was moody, and I was not sure what might set him off.

"Timmy, Monet would love your painting!" I told him.

Beaming back at me, Timmy paused and then stated with glee, "I'm not painting like the birds sing. I was painting like the stars shine!"

We had just finished our own *Starry Night* watercolor paintings the previous week, modeled after Van Gogh's famous piece. So, I understood the connection right away. "All right! That's great!" I patted him on the back, and he enthusiastically continued with his work. Before I knew it, another student, Sally, chimed in. Obviously, she had been listening in on our conversation. "I'm painting like the moon sings!" Then another student yelled out, "I'm painting like the sky glows!" Suddenly, the entire class became a chorus of "*I'm* painting like . . ." statements. Some were painting like flowers, and some like the sun. I laughed and applauded them all.

As the sudden rise of voices dissipated, little red-haired Charlie tugged at my shirt as I walked by his desk. "Ms. Bickett, Amy's copying me!" I heard this complaint sometimes from kids sitting by each other, not often, but occasionally it was an issue. Kneeling by his desk, I considered his work, looked back and forth between the two pieces, and it did seem they were similar.

"Charlie, they are similar but not the same," I began. "Besides, Amy was giving you a compliment if she's copying you." I tried to explain, "Imitation is the highest form of flattery!"

Then Amy retorted, "I'm not copying him. He's copying me. I started first!"

Before the argument went any further, I interjected. "Look, you two, focus on your own work, and remember it is OK to be inspired by someone else's painting. Just be sure you make your own, *your own.*"

Charlie then deliberately splashed some blue in the middle of his painting, covering over parts of his flowers. I didn't have any place else to move either of them at this point and instructed them to work it out, as we needed to clean up very soon. Ah, the joys of teaching!

After the great effort of cleaning up the desks and getting all my supplies back on the cart, Timmy proudly announced the names of the cart pushers for the day. He certainly did not forget my request for him to oversee this job this year. Setting the art cart managers off in the direction of my next class, little Molly approached me with a small orange heart she had made.

"Ms. Bickett, *I* painted like my heart sings." Molly gave me that precious heart, and I kept it on my art cart for a long time. It was a good reminder that the heart was always the best place from which to work.

As I noted earlier, I've always liked to sing and make up songs. When I was in my early teens, I wrote a song called "Diamond Wing Pony," a tune I'd always kept in my head. In the fall of my second year at Creek Side, my husband, a musician and composer, wrote it out for me and accompanied me on guitar while we recorded it. Initially, my sister Jane, who has a lovely voice, was supposed to be the lead singer for the recording. Unfortunately, she was unable to make the trip down from Oregon at that time. Later, my son and his wife embellished the recording with rhythm and their voices as well.

For fun, I brought in the "Diamond Wing Pony" CD and played it for the children. They caught on to the tune right away. Before I knew it, my second graders were singing "Diamond Wing Pony" as they created magical colored-chalk pictures of an imaginary scene.

Many of the children brought me their amazing abstracted works of art, and I asked if I could keep a few of them. They were so generous. I ended up with more than I expected! I was beyond touched. I told them I would like to write a book (unpublished as of this writing) to go with the CD, which I did a few years later.

To connect with the horse part of my song-story, I also shared how the Black Hills Wild Horse Sanctuary in South Dakota was rescuing wild horses. I showed pictures of the wild mustangs that I took the previous summer when Brian and I had visited the sanctuary.

"Oh, so that's where the Diamond Wing Pony lives!" called out several of the children.

I laughed and agreed, "Yes, indeed, sometimes the wild mustangs run so fast, they could be flying!"

The next day little Molly came up to me at recess and whispered in my ear, "I still have your song in my head!" That was, indeed, a priceless gift to hear.

To this day, I still have those drawings the children gave me.

(You can find the words and music at the end of this book.)

Lesson: Create magic!

Spiraling

It was November, and a third-grade teacher, Ms. Dall, and I worked on many projects related to the garden. I became very involved in the garden, volunteering (often with my adorable husband) on weekends, tidying up, weeding, doing repair work. I attended a workshop on composting and was able to donate a compost bin. Ms. Dall and I worked on getting composting worms in little (former Tidy Cat) bins for each classroom. This project infused me with joy and purpose.

We harvested homegrown gourds from the school garden, cut holes into them to make birdhouses, and Ms. Dall's class painted them. On the weekend, I covered them all with a sealant so the gourds would be ready for Monday. The children were excited as we made our way to the garden, lively and colorful birdhouses in tow. I turned to watch them and listened. This was what education should be, I reminded myself, this happy chatter of children ignited by a lesson. I had a bin of clipboards and markers ready in the garden ahead of time so, after we hung our gourds, we created some drawings. Also, there were lizards and a baby gopher snake I'd found that morning for the children to hold and draw if they so choose.

Third-grade boys and girls, bubbling with enthusiasm and joy, hopped about, finding little niches for their gourds. When they finished, I asked Ms. Dall if it was OK for us to form a circle. Spontaneously, I decided we needed ceremony, a dedication to the birds for their new homes, and for this perfect day. We gathered the children in the center of the garden.

"Everything we've done matters today," I began as the class was serenely quiet. "Today, you made a difference. The birds will come and live here, and we can listen to them sing."

We stood in silence as the sky seemed to respond with a gentle breeze, swaying the little gourds, ushering in a few wispy clouds.

As the children enjoyed holding and drawing the blue belly lizards, Ms. Dall informed me that she was supposed to be having the students prepare for STAR (California Standardized Testing and Reporting) tests during this period. We laughed together in agreement; this was a much better deal. Lizards were very proficient teachers! When class was over, we happily released our little reptilian guests with gratitude.

I brought my "Kelp Doll" story to school for my second graders, along with some dried kelp to give to the children. Giant kelp beds sway in the sea along California's coastlines. These submerged forests provide a plethora of fish and marine mammals with food and shelter. Sea otters can often be seen from shore with the long strands wrapped about their waists to anchor them in place. The kelp washes up on shore when their holdfast (what anchors them to the seafloor) is uprooted. The giant kelp arrives in entangled masses that dry in the sun. The top part of the plant looks like a balloon. Its function is to keep the plant afloat. After it dries on the beach, the kelp can be broken off the strand and clearly resembles a doll, sans face. Ohlone children once used these faceless dolls as toys. The curly locks of reddish hair on its head make amazing hairdos! I enjoyed several years of creating kelp doll gifts for family and friends by adding cloth and beads to create unique characters.

It was no small task as Brian and I collected nearly a hundred pieces of kelp at the beach a few days before. The students loved the dolls, except for a few fussy girls who insisted they were ugly. Sadly, one little girl confessed to me the next day that her mother made her throw "that horrible thing" away.

In the spring, I brought seashells I'd collected over the years for my older fourth- and fifth-grade students to draw and then paint pictures of later on. I loved seashells. The bulk of my collection was from a trip to Sanibel, Florida, with my friend Rose. They became the focus of contour line drawings, overlapping, and shading; rendering shapes and textures; and, finally, sizeable colorful O'Keeffe-style paintings. Reprising my role as the famous American painter, I arrived as Georgia again, and the students reveled in it. I reaffirmed how much I loved teaching and how much I loved my students.

It was now April of my second year, and it had been a long winter. The creek walks were alive and well with all kinds of magic, and I recovered from a long illness, coughing my way from subsequent asthma through wind and rain, sun and clouds.

April produced an abundance of flowers. Taking advantage of the season, I engaged my students in all kinds of blossomy lessons, bringing in seedlings from the local nursery. The students took home the tiny plants once we completed the project.

One memorable sunny and carefree morning, Timmy sent out the art cart helpers as I finished in the classroom. I shouted to the two little children to take the cart to Room 9 as they headed out the door. Standing to inspect the room before I left, as I waited for the teacher to reappear, I felt grateful that everything seemed to be going well that day.

Once Ms. Sunn returned, I dashed out to Room 9, thanking the two little children who were skipping back to class after delivering the art cart. All was well, life was going as it should, and the earth was spinning in synchronicity with all things. When I arrived in Room 9, I was greeted with hellos, but the children looked puzzled.

I focused on their faces and asked, "Hey, what's up?"

"Ms. Bickett, why haven't you brought the cart today?"

Stumbling back a little, I turned to my right and left, and sure enough, no art cart.

"But I saw the children returning to the last class; they headed out with the cart and were going back without the cart . . . so I thought it came here!" I explained with confusion.

Where was the art cart?

"Buddy," I said to a blond-haired boy sitting nearby. "Will you please kindly go to Room 23, where I just came from, and ask the children where they delivered the art cart?"

Buddy dashed off, and I sighed. The case of the missing art cart, however, was short-lived. We all turned to face the open door when we heard the clickity-clack of the art cart's wheels with two fifth-grade girls pushing it along. They walked right past the doorway, so I stepped out and shouted, "Hey, you two going someplace with my cart?"

The two young women stopped, and when they saw me, their faces lit up.

"We didn't know where you would be, Ms. Bickett, so we just started pushing the cart back to Room 5."

Suddenly, the two little helpers from Room 23 came running across the blacktop with Buddy. Once they reached me, I queried them, "OK, so, why did you take the cart to Mr. Willow's class? Did you not hear me when I said Room 9?"

I was asking with a smile, so they knew they were not in trouble. I was curious!

"I didn't hear you! And Becky here," little Mary said, pointing to her classmate, "was sure you said Room 12!"

I laughed and patted them both on the back.

"The cart has been found. Thank you for coming, now scoot back to class!"

Off they flew as the fifth-grade girls steered the cart into Room 9. I bowed to them with gratitude and checked the clock. We lost about ten minutes! No matter; everything went well. Fortunately, this class was before lunch, so I had a few extra minutes without rushing to tidy up. And, from that day on, I made sure I was very clear about the art cart's destination before it disembarked from one room to the next.

To make the year special, I had written and received a grant from an education foundation so that an artist could come to repaint our school mascot, the peregrine falcon. My fifth graders participated in creating bird designs and helped the artist complete the mural. The peregrine falcon is still on the wall by the office in front of the school.

Lesson: Teach what you love.

To summarize my second year at Creek Side, I composed a poem about an experience I had with a fourth-grade boy:

"Spiraling"

A fourth-grade boy
Came to me and said,
"You know, Ms. Bickett, when you
put a seashell to your ear
it's just your blood flowing in your head
making that sound. It is not
really the ocean."

I smiled at him,
His hands clutching the seashell,
His eyes fierce with knowledge
As he walked away
Pleased with himself.

One day, I pray,
He will
Discover the sea inside the shell
Once again.

The Third Year, 2008:

RENEWAL AND GROWTH

Our Flea Adventure

In August, just before school was to begin, I wanted to get into the school garden before classes began. Brian and I were working on some repairs (he was fixing a broken archway) while I did some weeding in the raised beds. The day had been hot, so we had headed over to the school in the early evening after dinner when the air began to cool. Lizzie accompanied us and waited with some impatience under a shady tree in the garden. With her tennis ball in her mouth, she watched us as we worked for a little over an hour.

"Brian, time to call it quits!" I said, brushing off some dirt from my shorts. Eyeing the sun's angling toward the horizon and Lizzie's expectant expression, I realized we owed her a few ball tosses in the field before heading home in the dim light of dusk.

Tree frogs were beginning to chorus by the creek, heralding a giant wave of relief from the relentless heat of the day. We locked the gates to the garden, and Brian proceeded to throw the tennis ball for Lizzie to retrieve. I was captivated by the sky, watching the sun slip away behind the mountains, and felt great peace in my heart. The warm glow of sunlight illuminated Lizzie's golden hair in a bright halo. How I treasured the sight of her prancing across the field with complete abandon. It doesn't take much for a dog to be happy!

My thoughts drifted from Lizzie's rapture to my work. I was excited about my third year at Creek Side and looked forward to seeing the children again. Immersed in my bliss, I was awakened from my reverie by Brian's voice.

"Hey, she's rolling in something!" he called.

Turning to see what he was talking about, my eyes widened in horror as I saw Lizzie happily rolling in something over by the fence. Something instinctually warned me this was not a good sign. She was way too exuberant. It could only mean one thing. As I ran toward her, I could smell a terrible stench, most likely from something quite dead.

Off we rushed toward our deliriously happy dog. The smell was beyond comprehension as we dragged Lizzie off of the decomposing body of a baby possum! The blue shadows of evening began to darken as we ran home with our horrifically pungent dog in tow. In the dark, I did my best to hose Lizzie off in the backyard. A little shampoo, brushing, and conditioner with fragrance, and I figured it was all over. Not so. Within twenty-four hours, much to our horror, our lovely golden gal was covered with thousands of fleas.

To make matters worse, we discovered Lizzie was allergic to fleabites! Months of pest control visits (I even found fleas in our bedroom!) and a hefty vet bill followed our flea adventure. The flea treatment I always gave Lizzie every month wasn't strong enough to take care of all the fleas that overwhelmed her body. While researching fleas, I discovered that fleas reside on possums with a vengeance. The mother possum has to keep moving her babies because the nests are so infested. I read about all the diseases connected to fleas and fleabites. I looked at a flea (dead, of course) under a magnifying lens. The devil himself could not look more wicked.

Brian promptly visited the schoolyard the day following our flea experience to scoop up the dead possum with a shovel. He then put it in a garbage bag and threw it into the nearest dumpster. With the start of school just days away, we didn't want children to encounter the sight (and smell!). I could imagine other mischiefs that could well occur with curious elementary children.

Once again, I was assigned to teach second, fourth, and fifth grades, along with my two enrichment programs. After doing a little traveling over the summer, I felt stoked (as they say in California) and ready to rock with new art lessons and, of course, creek walks.

There was the usual meet and greet with colleagues before the first day of school as classrooms were being readied, and I prepped my art cart once again. Ramona and Melissa teased me about my wacky cart as I decorated it with pride. By this time, I rather liked the idea of being a traveling teacher and not having the responsibility of maintaining a classroom. After all, what choice did I have? Since I had decided to view the cup half full instead of half empty, it made my job easier. Although, I reminded myself that I would wish for my own room again when the wind and rains returned that winter as I pushed the cart through puddles and battened down the hatches. I paused as I completed the refreshed cart and envisioned myself on a small watercraft, sailing across the lake of the playground to my next class during a storm. Maybe an art room wouldn't be so bad.

Many of my second graders had been in my first-grade enrichment program the previous year, so I knew at least a few names and faces. As I entered my first class, all fresh and excited, a student I did not recognize jumped up.

"Hey! You came as another lady last year. You cut your hair and dyed it black!" she yelled.

"Really?" I replied, pretending not to know what she was talking about. The little girl tilted her head and pressed on.

"Yes, and you were also a bat and someone else who looked very old!"

I shook my head and smiled with a wink. Funny to think of what the kids remembered, even the ones I didn't have in art classes.

We started out drawing summer memories into the shape of a mandala. A petite dark-haired boy from India was stumped; he just didn't know what to draw.

"Reyansh," I began, trying to encourage him. "What did you do this summer?"

We talked about his trip to India, his visits with relatives, games with his brothers and sisters, yet nothing seemed to appeal to him. Looking at the time, I shrugged my shoulders.

"Well, if you can't think of anything, just draw a cow!" I said jokingly.

And you know what? He did just that!

A perky red-haired girl hopped up to me as I was about to leave at the end of class. She tugged at my shirt and handed me a little picture of the sun. Her name was Rebecca, and she was one of my first graders last year.

"Ms. Bickett, I made something this summer because you inspired me about the sun last year," she said.

I hesitated, as I didn't recall exactly what I had said about the sun. Still, obviously something I said stuck with her. Rebecca told me about a sun painting she made at home and how much her mother loved it. I was so glad she remembered even if I didn't!

The first week flew by with renewed encounters, like the one with a now-fifth-grade student. Will caught me outside during recess, and we engaged in a discussion about Leonardo da Vinci. I teased him by saying, "Well, you never know. He may come for a visit this year!"

Will stepped back with a puzzled expression as a couple of other students joined us.

"But he's dead!" he announced back to me.

A girl who was next to him blurted out with a sly smile, "Oh, you know, like Georgia O'Keeffe came last year . . ."

Suddenly, the students were all smiling and winking at each other and then at me. I realized I was going to have to reprise all of my 'aka roles' this year and maybe invent a new one!

It felt like a new beginning, even though I'd been at Creek Side for two years. I was delighted with the chance to start all over again. I recognized my renewed energy and enthusiasm as a gift, and I prayed the joy would stay with me throughout the year. There were experiences, though, that could weigh you down and misdirect your focus from the children.

Every year I requested a copy of class lists from the teachers I would be working with. At that time, I wasn't aware I could have obtained this information from the secretary, who always seemed way too busy to stop and do anything extra anyway. Therefore, I wrote a polite note and put it in teachers' mailboxes, asking for their student lists whenever they had them, no hurry.

One afternoon before I left school, I encountered a teacher in the workroom who was furious about my request. I stood and listened to her tell me, in detail, how she was *way* too busy to make one photocopy of her class list for me. In the time it took for her to tell me this, she could have made a hundred copies. We're all human. Sometimes we just need to feel heard. Teachers have a great deal to do. I completely understood her feelings, regardless of how little sense it made.

Lesson: Learn to laugh and let it go!

"Excuse me, would the owner of . . ."

I had a little sandy-haired boy, Shane, in my second-grade class. Like Timmy, who wasn't in my classes that year, Shane was very sensitive and had emotional difficulties. I was often drawn to children like this, feeling the need for an individual, tender relationship. Everyone benefitted, as behavior issues that could and did arise in class could be more readily resolved if I knew how to connect with the student and redirect a potential outburst. Hence, Shane and I sometimes walked together at recess or at lunch. I began to see his incredible artistic talent and intuitiveness. He just couldn't handle much frustration and didn't get along well with the other students.

On our first creek walk that autumn, Shane fell in love. He was simply enamored with the creek, the trees, and the animals there. I listened to him talk as we strolled along the trail, and I was tickled by his attempt to share an experience with me.

"When I was a little boy . . ." he began.

Listening carefully to his tale, I couldn't help but smile at the thought that he was apparently no longer a "little boy"! For the next few months, Shane always talked about the need to name the creek. He wanted a contest, then, no; *he* wanted to be the one to name the stream. Finally, I asked him to tell me what he'd like to call the creek, and he replied, "Grandfather Creek." And that sounded good enough for me.

One magical day, as we sat in the arms of Hummingbird Hollow, I overheard two girls talking. Mary Beth said, "The creek is like a museum!" Alyssa countered, "No, it *is* a museum!"

How lovely it was to listen to their heartfelt dialogue! Just then, little Ricky came up to me and proudly displayed his steel-toed boots and said, "I wore these just for today!"

A few of the children in this class came to the creek with me last year as first graders in my enrichment program. I was most impressed with the things they remembered.

"Hey, where's the tea tree?" Rebecca asked. She remembered the elderberry tree where I had pointed out that I made tea out of the elder bow blossoms.

I read the Onondaga story, "The Earth on Turtle's Back," from the book: *Keepers of the Earth* by Michael Caduto and Joseph Bruchac, to my first-grade enrichment students later one warm day in September. We explored creation stories, and I developed questions to ask for comprehension practice. The meaning of this story was very poignant for me. A tree had to be uprooted because of a dream the queen had. The queen leaned over, curious to see what was in the hole in the sky. Then she fell into the water world.

According to the Onondaga, the earth was created on the back of an enormous turtle. Various water animals attempted to bring up some soil from the bottom of the ocean, where the pregnant queen lived and thrived. Destruction was an integral part of how life recreated itself. Straightforwardly, I showed my students how destruction in nature nourishes the earth for new things to grow. The amazing thing was how simple this seemed to be for the first graders and how easily they grasped the concept.

The weather that September and early October was scorching. I was waiting for a class of fifth graders to return to their class after a PE session outside. How refreshing it was, for a change, to enter a classroom before the kids; the silence was soothing as I waited for them. As the children clamored into the room, I was forewarned, "Ms. Bickett, we're all smelly!" I was hesitant to tell them, as parents began to arrive to chaperone, that after they quenched their thirst, we were heading back out into the heat to the creek.

The news that the art class was to be at the creek that day (they were told last week, but not everyone remembered) was greeted with happy cheers. No problem with the heat! I guided them to the delicious shade under Grandmother Oaktree. I pointed out birds and shared how many kinds of hawks and falcons hung out here. We talked about why the birds of prey might like this area (voles, mice, squirrels, and other birds). I shared with them some anecdotes of hawk encounters I'd had in the past when quite out of the blue, a girl, Liza, shouted, "Look!"

We looked up to where she was pointing and lo and behold, on a low, thick branch of Grandmother Oaktree, sat a Cooper's hawk! All that time, the bird was listening to us. The raptor eyed us with great interest. She was not a bit startled by our presence. Everyone was silent and as still as the bird. I had to interrupt this serendipitous encounter with the sad news that it was time to leave. We tiptoed away as the bird watched us.

Liza asked me on the way back to class, "What was she doing up there?"

"Hm, maybe wondering if we were edible or not!" I joked. Talk about timing!

Finally, the weather started to cool off in October. I was in a second-grade classroom, and it was the first class of the day. The children were getting settled after the teacher took roll, and I was unpacking the art cart. We all stopped what we were doing, as there was an announcement over the intercom. The classroom teacher hadn't left yet, so she and I were standing by each other as we listened. "Excuse me. Would the owner of the white vulva please move their car . . ." the voice of the principal trailed off, and there was a stifled silence.

Mrs. Swanson and I looked at each other wide-eyed and did our best not to giggle. Then, the loudspeaker came back on with some muffled laughter in the background, and the principal began again.

"Would the person driving the white Volvo please move their car? You are blocking the main driveway."

Mrs. Swanson scurried off in a hurry, suppressing her laughter as I began the art lesson. I thought of the fact that folks in the surrounding neighborhood could often hear announcements over the loudspeaker. I wondered if anyone was drinking their morning coffee and listening to this one! We all laughed about it later with the principal, who was utterly embarrassed at her slip. I was driving my car later in the day and had to pull over because I was laughing so hard as I remembered the funny way the day got started. Luckily, the joke was lost on the second graders!

The next class didn't go as well though. The same teacher who gave me grief about asking for class lists was someone who, shall I say, could be a bit terse at times. I did my best to work around her as she often stayed in the classroom when I was teaching. From time to time, she would shout out a comment to a student—most usually a scolding—while I was teaching. I didn't particularly appreciate her doing that, though I never said anything. I reminded myself to pick my battles and let this go. Ms. Lang wasn't someone I cared to tussle with. She was very condescending at times and quick to argue. I sighed to myself: *Oh well, that's just her.*

This morning during the art class, Ms. Lang, without my knowledge, permitted Shane to leave the classroom for some reason. I was presenting my lesson, and up and out he started to go. Without any time to consider the situation, I asked Shane where he was headed. Shane appeared upset by the confusion. As I said, Shane was easily shaken, so gently, not forcefully, assured him that I just needed to know when any child leaves the room.

Suddenly, I saw he was getting rattled as he paced back and forth and said, "Well, Ms. Lang said I could leave . . ."

The teacher was staring at me with stern eyes. Realizing we were in an awkward situation, I nodded to Shane, saying, "Of course you may leave, Shane, I didn't realize you'd already asked Ms. Lang."

Fortunately, this problem didn't happen every week, but it occurred enough times with other students in her classroom that it became uncomfortable for me. I wrestled with the fact that students could get caught between two teachers and did my best to stay alert to what she was telling them. Eventually, I found time with her and mentioned softly how much I'd appreciate it if she'd let me be in charge when I was there. I offered how great it was for her to not have that responsibility during her prep time. And you know what? It wasn't a problem after that. I realized how my ego had been a little bruised. After all, I was a seasoned teacher with thirty-five-plus years' experience and wondered if it was a matter of her not trusting me. But my competence wasn't the issue, and it felt so good to be free of the whole affair. Too many cooks don't work well in the classroom or anywhere else for that matter.

As I walked home from school that day, I encountered shards of glass from a beer bottle on the path behind the school. I was happily tired, so I wanted to go home and ignore the mess. Taking a deep breath, though, I went back to find the custodian and then returned to the scene with a broom and dustpan, a garbage bag, and some gloves. Muttering to myself (it was long after school was let out, there were no children nearby), I thought of all the times I'd witnessed parents literally stepping over trash as they walked their child to school over the footbridge area. I couldn't always pick up trash because my hands were full, or it was too messy at the time, but I did my best to return and clean up what I could.

Children need to see that someone cares. We are living models for our students and children. What does all the trash say? When I was done with my chore, I completed my walk home with a sense that what I did mattered. I hope so.

Lesson: Show you care.

Art Sans Glue

It was now nearing Halloween. I mentioned to my fifth-grade students that we would be creating *nichos* (little shrines) in celebration of the *Dia de los Muertos*, Day of the Dead. In classes where I taught this lesson, it was always so gratifying to see the faces of my Mexican American students light up. Little Enrique, who barely ever spoke up in class, became animated and eagerly told his classmates the story behind the holiday.

"The nichos," he explained, "are little altars where you put pictures of someone you loved who died. And then you decorate it with things they loved. Sometimes the nichos are small and others can be bigger."

He was just beaming and full of pride. I thanked him in Spanish and brought out photographs of nichos and a few examples I had made. My Spanish-speaking students really liked it when I spoke in their native tongue, as I also attempted to teach some Spanish words to the rest of the class.

The day we created our nichos, I was walking around and discussing with the children their work, as I often did. Jim, a talented art student, explained to me after I ask about his piece, "This one is for my mother. She just died before school started this year of lung cancer. When I grow up, I am going to become a doctor and find a cure for cancer."

His nicho had a little airplane on it, and Jim further explained, "It is an airplane taking my message up to heaven to her."

Moments like this one affirmed why I became a teacher. This profoundly touching encounter opened and broke my heart. I will never forget Jim and wonder if he ever became a doctor.

To put the icing on the cake of the season (pumpkin cake, that would be), I dressed up as Frida Kahlo again. As I walked across campus, I heard a nonstop chorus of voices yelling, "Hey, Frida!" The children who remembered Frida from last year sparkled with smiles. In fact, it seemed everyone I passed smiled at me. How nice! Being Frida seemed to make everyone happy. I thoroughly enjoyed the day, and when I rubbed my aching feet at home, I was pleased, too.

For my little language development children, I brought my raven puppet to school. Brian had bought it for me on a trip to Santa Fe a couple of years earlier. We often listened to the crows when we were walking around campus, and I taught the children how to 'talk crow.' One day, the principal and a guest walked by as we were all cawing at some birds in a nearby tree. Little Albert turned to me and said, "Ms. Bickett, I heard the crow talking, and he was telling me he was going to his school!" When we reached the classroom, I got out the raven puppet that talked to the children.

Our guest raven captivated the students. A little boy's hand went up, and I called on him. His question, "Is he real?" took me by surprise.

"Well, he's a real puppet!" I replied. I ended up keeping the raven puppet at school for not only the rest of the year but until my very last day at Creek Side because he was such a great hit with the children.

After Halloween, I dressed up as Georgia O'Keeffe again, reprising her role with a new art lesson. The questions were hilarious, "Is that make-up?" "Is that your real hair?" This question was particularly funny because I was wearing a long gray wig. My real hair was dark brown and shoulder-length! And the fact that they had to ask if I was wearing make-up as well was perhaps a bit telling of my age as I drew in lots of wrinkles.

In November, we watched Andy Goldsworthy create his sculptures again, this time, with new students, of course. The artist worked painstakingly on his ephemeral pieces that melted or floated away or got carried away by the wind.

At the end of the video, Henry, a curious and intelligent boy, raised his hand. I called on him, and he asked with great amazement, "Why does he *do* that?"

I didn't answer him. Instead, I suggested that the entire class could think about the answer to Henry's question. We would talk about it next time. I wanted the students to come up with ideas. Besides, I could guess why Goldsworthy created his temporary sculptures, but only the artist could enlighten us.

We went outside the following week after working on ideas with partners, and Henry came up to me and declared, "I guess he did all that work because it was fun!"

His face was joyful as he hopped and skipped back to join his team, which was assembling a large pile of rocks into a giant circle. None of the other students appeared to remember we were going to discuss the matter of the artist's motivation. It was OK because they were very engaged in their creations, and we didn't have time for a group conversation that day anyway. And I was impressed that Henry seemed to deduce a plausible reason for the artist's transitory creations.

Later that day, Nell, a girl in another class, came up to me after she finished her sculpture with her group. They created a lovely piece comprised of branches and leaves.

"It's fantastic to assemble something without having to use glue or anything else," she said. We agreed; many times, simple is best. The echoes of joy from this day are still with me, a treasure.

It was a warm November afternoon, and I was walking home, tired but grateful. Besides all that I had to do, something heavy had been weighing on my mind that month. I was sad about my sister Betsy, who had recently been diagnosed with breast cancer. I was born in January 1956 and Betsy was born on December 31 later that same year, so we were often referred to as "the twins." Being the older sister, I felt a protectiveness for my sister and offered prayers for her recovery and well-being. That next spring, for Easter, I would visit her in Minnesota. Suddenly, a graceful white egret flew overhead and glided through the trees along the creek before it disappeared. This was the first time I'd ever seen an egret by the stream behind the school. The bird's presence was like a dream. Its angelic wings seemed to lift me along to my home, and it felt like a good omen. Indeed, my sister survived her painful ordeal with cancer and now enjoys her grandchildren in good health.

Lesson: Behold the moments of grace.

Careers

We were exploring various careers of people at school in my kindergarten classes. I had the usual curriculum that explored what it would be like to become a doctor, lawyer, nurse, librarian, firefighter, etc., complete with great photos. However, I felt that for authentic learning to take place, the lessons needed to be personalized and relate to the children's experiences.

My son Jacques came as a guest to give the unit an engaging start. He brought his bass and played for the children and gave them each a chance to play the instrument. It was so cute to watch them 'play' the bass, and I couldn't help but notice how patient my son was with them. From then on, the children asked about Jacques a lot. Later, I commandeered him into coming to school for Thanksgiving dressed as the turkey! Brian decided to abdicate his role, and I was delighted when my son stepped up to the plate . . . so to speak.

The following week, my flock of kiddies and I floated around the school, interviewing any adult willing to give us a few minutes of his/her time. The children were excited. The personnel on the campus, including custodian and school librarians, were very accommodating.

We came up with questions we wanted to ask each person we would interview. Before we were to meet with the principal, Mrs. Heart, to discuss her job (the children found it easier to say "job" than "career"), I thought I'd go over what we had discussed in class.

"What does Mrs. Heart do? What is her job?" I asked the children as we huddled in a circle while we waited to see her.

There was a long silence, and I inquired what their little brains were thinking. They seemed to be having some difficulty answering my question. Finally, Miguel, who really seemed to be struggling with the answer, piped up.

"Well, she always helps us at lunchtime, so she must be the lunch lady!" he exclaimed.

"Mrs. Heart helps tell cars where to go to let children off," announced Abeba, a quiet girl whose family had recently immigrated from Ethiopia.

"The principal lady picks up trash at recess," offered Tran, a sweet Vietnamese boy with a bright smile. "I know, I've seen her!"

Smiling, I realized that, of all the jobs at school, the principal's career was an enigma to these students.

"Why, you are all correct!" I confirmed. "Mrs. Heart does all those things. I wonder what else she might do?"

They truly did not understand what exactly she did. When I asked about the other positions at the school, they had difficulty responding. Later, when I shared with Mrs. Heart the children's perception of what she did at school we both laughed.

The children came out of the interview with a much more unobstructed view about what the principal does all day. Though Miguel queried me as we left, "Mrs. Heart does all that *and* helps at lunch?"

The children were genuinely impressed with the myriad of tasks she orchestrated throughout the day.

December at Creek Side was always a lot of fun. With the holidays looming ahead of us, it seemed everyone was in a good mood. I truly enjoyed the staff. My fellow teachers were thoughtful and kind. So far this year, they were very accommodating in terms of some art space in their rooms, and the children were ready and waiting in their seats when I arrived to start the art class. I began to form individual bonds with a few of them and felt at home at Creek Side.

Melissa, the PE teacher, and I sometimes ate lunch together and got together occasionally with another teacher for tea. When possible, I would join the other teachers for lunch in the lunchroom, though most often, my lunches were at home to take care of Lizzie. Teachers would pause in the hallways to chat briefly, and I frequently received encouragement from them. There was a Christmas party planned with gift exchanges. I glowed at the thought that I was a part of this dedicated staff.

I planned a lesson with my second graders after my friend Jan Pitcher came and read from her book, *Where Do the Stars Go?* Everyone decorated a cutout star and wrote their wish on the back. The stars were hung about the classroom or on the student's little desks for a couple of weeks before they took them home. Their wishes were touching. The children wrote things like, "I wish we had more art." "I wish no one would ever be left out." "I wish I had three moms." (Written by a little girl who was adopted). "I wish I could get my dog back." And "I wish everyone had peace in their heart."

These wishes encouraged many stories as we shared our work at the end of the lesson. These kinds of activities always gave me more insight into the lives of my students and helped me to get to know them better. Indeed, though, this was not listed as one of the standards we were required to teach.

As I walked home one cloudy, chilly day that December, I composed the following poem:

> A Day in December
> Sunlight dresses vacant meadows . . .
> Who will see the verdant grasses bathed in soft light?
> A little boy lingers by the creek after school,
> To pause, to wonder . . .
> Who will see this and remember?
> Who will feel the slight breeze and breathe?

In my first-grade enrichment class, we planned a winter party. It was the last day we would meet until January, so I had chosen some entertaining word games to play and some music—I was all set. One of my room moms arrived with chocolates for the children to enjoy. I asked her for the container, first, so I could check the ingredients, as I knew I had a few children in the class who had food allergies. Everything looked OK except for the fact that some of the candies had peanuts. I knew there was one little boy who was allergic to peanuts. At first, I told the mom we could not use the candy. I had small prizes I'd bought for the children as I had tried very hard to avoid giving out food. There were too many allergic kids, and I didn't want to deal with the matter. I left that to the classroom teachers to struggle with.

However, this mother did not give up. After listening to her pleas, I finally acquiesced and agreed on a strategy. I would explain to the allergic child that, although he couldn't eat any of these candies today, I would personally bring him a unique candy cane tomorrow. He seemed fine with the deal. At the end of class, the mom distributed the chocolate morsels to the children. I was busy but also trying to keep an eye on our peanut guy, just in case. I glanced away to monitor two students working out a conflict about their treats. When I returned to my vigilance, the little peanut-allergic boy gobbled down a piece of candy he had appropriated from another child. It happened very fast, and I didn't have time to snatch the forbidden treat.

My jaw dropped as I raced toward him. I had him spit it out and rinse his mouth quickly at the sink.

"What were you doing?" I asked, perplexed, as he clearly understood there might be peanuts in the candy and that we had an agreement about the candy cane.

"Sandy didn't want her piece, so she gave it to me," he explained.

I shook my head and realized I was to blame. How foolish it was for me to think a little first-grade child could resist a piece of candy, regardless of what he'd promised. I'd allowed the mother's wishes to override my gut feeling about the matter. I fell into my habit of not wanting to disappoint people. As a result, the allergic boy's mouth began to itch, so I rushed him to the office. Thank goodness class was over, and I could reach his mother at home. The nurse gave him some Benadryl, and all was well. But I swore never again to offer food or treats of any kind at school! And I learned to say NO (albeit politely) to a parent when I felt pressured!

The last kindergarten class before the break, I brought Lizzie to visit. Little Camilla was petting Lizzie and saying how afraid she'd always been of dogs. Tran was amazed when I told the children that Lizzie was the same age as they were. After thinking about it for a moment, he looked at me with great seriousness and said, "But Lizzie is older." I think he was referencing 'dog years'! The children always seemed to think of all the possibilities.

I was discouraged by something that happened with my fourth-grade art classes before the break, though. A poster depicting a woman that the students had examined was returned with some snickering. There were giant breasts drawn on the chest of the woman in the painting. At first in my mind, I downplayed it as an innocent prank. But then, I wondered. Perhaps this could be a teachable moment.

I tried to make the students aware that drawing the breasts was disrespectful and we talked about how important it was to respect women (and works of art, for that matter). Of course, no one accepted responsibility for this action, and I left the classroom quite unsure that anyone understood my point. With so much misogyny in this world, I wanted to help the children be aware of even subtle, and perhaps unconscious, negative attitudes about girls and women. I felt at least I did my best to bring up the matter with the children in the way I could in a public-school classroom. I didn't scold or make a big fuss out of it, but I did make it clear why it bothered me.

I dragged my feet at the end of the day, still bothered by the whole issue. Then the happy, smiling faces of children getting ready for winter break, along with the many hugs I was barraged with in the hallways, helped me to let it go. It was that mixed bag of life and teaching, for school is indeed a microcosm of the world we live in. I dealt with the unpleasantries along with the joys. They seemed to interplay continuously every day, side by side, as I walked through my life as a teacher and as a human being.

Lesson: Listen to your inner guide.

A New Year

It was January, and my birthday was on the sixth. Unfortunately, I came down with a stomach ailment that kept me home that Wednesday. The next day, when I returned to teach my older students, I was bombarded with a vast entourage of kids asking me, "Were you *really* sick on your birthday?" I had no idea that the teachers and students knew about my special day, let alone that I had called in sick. Funny, again, how word got around fast! I answered their questions truthfully.

"Yes, I was home with a tummy ache," I replied, only to witness their heads shaking, smiling faces, and winks at each other as if they comprehended bluff. With exasperation, I endured the day's inquiries and muttered to myself, "If only I hadn't been ill!"

The Vietnamese New Year arrived, and the kindergarten teachers arranged an exuberant parade around the blacktop area of the playground and invited everyone at school to come to watch. It was such a lovely sunny day, and I had just finished teaching my first-grade enrichment group. I stepped out to watch the brightly clad kiddies proudly walking around, following their teachers like little ducklings. My kindergarten students waved at me with precious broad smiles. I was so proud of them! Most unexpectedly, little Leon broke from his line and came running up to me, gave me a big hug, and said, "Isn't this a beautiful day?" He trotted back before his teacher saw his detour and beamed back at me with a big wave. What a gift!

HeArt: it was nearing Valentine's Day, and my second graders were energetically painting hearts with tempera paints. I showed the children examples of Jim Dine's work—colorful, boldly painted hearts. They created brilliant works of art that I proudly displayed at both the district and our school office. During the class, a discussion ensued about the philosophical nature of love, and Rebecca announced emphatically, "If you love someone, you won't disrespect them!" I thought that was excellent insight from a little girl.

February flew by, and in March, there was a talent show. There was a flock of teachers, led by Ramona, the music instructor, who would be dancing to the *Flash Dance* tune, "What a Feeling." I was tempted to join them, but I was quite busy. I had an art show to prepare for and needed to focus on an acrylic wolf series I'd recently begun. The teachers met in our shared Room 5 after school, so I paused to watch them learn their steps after I had finished putting away supplies. The show was only a few days away, and they were working diligently so they would be ready. As I was about to leave, I got cornered with an urgent request to step in and dance with them.

"We've just lost someone who had to bow out due to illness," Ramona explained. "Won't you join us?"

I sighed and realized I really would enjoy the opportunity, as I loved to dance. I replied with an enthusiastic "Yes!" Perhaps I had been waiting for them to ask me to join in all along. I put down my carrying case and jumped in right then and there. We needed to practice every day after school if we were going to be ready.

The night of the performance, I couldn't believe I was really dancing in front of the entire school, but I admit it was great fun. My colleagues were impressed that I picked up the steps so quickly. I didn't tell them I once took ballet and modern dance years ago. The curtain opened, and we swirled and hopped about in unison. It was exhilarating! I saw familiar faces in the crowd and smiled. Apparently, no one knew we would be dancing that evening, so the group was especially surprised to see teachers, and the principal, all dancing on the stage! After the show was over, children came up to me to say, "I *knew* it was you!"

The fierce March rain and wind also performed for us that evening. I bundled up and ran for my car as parents and students caught up with me to tell me how great the dancing was. I felt like I was on the Red Carpet for the Academy Awards! For weeks afterward, I heard over and over from my students how happy they were to see us dancing. I never knew it would mean so much to the children. I think it gave them a chance to see us as something other than their teachers in the classroom, offering them a different side they didn't often see. Teachers are, after all, human beings who like to have fun, too.

All the following week, it rained heavily, so I wore my oversized rain boots and trench coat. As I was struggling to hold down rustling papers and materials on the art cart, once again, a student bounded up to help me. On these stormy days, I didn't allow the children to push the cart to the next class, as I didn't like the thought of them getting all wet. The playground blacktop became quite saturated with water, and I trudged through the black lakes like a heaving barge. I asked little Amy where she was going, and she replied, "I'm on my way to the bathroom, and I just wanted to ask you something."

"OK," I replied. "What's up?"

Amy pushed her hood up so she could see me as we trudged along and said, "What if you didn't come one day? What would happen? What would we do?"

I stopped in my soggy tracks and looked at her, surprised and curious. Where was this coming from?

"Why, Amy, if I was not here, I would get a substitute, and I would be back the next week." She smiled as we continued with our trek. When we parted under the eaves, Amy looked relieved and waved goodbye as I thanked her. I didn't have time right then to explore this further, but her anxiety was quite palpable, quite real. I never did figure it out, and I didn't bring it up again, and neither did Amy. Perhaps she loved the art classes so much that she couldn't imagine them not being a part of the curriculum. Maybe she just needed reassurance, or perhaps she had bonded with me in some way I didn't realize.

A Friday in March, when things were drying out a bit, Lizzie and I went to the local dog park. Of course, my golden girl was always attracted to children, so I was not concerned when I 'lost' her to a little boy. As I watched him toss the ball for her, I started to wonder why he wasn't in school. I had Fridays off because I worked only Mondays through Thursdays. I knew why *I* was there, but this little guy was about seven years old, and either he was being homeschooled, or he was sick. His mother was nearby with their dog, chatting with some other women, not paying too much mind to her son. The child noticed me watching him and approached me with a question.

"Why are we here?"

I opened my eyes wide with surprise and confusion, not sure what he meant.

"What do you mean? Here at the park?" I asked.

Scratching his little chin, he paused and then continued, "No, just *here*, I mean, what are we doing *here*?" Before I could engage this most extraordinary child any further, his mother called to him.

"Bye!" He waved to me as he ran up to her, leaving me standing there to wonder.

Did he mean *here* on the planet? In this life? In San Jose? I will never forget the look on his face and the genuine earnestness of his inquiry. I never would expect such a question from a child, but then, this event caused me to reconsider that notion. This experience, for me, has fallen into the category of one of those angelic moments when I felt I'd been visited by someone/something special that brought a message to me. Trouble is, I'm not sure I got the message. Perhaps he really wanted to know why we are here on this earth. Maybe he figured *I'd* know. Who knows?

Lesson: Let them see your humanity.

Another Chapter

On a particularly hectic morning, I was following the art cart managers down the hallway with only a few minutes to spare. I had five minutes between classes, and on this day, I felt rushed and tense because I felt like I couldn't keep up with the schedule. It was a Thursday, and I had encountered some behavioral challenges with a couple of my fifth-grade students that delayed my departure from my first class. I needed to mediate an argument between two girls who seemed much too sophisticated for fifth graders in terms of their language.

Some of the girls seemed to be growing up too fast. I shook my head as I considered they were beginning to look like seventh graders! A few, as I had to look twice, appeared to be wearing eye make-up and lipstick! *I* didn't even wear make-up to school! I was heading down the hallway caught up in the resolution of their conflict and not really paying much attention to the children blurring along. A class of first graders was passing by on their way to the library. Little Robby stopped right in front of me, so I had to stop and focus on him. I was partly irritated because I was in a hurry to get to my next class, so I hoped whatever he wanted was quick.

"Hey, Ms. Bickett, you look like you are having a good day!"

Suddenly, everything shifted. I didn't know what to say as Robby skipped off to rejoin his class. I stood there, almost dropping the folder I was carrying, and watched him disappear into the library. Turning to continue my walk, somehow, everything felt softer, more at peace. I didn't hurry and still reached the classroom on time. Instead of seeing a room full of challenges and potentially naughty children, instead of feeling discouraged, I saw a room full of eager faces brightening up when I entered. I realized how they might actually be looking forward to seeing me and that I had power over how things would go that day. A cup was sitting on the teacher's desk, and, quite clearly, it was half full. How welcoming it was to get an attitude adjustment before I let a few disheartening issues destroy a perfectly good day.

The rest of the day went quite smoothly, and I was reminded how my own attitude really mattered. I was disappointed in myself for letting the girls' quarrel get under my skin. I thought back to what had upset me, and I realized I still took things too personally. They were just kids, after all.

The next week with my kinder kids, Leon announced, "I am getting a lot of new brothers today!" His family was from Mexico. Apparently, a few cousins were arriving that day to live with Leon and his family. We engaged in a discussion about families as I listened to each child share something about how many siblings they had, brothers, sisters, stepsiblings, and cousins. Kyle said to me that his older sister was quite definitely a hundred years old! At first, I thought Kyle must be talking about a much older sister. Kyle assured me, however, that he was talking about his older sister, who I happened to have in fifth-grade art class! I didn't even want to guess how old he thought *I* was.

I read to the children a book called *Grandmother's Dreamcatcher*, the tale of a little child who visits her Chippewa grandmother in the Midwest. This is a delightful story that focuses not only on the tender relationship this child has with her grandmother but the traditional story of dream catchers. The story goes that the catcher traps bad dreams like a spiderweb catches insects and prevents them from seeping down while you sleep beneath it at night. Only the pleasant dreams find their way to the sleeper through the string and feathers.

I gathered willow branches and created twenty little dream catchers (for all my kindergarteners), trying to make them look as authentic as possible.

Years ago, I taught my seventh graders how to make dream catchers using grapevines. This was no easy task, so it would not have been appropriate to even try to explain the lesson to the kindergarten children. Each dream catcher I made with love for my little ones. I was excited to give the children their presents.

The following week, Kyle came up to me, very upset.

"That dream catcher you gave me doesn't work! I had a bad dream! My mommy wanted to throw it away, but I told her I wanted to keep it!"

I felt terrible, never having encountered this problem before (and I've given hundreds of dream catchers away over the years). I struggled with how to help him.

"I'm very sorry that happened, Kyle. Maybe some bad dreams help us because they show us our fears, help us see and face them," I said gently. Then, I waited as Kyle thought about this for a little while before he replied.

"But I already *knew* I was afraid of monsters!"

Some things you just must let go.

This was a year I was being evaluated, and though, at first, I was not thrilled with the idea, I had to admit it did make me stop and think about what I was teaching and how I could improve. Our wonderful principal evaluated us not only for our personnel files but to help us grow and be the best we could be for the children. I appreciated Mrs. Heart's suggestions and feedback. The days she observed my art lessons, I felt nervous that she was noticing every little detail, writing away while I was teaching. She didn't miss the humor, either, as we laughed about some unexpected things the kids did, always something to smile about with a roomful of young students!

Teachers were supposed to be evaluated every other year. Still, I was told, after so many years of excellent evaluations, we could choose to go to the five-year rotation. I found out that this was not, in reality, even an option. I had to go through the process once again. I didn't mind so much in the end. I was grateful for the insights and did make changes based on the principal's suggestions.

In a second-grade class, we were reviewing the color wheel before we started a new lesson. Teaching—and learning—involves plenty of reviews and remembering concepts taught previously. It can be a challenge for teachers to keep ideas fresh and reinforce the themes before introducing new lessons. So, after I went through a review, a little girl, Bina, asked, "Who invented the color wheel?"

I replied jokingly, "Well, I did, actually."

The class sat staring at me, and I was reminded that I needed to watch my dry sense of humor with the younger ones. After a chastising by Bina, who frowned at my poor joke, I went on to say, "Well, nature actually did."

This discourse took us on a long journey—from examining colors in nature and where pigments originate to color light theory. How I loved questions like the one Bina asked that day!

In the last week of March, I headed out to the creek with a group of fifth graders. In the mid-morning light, all the birds seemed to be coming alive. We enjoyed standing on the trail and listening to their cries as I announced what kind of bird was making each sound. I was delighted that I happened to know all of them, from the chickadee, the towhee, and the phoebe to the scrub jay. *It was easy,* I thought.

One boy, Arnold, asked me, "How do you know the birds by their song?"

Replying with joy, I answered, "Well, I've spent many years just listening, and eventually, you figure it out. You can do it, too. It just takes time."

Arnold asked what was making noise in the bush next to us. I saw some sparrows hopping around from branch to branch. I showed him.

"You see, you listen for the sound, look for the bird, and if you can, then you recognize, 'Oh, that's a sparrow,' and the sound and the sight get imprinted in your memory," I explained.

I often wondered if Arnold learned a few bird songs over the years.

We had a lot of rain in the third year at Creek Side. I was aware of all the pollen that seemed to be, as my husband said, "All mating in my nose at the same time." I sneezed and heard a chorus of "bless you" as we moved along, the birds chattering around us, the magic as bright as the blue sky above. How I loved the creek walks.

As I was leaving school that last week of March, I was gratified at having done all I could to give my students rewarding and memorable experiences. A little girl named Jesse bounded up to me and gave me a bear hug.

"I just *love* Lizzie!" she said and then skipped away. The funny thing was, she had never met Lizzie. I forgot how popular my beloved golden girl was with the kids at school, even the ones who hadn't met her.

Lesson: Sometimes the magic works; sometimes it doesn't.

Drawing to a Close

April of the third year at Creek Side found me weathering a sinus infection that had sprung from my allergies. Nonetheless, spring was gorgeous, and after the April break, we rode the year-end slide to the final 2008-2009 school year. STAR testing took up a few weeks, and the prep teachers—those of us teaching art, music, and physical education—worked around the schedule as usual.

One fine spring morning, as I walked toward my first class, little Stephanie came up to me and said, "I always have so much fun when you are here!"

I gave her a big thank-you hug and puzzled over her comment. She was in a class that was a challenge for me. I felt I needed to work on my attitude about this group, and her comment created an awareness in me that helped when I taught her class again. When I focused on the present and not on all I had to do, I found it was more fun. Stephanie beamed at me when I came into the room, and I bowed to her and thanked her again.

"I have fun when you are here, too!" I said with gratitude in my heart. Even my sinus pain seemed to diminish, and I felt a little bit of spring fever moving in as a welcome replacement.

My fifth-grade students, with a handful of problematic behaviors to manage, seemed to be more relaxed with all the blossoms and blue sky. Monica, a vibrant and loquacious young lady, slipped me a note with something written on it with a drawing as I was leaving class. She had been mischievous during class and seemed to have excess energy that day. Her teasing of the boys got a little out of hand. All I needed to do was look at her once with a long gaze, and she got the message.

"I love having you as an art teacher," the note read.

It was difficult to see the drawing right then because I exited the room with tears in my eyes. How gratitude does change everything.

My kindergarteners were blossoming as well, quite a change from their shyness at the beginning of the year. I chuckled at their chattering. Kyle, who seemed to have forgiven me for the dream catcher mishap, commented to me sweetly, "I always like the days when I get to see Ms. Bickett. Those are the good days!" Comments like these were something I cherished and remembered when I started to feel frustrated.

My second graders won the Long Marine Lab's contest, first place in the group section that spring. We created *See Lines on the Sea Lions* on large craft paper, featuring marvelous drawings of sea lions as they were resting together. The winning piece was a collage of each child's sea lion created with oil pastels on black or brown papers. The Marine Lab representative assured me each child would receive a prize, albeit a small token. I knew how much it would mean to the children. The problem was that when I got back from driving over the hill to collect the prizes, we were short; there were not enough prizes to go around! Not all the children turned in their permission forms, I realized, so actually, the Marine Lab did send prizes for all who turned in their forms. However, I didn't want to penalize the unfortunate ones in class who didn't get their paperwork in on time. I improvised and bought some little prizes from the Affordable Treasures store.

And yet, after every child in my second-grade art classes received a prize, many of them complained. I was baffled. Apparently, they were disappointed in my little erasers. I simply could not afford anything more; I ended up having to buy quite a few.

This time of year, there was no money left in the art budget. Many expenses came out of my own pocket. I thought of all the effort of driving back and forth over winding Highway 17 several times and going out of my way to buy extra prizes. I felt a bit unappreciated. Then again, it was always best to remind myself they were just children and not to take it personally. Sometimes, you can't win, and you move on.

The second graders worked in teams for a new lesson to create Matisse-inspired compositions with lines, shapes, and colors, using yarn, paper scraps, and posters. At the end of class, after we shared our work, I challenged them to take everything apart so I could reuse the same materials again in the next classes.

"This was the most fun. Thank you!" I heard over and over. The children didn't seem to mind that the entire focus was on the experience, the process of working together on a temporary product. I enjoyed listening to them, laughing, and seeing their enthusiasm. Some misguided administrators consider an excellent classroom to be a quiet one. As I watched the children learn and laugh, I wondered why learning couldn't be more fun.

Of course, emotional engagement facilitates learning. We know that now.

What we experience with our emotions creates lasting memories. It would seem better lessons are encased in joy rather than resentment or drudgery.

At the beginning of the year, I posted a Rumi quote near where the art cart was parked.

It read: "Wherever you are, be the Soul of That Place."

It had been a good reminder all year.

The month of May snuck up on us quickly, and I always liked to ask the children what they liked the best about the school year. One day, while we were returning from a creek walk, I queried my fourth graders.

"What did you like the most about the creek walk today?"

"I loved Hummingbird Hollow."

"I loved the swallowtail butterfly that followed us around."

"I loved the squirrel."

"I loved the rocks."

And last, the most interesting:

"I saw a large branch upside down, and it looked like macaroni and cheese and made me hungry."

Every May, the school PTA treated the faculty to a fancy lunch someplace, usually in downtown San Jose. I arrived late for the event for some reason I can't recall. All the teachers were instructed to choose raffle tickets, and I commented as I drew mine out of the basket, "I never win!" Then, I corrected myself silently, *Oh, no, I didn't think that! Today, I win!*

And I won a movie theater pass, much to my great surprise and glee! I thought of the fact that I was late and couldn't find a parking spot at first, only to have one open right in front of the restaurant. It was a relief to feel things working together in synchronicity.

The last day of school was very hot. As the blazing sun stared down on us, emotions seemed to run high. Daisy, a shy second-grade student, sat crying alone during recess. I figured by now, after an entire school year, conflicts would dissipate.

"What's the matter, Daisy?" I asked tenderly, kneeling beside her.

"No one likes me!" she cried. Daisy told me she played alone most days, and I felt my heart break for her. Here we were at the end of the year, and she had no friends. How did I not notice this? I saw two girls nearby playing jump rope, and so Daisy and I got up and walked over to them.

"May she join you?" I asked.

"Oh, sure!" they responded happily.

As I walked away, I turned to see Daisy smiling as her feet left the ground in the blur of the swinging rope. I hoped that next year I would pay a little more attention to such things as I walked about with the children on campus.

The year's "End of Year Poem" was printed out and given to the teachers. So here it is:

I gaze at the room full of teachers
Talking and laughing at the end-of-year party.
Time has blurred by so fast.
I think of the year, of graciousness,
of being a part of the intricate interplay of humanity.
Each year seems to spin a little faster.
Every moment, a breath.
I ask myself now, how many breaths
did I take this year?
Did I take it all in, or did I push it away?
Did I let things go or hold tight?
Did I frown or smile?
What child did I miss who needed me?
And when did I care too much?

It is all an echo now,
2008-2009 lingers at the corner
then vanishes in a wisp of a breeze.
Or was it a tree branch nodding,
guarding the mystery of time?
A secret in the newly formed blossom,
the cycle complete.

The chatter of voices drifts along,
and sways to summer's lure.
I think of a summer's day, reaching for the
hammock, the novel, and for ice spinning
in golden sun brewed tea.

Once again, for the third time, I parked the defrocked art cart in a solemn corner, but this time in a new room. We, the three prep teachers, had to pack up everything and move to another room, and it was a lot of work at the end of the year when all we wanted to do was go home and be done with it. We were not the only ones who had to move, however. The entire staff eventually got juggled sometime during the next year due to renovation at the school. Finally, every room had air conditioning—a huge factor, in the heated afternoons, in facilitating student learning.

I did my best to leave things organized before I went so that when I returned in the fall for my fourth year at Creek Side, I would be welcomed with ready art supplies. I made out my order for the secretary so some things would arrive before school started. PTA gave me a budget every year that I wasted no time in spending. After teaching well over three hundred children a week, the supplies were in dire need of replacing.

Another year was over. I anticipated a rewarding journey back to South Dakota during that summer to see my mother again. I was looking forward to time swimming at a local pool. But, most of all, I relished the idea that I could rest and replenish my own energy. As I stepped over the threshold into my beautiful home, Lizzie greeted me with her lovely golden smile. I embraced her with a sense of relief and gratitude that lasted me all summer long.

Lesson: It was enough.

The Fourth Year, 2009:

THE YEAR OF MY UNDOING

Begin Again

Taking my large pad of newsprint and setting it up on the easel, I then assembled my Conte crayons, charcoal pieces, and graphite sticks. The artist I was in my twenties, who aspired to master the human figure, was resurrected during weekly figure drawing sessions downtown.

It was a Thursday just before the beginning of my fourth year. Though I was anxious about the many things I needed to accomplish before the first day of school, I happily attended a session to draw with my artist friends. Elizabeth, an extraordinary artist who sat next to me, asked, "How do you do it? Teach and have all that energy?"

I thought of the hours and hours of standing (I never had, in all my years of teaching, ever sat down while teaching other than for a few brief moments), my aching feet, my thirst, and tests of patience . . . then I looked at Elizabeth and said, "I don't know. The summer is just enough time to get revved up again. By late August, you get excited to see the kids and start over again."

I shared with her that, at least this year, I would have the same grade levels again, so no significant changes. That always helped. We drew vigorously together, and I found the intensity and challenge most rewarding. Throughout the year, I frequently met to draw with other artists. Not only was it a great stress reliever, but also, the figure drawing sessions connected me with artist friends and kept my drawing skills sharp. I did find out, however, that this year, I would not be the only art teacher at the school.

There was an art teacher who was at Creek Side before my arrival and was asked not to return due to credential issues. Due to the *No Child Left Behind* legislation instigated during the George Bush era, teachers were given ample notice to become "highly qualified" in their area or they faced either relocating to a different subject or firing, if not tenured.

Mrs. Gibson, a talented and dedicated teacher, was only hired on an hourly basis, and hence, along with other prep teachers, let go. In my fourth year, she was invited back to Creek Side to teach art classes so that every grade level could have art. I thought it was a great idea because I could only teach part-time, and the more art, the better!

They gave her a cart as well, and so from then on, there would be two of us pushing art carts around campus. It was amusing to envision us pushing our carts across the campus, like ships passing each other atop a black sea. However, mine would be the only decorated one. I always admired the quality of the art her students produced and did everything I could to make Mrs. Gibson feel comfortable.

Mrs. Gibson told me a year later how much she appreciated the way I welcomed her back. She seemed almost surprised that I would be so accommodating. Why not? From my point of view, Mrs. Gibson's reappointment at Creek Side was fabulous for everyone. Hooray for our PTA, who paid for her position out of their discretionary funds.

The sparkling new year was about to begin, and we had our first school meetings. I unpacked boxes of supplies I'd ordered before I left in June. Our schedule was completed, and the art cart was shiny and colorful. Everything was ready to go.

Finally, the first day arrived.

A habit I fell into while teaching middle school was to wear mismatched earrings. It was always something that seemed to shake up my students a bit, and this time, it did just that. My awkward, asymmetrical embellishments seem to perturb most of the students.

"Why do you wear two different kinds of earrings, Ms. Bickett?" a fourth-grade girl, Molly, asked me.

I looked at her with a broad smile and replied, "Well, why not?"

Molly smiled back and said with approval, "Oh, I see now!"

By accident once, in my earlier teaching years, I wore mismatched socks, and it also became a sort of game between my students and me. When I arrived, they always checked which socks I had on that day. I decided it would be fun to resurrect this ritual with both earrings and socks that year. In the weeks to come, students, especially my fourth- and fifth-grade girls, quickly checked my ears and socks when I entered the classroom. It almost seemed they were disappointed when my earrings matched!

I obtained large pieces of paper from RAFT for all my students to fold in half to decorate and use as portfolios. After worrying about where we would find space in the classrooms to store them, this time, I somehow managed to secure a spot in every room with the teachers' help.

In one of my second-grade classes, I explained to the children, who were still working on how to fold, that it was kind of magical. It's funny how we take something simple like that for granted. Most of the children struggled with the task.

"Watch and see. I'll show you!" I carefully folded the paper, describing exactly how it was done, and then said, "See, like magic! *Voila!*"

The children gasped, and one astute dark-haired boy said, "She *just* folded it!" as if to contradict any possibility of magic. He looked somewhat exasperated with his classmates; obviously, this little guy had no trouble folding at all!

Every year, in September, I taught an art lesson that connected to the International Day of Peace. I liked to present a different experience each year, so I came up with having my fourth and fifth graders create a surfboard. Many of my students either surfed or boogie boarded, and so I thought it would be fun for them to design their own surfboard. However, there were some requirements: somewhere on the board, they needed to have the peace sign, and they were also to use symmetry. I had some examples drawn up with many photos of surfboards. If I had my own classroom, I would have brought in a real surfboard (which I'd done in the past as a middle school teacher). I gave my students a lot of freedom in this lesson as we considered the meaning of the peace sign. After researching this symbol, I discovered it had a gruesome beginning. The peace sign we know today started out as a symbol people would paint on safe places in case of a nuclear holocaust.

In the second week of this lesson, I brought a book about the peace sign and shared this information with the children. This seemed like a straightforward lesson, and things appeared to be going well. That is, until Wendy raised her hand as I was walking around the room watching students work and talking to kids.

"Hey, Wendy, what's up?" I asked her as I made it to her desk.

"I can't do this lesson. My parents would never let me draw the peace symbol," she confided in me.

I was surprised and asked why not.

Wendy went on, "My mother forbids it because it is from the devil!"

My astonishment led to great sadness for this child, but I did not want her to be uncomfortable, so I told her it was OK for her to do as she wished. She did not have to put the peace sign on her surfboard. I asked her to maybe make her own symbol of something peaceful on the board.

Wendy considered this for a moment and then said, "I want to draw the peace sign. I just won't tell my mom!"

I was not very comfortable with this either, and I responded, "Wendy, these will be on display, and your mother may see it. I think it is best not to hide things. If this will upset your parents, then you need to abide by their wishes. I don't understand their objections, but I do need to respect them. Think it over, OK? Maybe talk to your mother about it. See what she says."

I thanked her for letting me know, and then I moved on, a bit bewildered. I was not sure I handled this unexpected issue very well. As teachers, we sometimes have to react immediately to awkward situations and respond as best we can. This reminded me, as I got ready to leave for the next class, that no matter how many years I had been teaching, I had *not* seen it all—absolutely not. Perhaps this was an omen, as the fourth year at Creek Side would present me with many firsts, some good, some not so good.

In the end, Wendy decided not to use the peace symbol on her surfboard design.

The classes talked a lot about peace and what made us feel peaceful in the days and weeks ahead. Some of their answers were quite sad to hear. Mainly heart-wrenching was that a few of the boys said they never felt peaceful. I talked to them a great deal about this, concerned that they either weren't aware of times when they experience peace, or they honestly never really had that experience. I hoped that this would change for them. I made it a point during the year to watch these boys, and it seemed to me, in contradiction to what they said, I thought they appeared peaceful when we were at the creek.

My little second graders were cute, refreshing to me as a contrast to the more sophisticated fourth and fifth graders. One of my first lessons with the second graders was a review of basic shapes as we explored the art elements. I prompted the children in one class, "Tell me some shapes." Up went many hands, and I gleefully called on them one at a time. "Rhombus!" "Trapezoid!" "Hexagon!" I started to laugh and asked, "Anyone know what a circle is?" I was not expecting such sophistication from my young students, and it was a delight to witness their enthusiasm and vast knowledge.

Once all the forms with parent signatures were collected, we headed to the creek. I dangled the proverbial carrot in front of each class. I assured the students that once all the permission slips were returned, I would set up a creek walk right away. This incentive really worked well, though I had to round up a few stragglers. The children were always amazed when I told them (after having them guess) how old Grandmother Oaktree was.

They always gasped when I said, "Over three hundred years!"

A sweet second-grade child, Melanie, was hugging the tree, and I, along with the parents, was smiling and snapping photos. She turned to me and said, "You can tell Grandmother Oaktree loves children!"

It just so happened that her mother was standing close by.

"How can you tell she loves you?" her mother asked Melanie.

The child looked up at the full branches and said thoughtfully, "Because she always has her arms open for us." Her mother and I exchanged *Wow!* smiles.

On creek walks, it seemed the children connected with many memories of other places and experiences they had with nature. Building on prior knowledge is a fundamental stepping-stone to learning, so I always enjoyed listening to their stories. One day, we discovered some ladybugs, and the children excitedly talked about other times they held ladybugs. We saw Buckeye butterflies that danced among the wild fennel, and all kinds of previous butterfly experiences emerged from memory. Stopping by Grandfather Redwood Tree (in the school-yard on our way back to class), the children shared stories about redwoods in their yards or ones they saw hiking. Trees and other living beings seemed to bring out the best in everyone.

Lesson: Access prior experiences and knowledge.

Is He Real?

Once I got my art classes settled, I began the kindergarten English language program and first-grade reading enrichment. We had already met a couple of times, and it was now mid-October with my new little flock of bright-eyed kinder kiddies. Fortunately, this year, like the year before, I had a real classroom to bring the children to for reading and any hands-on work. Our outdoor excursions were still the highlight of my program though.

We were discussing homes one day, and I asked each of them to share where they lived and to tell me something about their homes. I volunteered that I walked back and forth to school from my house. Immediately after I announced this, the entire group of ten children burst out laughing! I opened my eyes wide and pulled my head back with a grin, quite confused. A little boy named Arash offered an explanation.

"Of course, you walk to school, Ms. Bickett, you *live* here!"

Of course, I forgot, teachers *live* at school!

All of my elementary school teachers lived *at school,* I recalled with a laugh. Ah, youth!

As Halloween approached, we began fun art projects, and I had a great time decorating the art cart. The art classes helped with the cart decorations after I put a Frida Kahlo poster on the front. I noticed some of the fifth graders winking at each other and smiling when they saw it, then they looked at me and grinned. I wondered what they were thinking. I saw them whispering to each other, and I looked at the Frida poster again. *Hmm,* I pondered. Naturally, Frida would return this year!

Anyway, the art cart looked marvelously wicked, full of orange and black images. At a garage sale during the summer, I had purchased a miniature wooden carved Mexican man wearing a black shirt and pants with a black hat. He was sitting on a little wooden chair. Perfect for the art cart!

What I was not expecting was the barrage of questions I received regarding my little guest, who rode upon the top of the cart with my other supplies. My inquisitive second graders kept asking me, "Is he *real*?"

I explained that he was a real wooden man from Mexico. Yet, I was very perplexed when they persisted after that explanation.

"But is he REAL?" they asked again.

I couldn't figure out what they were after, and I asked them if they thought he was Pinocchio or something. Assuring them that he was made entirely of wood and would stay that way, I saw children coming up to the cart and touching the little wooden guy. They would lift his pant leg or take off his hat just to be sure.

Mid-October brought some not-too-surprising rains, though we had a deluge that left me soaking and miserable. Despite my efforts to cover the art cart with a heavy green tarp, the rain caused drips of color to stream down the sides. In keeping with my rule, I didn't allow the children to push the cart in the rain, so I trudged around with it, dashing from class to class. This day when I arrived in class, the teacher still had the door locked, and I had to pound on it a while before someone came to open it up. Little Suzie jumped up and came running to me as I dragged my sorry carcass through the door. It was after lunch, and I was feeling particularly worn out and irritable. Suzie grabbed me in a big bear hug.

"Ms. Bickett, you look so gorgeous today!" Wow.

By the end of the day, the clouds loosened up and scattered like little white sheep, innocent of the massive, dark, gray storm that poured the rain upon us earlier. A breeze kicked up, and I felt chilled but relieved I could walk home without getting wet. As I walked by the tall pine along the path to the creek and footbridge, a little boy, someone I didn't know, joined me. His mother was following close behind. I paused because this was the tree that always whispered, even with the slightest breeze. Its long, thin, green pine needles thickly filled each branch, providing ample resistance that created ethereal, subtle sounds. Suddenly, I became aware of the little child standing by me. He was looking up at the branches and listening, too.

"I love this tree," I told him. "It always makes me smile on my way home."

He looked up at me and said he always called the tree the Whispering Tree because it whispered to him, too.

Lesson: What is real?

A Big Little Frog

I looked out the window and saw low gray clouds, like the ones that rained on Lizzie and me on a morning walk earlier that day. I pondered these thoughts as I saw the past, the present, and the future. As they say, "No drop of water is ever lost." My students were always amazed and even partly grossed out when I informed them that the very water they drank today could have once been dinosaur pee. No new water is created; it is all transformed.

Thich Nhat Hanh said that we were manifested when conditions were right, and our lives are a part of constant change and transformation. The act of creation is really the act of recreation. In his book *No Death, No Fear*, the Buddhist monk likens the journey of water through its stages from liquid to vapor to solid and liquid again to our human experiences of life and death. I have found the wisdom of his teachings a great blessing many times throughout my life. The Hindus regard all water as sacred. I tried to instill in my students an awe and respect for water and how precious it is. In California, we often experience periods of drought, especially made worse with climate change. It was vital to me to teach our intimate connection to water, which sustains us, thanks to our creeks, rivers, and oceans. Without water, we would have no food or life.

The garden at Creek Side was a particular jewel. Lovingly tended and watered by teachers, parents, and other volunteers, each classroom had its own raised bed. The children planted seeds and nurtured them into various squashes, sunflowers, beans, peas, carrots, and cabbages. It was always a sheer delight for me to bring my students into the garden to make connections to the concepts I was teaching.

One morning, I took my little kiddies to the garden. It was a lovely autumn day. The sun was touching everything with brilliance, with a slight breeze that nudged the tumbling leaves on the ground to scatter and then come to rest against the long fence around the school. So far, little Amy had barely spoken a word. Her family was from Vietnam, and I did my best to encourage her to talk in her native tongue. I asked Amy to name some things for me in Vietnamese, for example, so I could learn.

Amy would, in time, open. She was sweet and very cute; they all were, my little ones. As we were discovering things in the garden, one of the children found a tree frog under a planter. Everyone gathered around as I gently picked it up for the children to see. We found a sunny spot to sit. After I moistened my hands, I held the little being carefully so they could all touch it.

There was a lot of excited chatter as the students explored the frog: how this little guy felt on his or her skin—cool, slimy, and surprisingly soft. Eventually, everyone wanted to hold the tree frog for a few moments. Much to my immense surprise and delight, Amy blossomed right before me. She eagerly held the tree frog and then started babbling out all kinds of sentences in excellent English. Amy beamed with a smile I had never seen on her face before.

It was a fantastic day. I remember it very clearly as the day I finally got to know Amy.

Thanks to the little tree frog, from then on, she talked all the time. It was like the little frog unwrapped her, showing us what a gift she was. The tree frog melted away her stern face and revealed Amy's beautiful self. It was a little frog in a very big way.

For my older students, I had arranged for a guest speaker to come from the San Jose Art Museum, part of their school outreach program, during a week in October. This woman enthralled my students, engaging them in visual thinking exercises, using posters of local and well-known artists from around the world. The students were invited to sketch or take notes as they wished during the presentation.

As we were packing up to move on to the next class, I noticed a fifth-grade student's art journal was open on her desk. At the top of the page, it read: "San Jose Art Museum: I WANT TO GO!" Only a few raised their hands when we asked how many of the students had ever been to our local art institution. I was pleased to see how much my students wanted to visit the museum after the presentation. Over the years at Creek Side, I invited the museum's volunteers to come and present at our school. I, too, learned a lot, not only from the content, but also about my students: what they responded to, what they knew, and what made them excited about art.

Since it was October once again, yes, I did return as Frida Kahlo. I began to realize the students and staff all anticipated Frida's visits, so I happily obliged.

It was recess time, and I was in Room 5, restocking the art cart and talking to Melissa, the PE teacher. Still wearing my Frida outfit, I went about my work. Two fourth-grade girls peeked into the room and called out to Melissa.

"Hey, have you seen Ms. Bickett?" they asked.

"No, she's not in here right now!" Melissa said as she smiled.

The two girls looked at each other and giggled.

"Hola!" I said to them in my Frida voice.

Letting out a hoot of laughter, the two students left, their giggles echoing back to me.

In my next fifth-grade class, I was going through my introduction, using some of Frida's paintings to engage the children in the visual thinking process. How wonderful to see art come alive and to hear their thoughts and questions about Frida's work, her subject matter, and style.

Suddenly, the door opened, and the principal entered with some highbrow guests. Mrs. Heart was giving them a VIP tour of the school that morning and chose my art class on purpose. She confessed this fact to me later that day. I was in mid-sentence, responding to a student's comment about the symbolism in Kahlo's work, and didn't miss a beat. Taking a deep breath, I continued as the students were all intensely focused on the artist's paintings. Ms. Heart cornered me after school.

"I knew you were in there, and I wanted them to see the art teacher. There you were, engaging kids in higher-level thinking!" My principal beamed at me proudly, and I thanked her. It was terrific to have someone pop in and see all your hard work paying off.

Since the weather was cooperating, in the last week of October, I took my second graders out to the garden to create little pinch pots. We collected twigs and other materials they had gathered to add as embellishments. I was well prepared for today's lesson because of the parent volunteers who helped me roll the clay into small balls ahead of time. They assisted me as we brought the supplies to the garden (not getting the art cart stuck this time!). I was grateful they were able to stay for the entire class time. How I loved those days in the garden with the children! There were many parents who graciously gave their time during outdoor excursions, making such experiences a success.

Into the second class of the day, I arrived full of exuberance. I hadn't told them ahead of time where we were going, so I wanted to surprise the children.

"How would you like to go create art in the garden today?" I asked excitedly.

I stood there with my arms open, smiling. Unlike my previous class that day, there was complete silence. I was greeted with stares and frowns! One little girl covered her mouth, and a few started to complain.

"What is going on?" I asked as the two parents in the room exchanged confused glances with me.

One of the girls, Missy, explained, "I have allergies. I am not supposed to go into the garden."

"My parents don't allow me to play on the grass. I get asthma. I have to stay on the blacktop at all times," another child added.

The funny thing was, I was sure I had seen her out in the field playing many times and recalled that she was in my first-grade enrichment class last year and went on several creek walks. Other children piped in that the garden was full of dirt and plants. It was challenging to pick up my jaw off the floor. In all my years of outdoor excursions, I'd never encountered this before!

"Gee," I started after trying to gather my wits about me. "I guess that means I need to cancel all the creek walks with this class. Too bad, I was planning to take you in early November." To this, the entire class chorused, "Oh NO!"

"But what about all that dirt and those plants by the creek? And the pollen and all that other messy stuff?"

The classroom teacher was at her desk and overheard this conversation. Shaking her head with dismay, she looked up at me. I shrugged my shoulders and grinned.

"Now, who would like to go to the garden today?" I invited them again.

This time, the entire class raised their hands desperately. And you know what? The lesson went just fine that day, without so much as a sneeze. The children laughed and chatted happily away as they created their small clay pots, nimbly forming them with eager fingers. The sticks, leaves, and acorns we had collected left interesting patterns of textures on the surface of the pots. I stood back and sighed with relief; I never heard mention of those elusive allergies again.

At lunch, I passed by a sweet third-grade girl, Lucy, who I didn't have for art that year, but who was in my class the year before. I always missed the children I no longer got to work with.

"It's good to see you, Lucy!" Lucy stopped and looked at me.

"It's good to see YOU!" she replied.

We both nodded and went on our ways, but I was touched by her authentic response. I really did miss my former students.

The previous summer, Brian and I had revisited South Dakota to see my mother, taking an excursion to the southern Black Hills to see a mammoth site. There were hundreds of the extinct woolly mammoths that were accidentally unearthed while digging to create an apartment complex in Hot Springs, South Dakota. I was thrilled to share my adventure with the children before we created our own cave drawings with charcoal, Conte crayon, and chalks. I asked the group of second graders, "What is a fossil?"

After some guessing by the class, my favorite answer was, "A creature that has been dead a long time." Spot on!

English Language Development lessons followed the curriculum I was given to use. Our next unit was about animals and pets. We were sitting together in a circle outside, and I queried the children to share what kinds of animals they lived with. There were various answers, and so when I came to Sandra, an outspoken girl from China, she growled! I waited, but all she did was growl.

"Is it a snake?" I asked her.

The children laughed, and she growled some more.

"Maybe a horse?"

Sandra's growl grew more and more ferocious.

"Let's see. I guess you have a cat!" I announced.

I was unsuccessfully attempting to get Sandra to say she had a dog, but she never said so. She continued to growl at me all the way back to class, and I finally asked her if she did, indeed, have a dog.

As she went into her room, Sandra turned and growled at me with a frown. I never did find out what kind of pet she had or if she even had one!

I was always so impressed at how children responded to art. Art posters came in handy in my first-grade enrichment class as well. I read a story related to the paintings, and we engaged in all kinds of conversations, questions, and writing lessons. It seemed to me that art always brought out so much in the kids. I learned a great deal about their previous experiences, attitudes, likes, and fears. A poster of a little boy wearing a yellow hat or a small black girl wearing a white dress ignited all kinds of responses from my young students to my fifth graders. The primary grades related more personally to the images. In contrast, the older children focused on the art elements, expressions, and the artist.

Lesson: Inspire!

What We See and Don't See

I heard a Zen saying once years ago that "... you really can't see a thing until you draw it." Thich Nhat Hanh said that "just because you can't see something doesn't mean it is not there." Seeing, looking, observing, watching, noticing are all processes that involve our eyes and our minds. You can also include the other senses, such as touching, smelling, and hearing. When we observe, sometimes we must use more than just our eyes.

Nonetheless, it seems we can look at something and not *see* it. That is where using our brains come in. How many times had I gazed in a particular direction and missed something? Many times, I must admit. And we can't see radio, TV, or computer waves flowing through the air, but they are there. Our senses cannot perceive them directly. We identify their existence by their results. This always makes me think of what we could be missing in realms beyond our senses. In our physical domain, learning to use our senses entirely is essential to learning, especially for art and science.

Since I had been practicing yoga and mindfulness meditation for many years, I found infusing the concept of awareness into my lessons a vital component. What better than an art class to model and create experiences that encourage children to slow down and become more aware of their inner and outer worlds? Along with teaching standards, we can also educate our young about how to live in this world with values that reflect respect for themselves, others, their communities, and the environment. We can help them learn what it means to be human.

When I took children to the creek, I always strived to get them to attune with all their senses as much as they could. Asking them to cease constant chatter was sometimes a challenge. I wanted them to just listen. And when we were successful, it produced amazing results. Students were elated at discovering sounds and creatures they would not have otherwise been aware of had they not listened with their ears, minds, and hearts.

In early November, as I promised, I took all ten classes to the creek, not all in one day or week, but within two weeks. I managed, with parent volunteer assistance, to get everyone to the stream before the rains began.

Each class kept a list of all the animals and trees we saw on each trip. By the end of the two weeks, we had seen a plethora of natural wonders. We witnessed a Cooper's hawk being chased by crows, tiny chickadees leaping about branches as we mimicked their "chick a dee" song, and giant sycamore tree leaves swirling to the ground in a kind of graceful dance. We discovered Buckeye nuts that were smooth and shiny, the lone bay tree with bay nuts (that local Native Americans ground for a kind of coffee drink), and blossoms. We saw an Anna's hummingbird's iridescent breast glitter in the sunlight as he made his little squeaky sounds (as one student put it). Tree frogs chorused along our way.

There were acorns all over, being gathered anxiously by black and gray squirrels. We found squirrel nests hidden in the oak trees and the children shouted with delight when we spotted them. When we came to a very tall eucalyptus tree near the end of the dirt road, with its undulating white branches dancing in the sky, one student remarked, "The eucalyptus tree looks like a painting!" As we returned to class, a fourth-grade boy made up a song called, "We Are the Bay Tree Kids!"

I was mesmerized by magic and joy. In subsequent classes, we discussed our journey to the creek, and I asked the children about their favorite part of the excursion. In a second-grade class, two students chimed together: "Our favorite part was just being with *you*!" I was deeply touched by those words.

The creek was a place many children had previously visited with their parents and then later with friends or their dogs. It became a trendy place in our neighborhood, and little wonder. Amid a metropolitan area, it offered respite into a wild world disappearing too fast. I hoped and still hope the school district, water district, and the city officials will open the gates to let everyone enjoy it, and I believe there would be less trash.

Sadly, older students from middle school and high school came and left beer bottles, cigarette butts, and other artifacts of their presence (including condoms) along the creek. They gathered there in the forbidden place to hide. If more people were walking along the trail, I didn't think they'd get away with quite so much. To make this whole scenario even more laughable, people were always cutting holes in the fence. For my first few years at Creek Side, I reported the breaches to the water district and the school district for repair. Finally, I threw my hands up in defeat; as soon as one hole got repaired, another appeared.

When I walked by, I simply smiled and said to myself: *Go for it!*

I also took my first-grade enrichment kids to the creek. The kinder kids were not able to go, as I only had about a half-hour with each group; we did not have the time. Plus, I would need to enlist parent volunteers to help, and it was too huge a task. But I was delighted to take my astute readers to the creek, where we composed poems and stories about what we saw, in addition to reading about riparian environments.

One little boy chimed as we walked (we were discussing the life cycle), "The life cycle at the creek just keeps going and going and going . . ."

We stopped to look at our reflections in a few large puddles, leftovers from a rainstorm over the weekend, on the main road. Peering into the still water, we saw clouds, trees, and birds fly by in the puddle world. The children decided to call it *Upside-down World*, and we became quite imaginative as we talked about what existed in this reverse world.

Another second-grade class went to the creek, and the children asked if they could pick up little treasures of acorns and sticks. I figured it was OK. So, the parent volunteers and I enjoyed listening to them squeal with delight as they collected a small handful of things. When we arrived back in the classroom, the teacher had already returned. This was unusual for this teacher, who usually got back late each time I needed to leave for the next class. The children were happily chattering and placing their sweet little treasures on their desks, not taking up much space. A few children pointed out their prizes to the teacher as she became aware of our return.

"I don't want to see them! Put that stuff away! NOW!" the teacher yelled.

The children were crestfallen. It was heartbreaking to see their disappointed faces. The magic vanished in an instant, and I was speechless; it was clearly time for me to leave.

Puzzled by the second-grade teacher's reaction to the creek treasures, I had to shrug it off; perhaps she was having a bad day. I hoped it wasn't how she always was, but I had never been in the classroom when she was teaching. Most of the teachers were great to work with. They were gracious about the fact I had to use their rooms for art.

I tried to leave the rooms spotless and did my best to be considerate. Perhaps this teacher saw the acorns and twigs as a dirty mess and didn't want to deal with the kids playing with anything into the next lesson. However, it seemed very unlikely that their little piles of nature collections would have caused any harm. I never figured it out, and I had to let it go. To confront her or even bring up the issue didn't rate high on my list of important matters.

As I closed the door to the room where the art cart was parked, a fourth-grade boy, Arnold, came up to me.

"Thank you so much for taking us to the creek. I have never been down there before and always heard so much about it." Arnold had gone out of his way to find me to tell me this, and I thanked him as well.

As I walked home, I remembered when I stood with the children in the center of the road by the creek, and I asked them to listen. We heard a vast universe. Then we walked along farther, and I asked them to just see things. And we saw new worlds where animals lived and thrived. We looked for the art elements in nature: for lines, shapes, colors, textures, and forms. Art came alive, and the children came alive. And, you know what? I came alive when I was with the children at the creek. It was quite simple and yet so intricate and full of subtleties. We looked at the trees and saw their unique textures, colors, branches, and shapes—triangles, ovals, and hearts—of their leaves. I began to think about the children creating field guides in the spring, and I was excited to work on the idea. We talked a lot about Leonardo da Vinci and his notebooks and Linnaeus's (the famous botanist, physician, and zoologist from Sweden, 1707-1778) plant drawings. The line between art and science blurred and connected.

I think of all those days with the children at Creek Side and what they heard and saw. And I wonder now, years later, what they remember.

Lesson: You never know what your students will remember.

To Say I Love You

Lucille Ball once said, "Love yourself first, and everything else falls into line. You really have to love yourself to get anything done in this world."

Halloween came and went. With my adrenaline waning, I always liked November's long, peaceful sigh with the days growing shorter and the air crisp and clean. The children became engaged in lessons about the early settlers, their encounters with Native Americans, and the change of the seasons.

As a learning strand, a kind of spiral lesson, I wanted to go back to basic drawing, straightforward and clear. I brought out the mirrors I had ordered and the charcoal sticks. Sometimes, these were my favorite art tools. Basic and freeing. I wanted my students to draw themselves, but first, we had fun drawing each other using the blind contour line drawing technique. I demonstrated with a "victim" at the front of the class so everyone could see. I held up a black marker onto the whiteboard and had my model sit still in a chair in front of me.

Then, I proceeded to draw his head, neck, and shoulders, starting at the top of the page, using flowing lines. I could not look at the paper, and I could not lift my charcoal stick from the paper. The results were always so much fun; this was the single happiest art lesson I loved to teach. Eyes were up in the forehead, lips off to one side, ears drooping by the chin—it didn't matter. We learned to trust our hands and the flow of information from our brains to the paper. We loosened up and created free-flowing, quality lines.

After the class stopped laughing, I then told my students they would draw each other in this way. The person sitting next to them would be their partner, and they needed to follow my example by starting at the top of the page (or else you run out of space too quickly). The laughter grew louder as the children took turns drawing each other. They held up their work proudly to display Picasso-like images. I thought their drawings were lovely. I couldn't wait to show them.

After this warm-up, I brought out the mirrors. Time after time, I marveled at how much the students enjoyed looking at themselves. A few clever ones picked up the mirrors and held them to their faces to create funny images.

As we were looking into the mirrors, I asked them to notice something (or things) unique about themselves. This was always a painful thing for me to see how difficult it was for the children to face themselves and think of positive attributes they each had.

"Now, I want you to look into your eyes and say softly or loudly. *I love you,*" I instructed.

The room was enveloped in silence as my students looked at me as if I'd asked them to jump off a bridge.

"No, really, right now, just look at yourself and say, *I love you, Bob,* or *I love you, Sally.* Go ahead," I urged them.

With great hesitation, one by one, the kids begin to say, "I love you" to their image.

There were murmurs all over the room, with an occasional joker shouting, "I love you, Babe!" to himself, breaking the ice a bit and encouraging the others. I walked around the room, listening. There were always at least a few children in each class who could never bring themselves to say these words, and I would let them know that it was perfectly OK; they could just think the words if they wished.

"No matter what, it is important to love yourself," I said with great sincerity.

A fifth-grade girl told me it was sinful to love yourself, and so I explained the difference between egotistical love and true, inner love of oneself.

We then drew blind contour line drawings of ourselves after I demonstrated. Once again, the results were just brilliant and very expressive. At that juncture, I brought out some of Picasso's contour line drawings and portraits to make my point. I loved the way the room filled with laughter on those days!

At the end of one of the classes while the mirrors were being collected, very spontaneously (with my nod of approval) students began assembling the mirrors on the floor into different angles. The results were intriguing! Everyone had a great time. We stood around the assembled, angular shapes where our faces were reflected. I remarked how this would be a great art installation in a museum. The bell rang just as we dissembled the structure. Those were the moments I loved when something unplanned invited us to play.

My second graders got a version of this lesson. I was, once more, dismayed at how difficult it was even for the younger children to say, "I love you" to themselves. I recommended that they practice at home while they were brushing their teeth or combing their hair.

"Just say, 'I love you' every day to yourself in the mirror and see if that changes anything," I challenged them. Funny thing is, I didn't even do that but vowed I should start as a practice, too.

Another day, I was returning from my quick visit home to feed Lizzie and grab a bite to eat. Little Ella, one of my language development students, ran up to me.

"Ms. Bickett!" she shouted wildly, waving her arms as she dashed up to me and stopped. "Would you keep this to show Kasey (one of the other students in our little group) tomorrow? I found a REAL dinosaur tooth!"

In her trembling little hands, Ella unfolded her fingers to show me a dark, triangular, sharp rock that resembled a shark tooth. I had shared with my students about the mammoth dig site in South Dakota (you can tour this indoor active dig site and view Ice Age fossils), and we explored what fossils were. Some old, fossilized seashells I had found last summer became prized possessions of my kinder students as I gave them each one to take home.

Lifting the "dinosaur tooth" gently from Ella's hands, I promised her I would keep it for her until tomorrow when we met again.

"It sure looks like a dinosaur tooth," I remarked, not trying to burst her bubble, and yet not telling her it was a real ancient tooth.

She happily bounded off to play, and I smiled at her preciousness. When my son was preschool age, I remember his fascination with dinosaurs. What a great time that was for me, as I loved them too! We visited Vernal Falls, Utah—twice—just to see the quarry of bones there. I was always amazed at how much children love dinosaurs. That next day, I brought out the "tooth" to give Ella. She then proceeded to explain to the rest of the group where she found the "tooth" (near the wild area behind the school) and how she was going to keep it forever. Kasey, her friend, held the treasure for quite some time before returning it to Ella.

Should I have told her it was not a tooth? What I decided to do was to encourage this precocious little kindergarten girl to do some research about dinosaurs and their teeth. Ella told me she wanted to become a paleontologist when she grew up, and I didn't doubt for one moment that she would.

Our next unit was about careers. I read through the books that showed various people in different professions. We also interviewed the staff who worked at the school, just like we did the previous years. I took photos of the principal, secretary, nurse, custodian, and lunch lady. I created a booklet that was site-specific and very personal. The children loved to see people they knew in a book.

This always reminded me of when I taught first grade years ago. My little students were absolutely astonished that teaching was my job. I asked each of my kinder kids what kind of role their parents had. As we went around the circle, I heard usual things like, "My mom is a nurse," or "My dad is a banker." Little Sandra was last.

"Sandra, what does your mom do for a job?" I asked.

"She stays home and takes care of me," she replied.

"Great!" I acknowledged, and then, I asked about what her father did for a job. Sandra, with a very intense expression, roared, "My dad's job is to make money!" As she finished her sentence, her fist went up firmly. I tried very hard not to laugh, but her expression was hilarious, and the way she said, "make money!" was so emphatic!

I engaged my fifth-grade students on a painting project, creating a parody of Grant Wood's *American Gothic*. I brought examples of Wood's work. Emphasizing the famous scene depicting a farmer and his wife standing in front of a gothic-style country house, I shared some information. The woman was his sister, and the man was presumed to be his dentist. We also examined some comical cards and posters that were a satire of the painting. There was one with Paul Newman and his wife on a box of popcorn as they posed as the *American Gothic* couple. Then, there was a birthday card I found with a man and his dog and several other examples. The students loved it, and we embarked on original, fun versions of the painting. They were to paint themselves as one of the subjects because this was a sort of self-portrait as well.

I was amused to see very talented renditions, including things like *Myself and a Piece of Cheese*, and *Me and Sponge Bob*! They all seemed to remember Grant Wood and his famous painting quite well after that!

Recess was an exciting time for me because I got to encounter students in a different context than the classroom. I had a chance to get to know them better individually. Students often wanted to talk and stopped me along the way. Frequently, I interceded in a conflict I'd noticed.

One day, I was walking down the hallway at recess when I heard someone calling my name from behind me, huffing and puffing. I turned to see little Andy, one of my second graders, whom I'd known since he was in my kindergarten class two years earlier.

Andy came up to me and stopped, bending over to catch his breath, before he lifted his head and said to me quite urgently, "Ms. Bickett! Ms. Bickett!"

"What is it, Andy?" I asked with great concern. "Is everything OK?"

He took in a deep breath. "You need to color your hair. It's turning white!"

Relieved he was OK, and trying not to laugh, I patted him on the back.

"OK, well, I'll see what I can do. Thanks for letting me know!" I answered.

Andy nodded and scooted off in relief. You just never knew what the children were thinking . . .

Seagulls had a great strategy during recess as they waited for the children to leave. The school building's roofs were pointed, and at the very top, the gulls would stand in perfect lines watching the children. I observed them as they arrived moments before recess as if they had a clock alerting them to the time. One by one, the gulls came and found their spot. I wouldn't be surprised if the same gull occupied the same place every day. I often thought I should bring my camera to photograph this. (I think I did once but have long lost the picture.)

As soon as the children were safely tucked back into their classrooms, down the gulls swooped to the blacktop and tables, gulping what they could, and headed off with small bags to pick at the contents later. It was quite a free buffet not only for the seagulls but also for sparrows and crows. One day, as most of the gulls and other birds had left, one lone gull was strolling around.

I was on my way to pick up my kindergarteners, and I paused a moment to watch him. He was walking around on his webbed feet, seemingly with nothing better to do. I worried about the gulls and other birds eating all the leftover snacks and lunch, as many of them also consumed the plastic bags the food was wrapped in. I warned the children about this many times, seemingly to no avail. Picking up small plastic bags everywhere, even as far away as the creek, became a regular chore for me. I explained to my students that urban wildlife doesn't have things as easy as they appear. They scrounge for food that is not healthy for them, and often they succumb to diseases and predators. I hoped to instill compassion for the two-legged and four-legged beings who need to survive and thrive like we do. But I'll never know where my words and actions may have led . . . or, are they still rippling somewhere out there?

Perhaps if we could love ourselves deeply, we could extend that love to all other living things on the earth. We have to start somewhere—where better than with ourselves?

Lesson: Model and teach self-love and compassion.

The Winds of Change

My fourth year at Creek Side (2009-2010) felt ominous. Despite things going relatively well, I felt unsettled, and I didn't know why. Something beyond the horizon eluded me. I tried to see it, but I couldn't. I could only sense the presence of a change in the winds. One day, change really kicked up its unexpected company before a real thunderstorm ensued.

As I walked to school, I excitedly pondered the clouds and felt the energy of a storm beckoning. When I was a little girl, my father would take me out to watch clouds roam across the plains. He taught me about cumulous, stratacumulous, anvil-shaped thunderheads, hailstorms, and my favorite, mare's tails.

It just so happened that our December theme was about the weather. I was thrilled the storm was occurring on a day I taught my younger children. After I gathered up my students, we returned to the classroom, and we acted out the weather. I assigned them each a role: lightning, thunder, rain, and lastly, a rainbow. The children had fun taking turns being different aspects of a thunderstorm, and just as we finished, the storm proceeded in the exact manner that we rehearsed!

First, there was a flash of lightning and then a rumble and bang of thunder. Rain poured down profusely for a few minutes, and then the clouds parted with the brilliance of the sun. I rushed the children outside because I was sure there would be a rainbow. Much to my amazement and gratitude, there was a vast, colorful rainbow! It arched over the school, opposite the sun, against the dark clouds. I congratulated my delighted students about their excellent play-acting, and they beamed. You absolutely cannot plan things like what happened that day; this was serendipity at its finest.

The winter break approached, and the rains came and went. I stood outside, feeling a part of the wondrous change, but then that unsettled premonition seeped into my awareness again. Sorrow filled my heart, and I attempted to get in touch with it. What was this?

Using my wolf images as Winter Solstice cards that year, I wrote to my family and friends. Being the middle child in a family of ten children kept me busy when the holidays arrived, and I liked to create my own cards and gifts, which took even more time. During the week before the break, I was overwhelmed with completing lessons at school and preparing for the holidays. Although my five older siblings were like a different family in terms of the age differences between them and me, the five of us in the younger set were close in age and as sisters. There was Patricia, or Pat, as we called her, who was the eldest of the younger bunch (two years older than me); then me; then my almost-twin, Betsy; followed by Kathy and Jane.

Pat and I had an extraordinary bond. When I was a timid, introverted seventh-grader, new to the school and to the city where we had just moved, she blazed a trail for me to follow. Pat showed me how to crawl out of my shell and be less afraid. I joined the "Declam" Club (poetry reading) first and went on to win first place in the regional contest when I read the poem "The Pencil Seller" by Robert Service. Next, in eighth grade, like Pat, I joined the Debate Club and was on the winning team in debating matches all over the city and county.

Pat's life continued to be an example of her bravery and courage. Over the years we had our disagreements and periods of distance, but we always managed to forgive and forget. The most tragic rift, however, had been during the time I taught at Creek Side when the entire family was split in disagreement regarding my mother's care in a nursing home. I had to step away from the fray, and that left me on the outside of the battle. Once again, I was distanced from my sister, whom I had emulated for so many years. We hadn't spoken in a few years, and my heart was broken.

The previous Christmas, Pat and I had a brief phone conversation. It was something, anyway, though disappointing. Clearly, she was still hurt about the family problem. I felt another urge to call her at her Chicago home, but I didn't think she wanted to hear from me, although a voice in my heart kept urging me to try. I never made the call.

However, I decided I would present her with a birthday gift. Pat's birthday was a few days after mine in January, so I began working on an acrylic painting of her at the beach. It was the last time I saw her, at Brian's and my wedding in 2006. I was confident she would love it and hoped it would break the ice between us. I couldn't wait for the school break to finish my surprise.

The children at school were at their usual best and worst before the holidays. The energy was palpable. My first-grade enrichment students often came late to class, despite the fact I had them make little clock pictures to put on their desks. Their teachers forgot to send them, and the children forgot to remind the teachers. One day, I lectured my tardy group of first graders that they needed to arrive on time. I emphasized that it was their job to help their teachers keep track of Book Club (as I called the class) on Mondays and Wednesdays from 9:00 to 9:50.

"Your teachers have enough to do!" I assured them.

Lucy, an astute little girl, answered, "Yeah, like they have to correct all that work they make us do!"

In the months ahead, they eventually began to arrive on time, with only occasional slacking. The children seemed to look forward to our advanced reading class—including our excursions to the creek, of course.

I was having a difficult time with the fact that Mrs. Heart, our beloved principal, would be leaving right after winter break. She announced her resignation to take a high-ranking position as a human resources director in another school district. I was distraught. I really liked her and felt she understood me well. It would be a challenge to get used to someone else. We met the new principal, and I was a little skeptical. She was only in her early thirties and very inexperienced, this being her first position as principal. I found myself crying at the thought of Mrs. Heart's departure, realizing the winds of change were upon us, and there was nothing to do but sail on. Little did I know just how much this would be true for me in the days and weeks ahead.

With my final goodbyes to Mrs. Heart, winter break arrived at last, and we were off for two weeks. I was really looking forward to completing my sister's painting, but I came down with a flu-type bug and spent much of my break coughing and trying to get well. The painting was nearly finished, and I was anticipating the day when I could ship it to Patricia. I imagined the look of surprise on her face, the phone conversation we would have, and the months ahead reconnecting with her.

But life had other plans.

The phone call I was hoping to make would never happen because of the call that did come on the evening of December 31, 2009. My sister Peggy from Minnesota called me around eight that night. I was still not feeling well and was planning a quiet evening at home, watching TV to hail the New Year.

"Patricia died tonight, Marianne," my sister blurted out as I literally fell back in disbelief. "They think it was a heart attack."

To this day, my heart still aches from the echo of those words. I lost my beloved Patricia, my sister, whom I loved beyond love and was close to all my life. We were always going to talk again. We were always going to make amends, I assured myself. And now, she was gone.

Her memorial a couple weeks later was impressive—there were hundreds of people there, a testimony to what a great healer Patricia was. Patricia ran her own acupuncture clinic on the outskirts of Chicago. My son and I flew to Chicago and arrived in a snowstorm. Jacques drove us the forty-five minutes north to where my sister had lived with her husband. I was deeply moved by the stories of all the people whose lives she touched, and I could see that my sister lived on through those she'd blessed while she was here. Sometimes, I still can't believe she's gone. I hear her laughter (she was a hoot to party with!) and feel her beautiful presence.

I honor my beloved sister Patricia by living my dreams and doing my best. Her courage has inspired me to see this book project through, to share my art cart experiences despite my doubts. That is why I dedicated this memoir to her.

To Patricia, who lives on through those she loved.

Lesson: Make that phone call.

Kindness and Victoria's Secret

I think of those days at Creek Side, how my fourth year was my most challenging and painful. Yet, the children touched me deeply with their compassion.

Mrs. Walton, our new principal, was kind but a bit too ambitious at first. She immediately instigated sweeping changes, perhaps from someone's misguided advice, to establish her authority over a staff much older in seniority and age. It didn't work well, and later, she had to back off some. I liked her, but at a distance. I was willing to give her a chance. I hoped she would do the same for me. That notion would become a reality much sooner than I realized in the weeks to come.

There was a day when I was in a classroom, a fourth-grade class, Mr. Say's, setting up during my lunch break. Two girls knocked on the door, and I opened it to encounter their excited smiles. "Can we help you get ready for the art class?" I took a deep breath and welcomed them in. I sure needed help that day. Because I had so many students, I never had many opportunities to get to know the children individually. That day, I learned Brianna was adopted and about Gale's hobbies. From then on, whenever I saw them, we had a special connection. How I wished I could have had a time like that with more of my students. Brianna and Gale volunteered on other days, too, and I happily enjoyed their company as we prepared the room for art. I was deeply touched by their kindness and grateful that I got to know them better.

One of their classmates was a girl named Victoria. Before class, Victoria said to me, "You know, I was named after three things: the city of Victoria, Queen Victoria, and Victoria's Secret!"

I asked her, quite predictably then, "OK, Victoria, what's your secret?"

"That's what my mom asked me when we saw the store in the mall!" she replied as she laughed.

Later that spring, we named the valley oak tree that stood near Grandmother Oaktree, Victoria Valley Oak, and Victoria was most pleased.

Valentine's Day approached rapidly as time seemed to slip by. I was not doing very well. Since the death of my sister, all I could do was muster my strength and courage to face each day. I was slipping into the sorrowful arms of grief. I wrestled with the loss, some days still in a state of shock.

There was a great deal of unfinished business between Pat and me. How could I go on? Enlisting the help of a former therapist, I plowed through family issues. I did my very, very best to arrive at school with the pain in my heart tucked away so I could be present for the children.

My first-grade enrichment class was working on a project for Valentine's Day, and I asked the children to write about the things they loved. I chuckled at some of the sweet things the kids said, and one little boy wrote: "I love my cute sister. I love my strict mom. I love my strict dad." You just never know.

The kindergarteners created large-scale self-portraits; I had them lie down on the floor while I traced them in a pose. Then, the children embellished their work with facial features, hair, and clothes and included favorite objects. We were learning about seasonal clothing and, at that time, focusing on winter clothes. The children drew on shoes, jackets, hats, and mittens.

Next, we created large red hearts with construction paper. I then directed them to glue their red hearts onto their self-portraits. Most of the children got the placement correct as a previous lesson was listening to their heartbeats after Lizzie visited them. I brought my golden gal to school often for my kindergarten children, as always. My beautiful dog worked like magic in getting the children to talk and relax. She was so patient with them. Bringing out the stethoscope, each child not only listened to their own heartbeat but also gently placed the receiver of the scope on Lizzie's big, broad chest. The children were always delighted and amazed at how similar Lizzie's heart was to their own.

We placed both of our hands over our hearts and closed our eyes, feeling our hearts beating in our chests as the children were finishing their large-scale portraits. Little Billy said to me, "We are gluing the hearts on our pictures so they can be alive!"

Their large-scale portraits were just gorgeous. It was a very successful lesson. The laughter of the students, the vivid images, and the narratives they shared—all treasures to behold.

In the following lesson, we focused on animals again. It was one of those spiraling lessons where we picked up where we'd left off in the fall. I interwove compassion for animals into this experience. I brought the booklet I'd created, based on Lizzie and Zelda, our elder cat, featured as they dialogued on how to take care of pets like cats and dogs. I asked the children to describe their animal family members. Most of them said they had a cat or dog. Little Ray chimed in, "I have two pets!"

"Really, Ray, what are they?" I asked him.

"I have a lizard and a worm!" he announced proudly.

Those moments showered me with grace and kept me going. It was the children who, I realized, nourished me and kept me from falling into an abyss. I had something meaningful to live for, a great job to think about, and it helped me get through my depression. However, there were days when I felt weary. My stamina waned by recess, and I began to feel I had to push myself to get through the day. As I crossed the footbridge over the creek on my way home after school, many days, I would stop and breathe and watch the sunlight reflected in the water. Learning to be with my grief and accept the significant loss of my sister would take time.

Lesson: Be gentle with yourself.

The Day of My Undoing

Valentine's Day was over, and there was a rash of stomach flu razing the campus. The weather turned cold, and the sky darkened as I rose one morning. During my morning meditation, I envisioned slipping on my soft armor. I asked for protection, as I was feeling particularly vulnerable that morning. Dreams left my sleep unsettled, and I woke up very tired. My stomach felt queasy as I dressed for the day, and it didn't help when I looked out the window and saw the threat of rain.

I stopped to breathe deeply and asked, "Please, gods of rain and thunder, will you hold off on your arrival until 2:50 today?" I pleaded from my heart, genuinely, hoping that the rain wouldn't start until the last minute of school. Just imagining the wind *and* rain while I pushed the cart around during the day sent a chill down my spine.

Despite feeling depleted when I arrived at school, I was determined to feel well. I tried to let go of things and focused on the positive. Regardless of my efforts, I thought I had nothing in reserve to get me through all I had to accomplish. I found myself wishing I had called in sick, and it would not have been far from the truth. I honestly did not feel well.

The first two classes flew by rather smoothly, and I was very grateful.

"So far, so good," I reminded myself as I pushed the cart to my third class, the one right before lunch. I insisted on managing the cart that day, much to my students' disappointment, because the wind was really kicking up. The clouds were indigo blue-black and hovered like giants looking over us. I peered up at the clouds and mumbled, "Please . . ." So far, so good, no rain yet, but it was predicted to hit any time and become very heavy.

This fourth-grade class was usually a challenge for me. The students tended to be rather chatty, not bad by any means, but very lively. There was a boy, Preston, who, up until this day, never caused any problems. I'd heard he had issues in music and PE classes and frequently had great difficulty getting along with other students. But, in art classes, I never noticed these things, and, in fact, Preston and I had a good relationship.

Perhaps it was the weather. It was always a good thing to fall back on, blaming the weather for errant behavior. I was not sure what had disturbed Preston. As I was explaining the lesson, Preston jumped up. He proceeded to run around the room, grabbing things from other students' desks, tearing up paper, and scattering it about. In a nutshell, I was stunned and most unprepared for what I saw—the situation was unraveling before my eyes. At first, I remained calm, despite the fact he was beginning to get irritating. I asked him to return to his seat quietly but firmly once I got everyone started on the painting lesson.

I didn't want to create a scene and did my best to engage him one-on-one, murmuring and asking him what he needed.

"Preston," I began. After about the fifth time he got up to run around the room, even once grabbing a paintbrush out of a girl's hand and painting a huge red stripe across her work, I asked, "What's up? Why are you doing this? Do you need to leave and take a deep breath? This needs to stop. You are hurting your classmates." Rather than connect with him, these words seem to fuel his wild attack in the classroom.

I had never seen Preston like this and immediately surmised something must have set him off before I arrived, either at school or at home. Regardless, he was taking over my class. Preston smiled and laughed as I did my best to put out fires. Damage control was all I could do.

Finally, I snapped.

"STOP IT!" I yelled at the top of my voice.

He had just left his seat after I had convinced him to sit and breathe for a few moments and tore another student's artwork to shreds. The entire class froze and looked at me, eyes wide with surprise. I had never yelled like this before, and I completely surprised myself, too. The class was nearly over, so I did my best to usher the students through the cleanup process, sending Preston to sit in the office to wait to see the principal, and later, me.

I called ahead to give the secretary a heads up about his arrival and then followed him there as soon as the bell rang for lunch. As I dismissed the class, Brianna, a kind girl who offered to help me many times, came up to me and said, "Don't worry, Ms. Bickett, he does this all the time. It was just the first time in the art class." I stared at her in disbelief and prayed it was not an omen for the future.

When I arrived at the office, Preston sat across from the secretary, smiling, and looking at me with complete defiance. How did this happen? How did I become his enemy when I thought everything was going so well? I took his behavior very personally, something I knew better than to do. Rather than doing what I should have done, like wait with him to see the principal, I started to berate Preston. There was no one else in the office other than the secretary, and

I did my best to keep my voice down. However, I felt myself snapping again, my cool unwinding, and my anger toward this child mounting.

"How could you do this, Preston? I tried to help you, but you didn't even try!" I went on and on about how disappointed I was with what just happened and that this must never occur again in the art class.

The secretary informed me it would be a while before the principal could see us. "It's OK, we'll get him something to eat while he waits. Why don't you come back after lunch?" she offered.

I realized she had a good point. I needed to take a break and gather my wits. My stomach was churning, and I felt dizzy. I wanted to go home and go to bed.

Escaping through the dark winds, I nearly ran home. After gulping down some soup, I had to stop myself.

"This is all wrong," I told myself. "I have to make this right."

I walked back to school, eyeing the sky, and pleading once again for the rain to hold off. When I returned to the principal's office, Preston was already in there talking with her. I knocked on the door and entered, and we had a conversation about the events in the art class. I did my best to keep my own feelings in check. Every button I had got pushed that day, and I was ashamed that I didn't handle the situation better.

Much to my surprise, then, after our talk, the principal asked me to stay. We had agreed on a course of action, and I'd figured that was that.

"Just a minute, Marianne," she began sternly.

Oh dear, I thought to myself, *I'm not starting off on the right foot with this new principal!*

"The office staff told me you were yelling at Preston," Mrs. Walton began in a very accusing tone. "We all need to vent, but you should never direct it at a student!" I was being reprimanded, and I knew she was right.

Apologizing to her, I confessed that I realized over lunch I hadn't handled the situation well at all, though "yelling" seemed a bit exaggerated for the lecture I'd given him in the office. I did admit I was rebuking Preston and was very angry at him. I felt a knife turn in my gut as I learned the secretary complained about me, someone who I thought would come to me first if I had done something to bother her. I'd never had anything like this happen to me in my entire teaching career. My huge inner critic launched an attack as I berated myself for messing up big time.

Nothing was going right. Every turn seemed to take me deeper into despair. Every hurt, every ache in my body and soul intensified, and I had come undone. I promised Mrs. Walton to make great efforts to connect with Preston personally and positively. My intention was to try to improve our relationship so that, at least in art class, he would not feel he needed to act up again. I had no idea that Preston was disliked by most of the teachers and staff and students at Creek Side. I had no idea how big the problem was because he had never been a problem for me before. I was shocked when the principal told me about Preston's history. Until now, I had no clue. As I left the principal's office, I turned to see her staring at me. I certainly hadn't impressed her that day.

I found Preston outside in the playing field before I went to my next class and asked him if he would like to help me collect sticks from around the creek on Friday (my day off) for art classes next week. Apologizing to Preston, I asked him to please tell me what was going on in his head. He shrugged his shoulders. Mrs. Walton explained to me that Preston's parents were divorced, and he lived with his father. She also informed me that difficult issues surrounded his home life. I saw a broken child before me, and I resolved to reach out to him.

"Preston," I told him before I headed to my next class, "I messed up today, and I made mistakes. We both did. Let's work together to make this right again, OK?"

He smiled, and I gave him a hug. It still didn't fix things for me yet, but I felt better.

As I made my way to Mr. Say's class, after the bell rang to gather all children indoors at the end of lunch, I stopped to face the wind. A small dust devil was heading straight toward me, and I stood in its path, unmoved. Seagulls were being blown off their course by the might of the air currents. I stood there, in the center of the swirling mass of leaves, and looked up into the sky. Tears streamed down my face, and I swallowed. Nothing felt right about this day, and I felt like I could be picked up by the wind and carried far away.

I sighed, turned toward the classroom, and began again.

The conclusion of this day arrived none too soon for me, and I put the cart away silently and quickly, not even bothering to unpack and repack for next week. I figured I'd be in on Friday to take care of that. Right now, I just wanted to go home.

As I left the classroom, the rain began to fall. I looked at my watch, and it read 3:00. It was ten minutes later than I'd asked for. Whispering "thank you" as I walked through the downpour, I felt deeply held by Grace.

I realized that it was and wasn't about Preston that cold and dark day in February 2010. It was also about losing a sister and being stuck in a cycle of grief. It was about what I could not control, like the unexpected death of my sister and a wounded little boy's behavior. I needed to find a more constructive way to manage my emotions, bring them into the light, and gain my own inner resolve to move on. Accepting that Patricia was gone forever yet coming to know she would always be with me made a huge difference. Even now, I still feel sad about her early departure, but I also feel joy because of the gift of knowing her.

That next day, Friday, Preston, Brianna, and I headed to the creek at lunchtime. Brianna shared with me confidentially, "I know why Preston invited me to go with you guys. I am the only one who treats him like a normal human being."

I shared with Brianna that Preston was, indeed, a normal human being and that it was unfortunate many kids didn't like him. Still, I appreciated that *she* was kind to him. We both agreed Preston was a good kid. We had a delightful time at the creek, collecting twigs and sticks, and I showed them how to make oak gall toys. I came to school on my own time, volunteering to go with Preston to the creek, accompanied by his only real friend, Brianna. Our time on Fridays lasted for a couple of months, stopping only because the school year was drawing to a close.

I fell apart when Preston needed me to hold it together. It took quite some time for me to forgive myself for slipping up, and perhaps it was, after all, a relief. Being a perfect teacher isn't much fun, and it was not realistic. By connecting with him after the episode and apologizing and offering to help him, I hope he saw I was human and learning right along with him. Author and former preschool teacher from Saratoga, California, Betty Peck once said to me (regarding being a teacher): "Your students just need YOU." By being my authentic self, I was able to connect with Preston in a more meaningful way. Preston and I (along with Brianna) had some wonderful experiences at the creek after that. If I hadn't blown it that day, I would have never come to know the child. I was grateful for the lesson, though I wished it could have happened more easily.

I pray that, wherever Preston is right now, he has found peace and that life is better for him. The wounded teacher he encountered that day used the experience to take care of her feelings and let go of her sister, to live on, move on, and be well.

Ultimately, Mrs. Walton and I developed a good relationship. She was not very experienced, but, yet, she did have some wisdom, being a mother of two. To get to this point in her life, Mrs. Walton had to have jumped through the necessary hoops. I grew to appreciate her and the challenging job she had as a principal.

Lesson: We are all human.

Moving On

One cloudy February day after the school break, there was a beckoning invitation from the garden to come and be alive. My kindergarten students and I answered the call. The children had been begging me to return to the garden so that they could find a tree frog once more. Wearing my dangling, large frog earrings and bringing along my life-sized bullfrog puppet, it seemed the day was undoubtedly a frog day. We sat in a circle and sang frog songs we made up, and the children had terrific conversations with Froggie Frog, the name they gave my hand puppet. We listened but did not hear any tree frogs other than the ones we imagined.

The second group, though, hit the jackpot.

"Ms. Bickett, I think a tree frog is inside this bench!" little Elisa said to me. There was a large rubber bench out in the garden that had a seat that opened to store things inside. I had a quick hunch she was right, so we opened the bench and peered inside. Sure enough, there was a little tree frog in a pot! The children enjoyed holding him and then pleaded with me to bring the frog to show their teachers and classmates. We put some water in a little dish and carefully transported the little guy to each of their classes. They asked to leave it in their rooms as a pet.

"This little frog was so kind as to let us hold him and see him. Let's do the right thing and put him back in the garden where he can be with his family and be free," I explained. Once I said this, they acquiesced. I set the tree frog gently back where we found him. There was no doubt he was delighted to be home again!

Once again, Grant Wood's *American Gothic* painting lesson inspired my fifth-grade classes. I had awakened with a feeling of immense gratitude and joy. My energy felt great, and I wanted to do something different . . . an idea materialized before me. As I was getting dressed, I thought those hazardous words, *Why not?* I tossed my jeans and shirt aside and went in search of my wig and a suitable dress for the day.

Off I strolled to school, wearing the wig. As I arrived on campus, I was met with all kinds of stares and open mouths. I grabbed the art cart and proceeded to my first class as the bell rang. Once inside the room, I heard whispers, "Who is she *this* time?"

I unloaded the decorated art cart (Grant Wood's famous painting as a poster in the front) with a smile as I conjured up exactly what to do. None of this was rehearsed or planned. I was totally improvising. By the time all the posters of his paintings and various books about the artist were set up and the supplies ready, the entire class was wide-eyed with curiosity. Since I had decided to portray the role of Grant Wood's sister, Nan, I wanted the experience to be fun and provide information about the artist.

"Howdy, boys and girls! Whew! I just rode my mule all the way from Iowa, and I am plumb tired. My brother, Grant, says to me, he says, 'Nanny, would ya so kindly go visit them there kids in Californy way for me? I just can't leave this here paintin', and I did so give them my word . . .' Well, just so happened I got the week off my job as a dental hygienist, and I says, 'Sure, bro, just point me the way,' and off Selma and me here will go!" I blurted out in a very exaggerated Midwestern twang. The laughter was terrific, and my students played along with my ruse just fine.

Of course, someone noticed my shoes and asked why they were the same as Ms. Bickett's. I shrugged my shoulders.

"Them there's a mighty, what they call, a co-in-ci-dance!" I replied.

The student nodded back at me with a wink and a smile. I felt so grateful and happy I nearly cried. I was grateful I took the chance to play this character and had fun that day. I really got into the part, relying on my Midwestern upbringing to supply plenty of authentic cliché phrases, delivered in a bit of an over-exuberant accent—but that was half the fun.

During recess, I was bombarded the entire period with questions like, "Where's Ms. Bickett?" Or my favorite, "Is that your hair?" Little Andy, the boy who told me I needed to color my graying hair, saw me in the hallway and was in a kind of speechless horror as he stared at me. I walked by him, and he said to me, "Now, Ms. Bickett, you really need to color your hair!" I assured him that I would, and as I walked away from him, he yelled, "Be sure to color it dark brown!" Maybe this little guy was going to be a hairdresser!

The word got out about "Nanny Wood's" visit, and all kinds of students came up to me with huge smiles. As I noted before, the days I came dressed up as a character to school were the times I saw more bright smiles than usual. My head, however, began to itch terribly, so at lunch, I needed to remove the wig.

When I returned in the afternoon, there was a palpable disappointment. "We heard we had a guest!" the crestfallen afternoon classes moaned. I assured them that Nan Wood really wanted to stay, but she and her donkey needed to catch the next train back to Iowa.

"It was really you anyway!" they chimed back in indignation. We had fun joking about my character, and by the time school was over, I was tired in a happy, fulfilled way. I sat outside in my backyard with Lizzie once I got home, soaking in the sun during a break in the otherwise cloudy day. All I could feel was the precious gift of time and that I got to live a good day.

I laugh as I remember little Jake, one of my younger students, as he ran up to me another morning. He blinked and stopped to look at me before he seemed to recognize me. Then he grabbed my hand and patted me gently, saying, "Ms. Bickett, you are a good girl!"

What a shift in energy for me. Before the recent ski break, I felt undone and broken. Though the clouds were still dark, and the rain again poured from the sky, I understood I had been and always would be held by Grace. That day, I enjoyed the updraft of the wind as it lifted my wings upward and sky bound. When you choose life, it's important to embrace it all, the dark moments that either break you or teach you how to bend, and the light moments, when you remember you can fly. And that is what makes our lives so beautiful.

Lesson: Life loves you.

Humor, Sticks, and an Angel from Out of the Mist

To create the ambiance of a rainforest in a second-grade class, I played a Raffi CD. The song was "Apples and Bananas." I chose this song because I hoped the notion of fruit would fit well with tropical places. The song reinforced learning across the curriculum with its fun vowel exercises. The children enjoyed singing along; many of them were familiar with this tune. Later, as they worked on their Rousseau jungle scenes, I played a tape of birds singing. It really did feel like we were inside a jungle because the rain poured outside. The entire week was very stormy. It challenged my good nature toward being a traveling teacher as the wind and rain did their best to derail the supply-laden art cart.

I had a classroom for kindergarten and first-grade students on Mondays and Wednesdays, and it was a relief to have the shelter of the room those stormy days. As my first graders came into the room one day, a little girl stopped and sniffed the air, turning around and examining the room. "This room smells like my dentist's!" she said with a scowl. I shared the room with two other teachers. And maybe a dentist? It was funny because none of the rest of us could smell the "dentist smell," though we tried.

The following week, my fourth and fifth graders were studying Picasso. I played a DVD about him (a short animated one). I had brought in numerous posters and examples of his work. The art cart was decorated with student art and a Picasso poster. My diligent students took notes and drew in their art journals as I carefully wrote the steps to the assignment on the board. It would be a month-long lesson, and each week we were to work on different aspects of an abstract self-portrait.

Whenever I told my students it was time to pack up because I had to leave, they always moaned and groaned. We never had enough time for art!

"Well, you see, I don't know how to control the time yet, though I do control the weather. Remember last week I said today would be sunny? Sure enough, it is!" I teased them.

I laughed, and they snickered at me. No sooner had I spoken those words than I realized I had opened myself up to comments like, "So, what will the weather be like this weekend, Ms. Bickett? I want to go skiing." And on and on. Luckily, I happened to remember the weather report from that morning, so I predicted a great weekend. Of course, as I left the room, I prayed the weatherman was right!

On a Monday, after that lovely weekend, little Jake, one of my kindergarteners, said to me, "Ms. Bickett, Ms. Bickett!" most urgently.

"Yes, Jake?" I asked. He was timid, so it took him a few minutes as we rode our "train" along, picking up other children.

Finally, he said as we approached our room, "I like to see your face!"

Smiling back at him, I answered, "I like to see your face, too, Jake!"

Wow, it was a great way to start not only a Monday but a fantastic way to begin a new week.

It was the precious things the children said that filled my cup. It was those quiet, tender words I shall never forget. Moments, beautiful moments that connected to other moments in my life, created a tapestry of experiences over time. Maybe it seems like nothing, insignificant, to recall a little phrase here and there. But they were jewels to me, shining and bright.

That Friday, I came to school again. Brianna, Preston, and I gathered more sticks. I was planning an art/nature lesson for my students and took advantage of our creek time together to also collect small twigs, leaves, and stones. Over the past few weeks, unnoticed by me, young children playing in the field during lunch observed our coming and going.

That following Tuesday, I was returning to school after the lunch break. A small group of third graders, students I knew from the previous year (but did not have as students that year), came running up to me.

"We've been collecting sticks for you!" they cried with glee.

They asked me where to put all their sticks, and I suggested a spot in the corner of the grassy area where I would return to get them later. Well, I completely forgot the pile of sticks. That next Thursday, as I was returning from lunch again, little Amelia, one of the third-grade girls, ran up to me, calling my name in urgency.

"Ms. Bickett! We've been collecting sticks for you and have a big pile! They are waiting for you in the corner where you said to put them!" I turned, and my eyes widened as I saw a large pile of sticks by the redwood tree!

I was deeply touched by their efforts. This time, I did not forget, and that afternoon, when my teaching was done, I enlisted the help of a few students to assist me in bringing the sticks back to the room where the art cart was stored. I found a niche to store them with the other sticks we'd collected. I would use the sticks the following week. I had plenty of materials and decided stick collecting could cease.

Because the almond tree by the creek could be seen from the schoolyard, my little students and I enjoyed nature walks to notice signs of spring. The pink-kissed blossoms of the almond tree glowed softly in the light of morning, and we were taken by such loveliness. Hence, one objective of collecting twigs was for my little kinder kids to create their own tiny, delicate blossoming branches. We glued soft pink tissue papers, squished into blossom shapes, onto branches for the children to take home.

One of my students, Daisy, told me that her mother would not allow the stick in the house, that it would be promptly thrown away when she brought it home the next week! The twigs and blossoms looked very realistic, and they were beautiful. I could hardly believe a parent would say and do such a thing. But then, I remembered the kelp doll that a mother threw away once and realized some people didn't want nature inside the house.

"Maybe when your mom sees how beautiful the twig and blossoms are, she will decide to keep it," I suggested. I cannot recall how that unfolded, but I'd like to think Daisy's mom loved what her daughter made and did not throw it away.

March always seemed like such a long month when I taught. There were no breaks, and it seemed to go on and on. I saved long, more involved art projects for March that kept the kids' interest. As my second graders were working on their Rousseau masterpieces, I liked to walk around and converse with the children. They were creating gorgeous jungle scenes in oil pastels.

I overheard a conversation between a little girl and boy: "Hey, Bill, what's your favorite show you can't watch?"

I didn't hear his response as I had to step away to hide my sudden burst of laughter.

It was rainy again that day, and I was beginning to feel less than enthusiastic about the weather and pushing the art cart through the puddles. The art cart was beautifully ornate with jungle art created by students and a Rosseau poster.

I had a lot of fun changing the art cart to fit new lessons, but often the tarp I covered the art cart with didn't completely keep the rain off art and supplies. It was recess, and I headed to the restroom feeling a bit gloomy when a second-grade girl, Frankie, appeared out of nowhere.

"Ms. Bickett, I can't wait for the art lesson today!" she called.

She hopped off in the rain to her classroom as I stood watching her. *That little child,* I reminded myself, *deserves an art teacher who was not negative because of the rainy weather and resenting having to push the art cart around.* I realized the children were anticipating a great lesson, and it was up to me to be there with all my heart. I realized I owed it to them to chipper up, at least a little bit, and find something good about the day. No problem with that, because suddenly I felt very, very rich and grateful to be there—and very thankful to little Frankie for being yet another angel.

I managed to have fun in the last few classes of the day, though I was fatigued. As I walked home in the wind and rain (the storms returned after a brief pause), my muscles begin to ache, and I felt very chilled. I felt tender and sore all over. I realized this was the first fibromyalgia flare I'd had in some time. When I enjoyed periods free of pain and relatively more energy, I sometimes fell into the notion that the mysterious body aches would never return.

Things always change. The optimist in me, however, notes that, often, things change for the better. So, I endured a brief resurgence of an old, unwelcome visitor. But I knew it wouldn't last. Sure enough, I felt renewed as spring came into full bloom again.

Lesson: Everything changes.

Nature Was My Classroom

When I was outside with my kinder kids, we always made so many joyful discoveries. On a particularly lovely spring day, I led my little flock of bright and cheery "chicks" to the classroom, but the day was just too beautiful to be indoors. After our greeting song, we lined up to go on a walk. "Today," I told my eager flock of spring faces, "nature is going to be our teacher, our classroom. Let's go see what she has to show us!"

Annie looked at me with a confused expression. "What is nature?" she asked.

I sighed with a smile. "Well, let's go see!" I replied.

We followed our leader of the day, Henry, to the vast green playing field behind the school.

"OK!" I said, halting the children. "Everyone close your eyes. Open them on the count of three."

When we all said the number three, and everyone's big bright eyes were open wide, I pointed all around us.

"There's nature!" I announced.

"OH!" Annie said with delight. "Let's go there!"

So, we did.

Often, I forgot to photograph the art cart. Every month it transformed, from Valentine's Day hearts to St. Patrick's Day banners, four-leaf clovers to Christmas trees. It was like pushing around my own parade. Frequently, when I entered a classroom with the newly decorated art cart, I heard "oohs" and "ahhs" and "wows!" The children told me they loved decorating the cart. Every month a different class had the chance to embellish it with their marvelous artwork. During March, Mr. Smythe's class enhanced the cart with rainbows, pots of gold, and leprechauns.

Sometimes I remembered and took a quick photo of the cart. I am happy to be able to share some of those photos at the end of this book.

One day when I was leaving school, I heard someone call my name. A little boy ran up to me, hugged me, and ran off. Another angel's visit to be sure, because, as before, I didn't know who this child was. Of that I was very confident because, though sometimes names would elude me, I never forgot a face. I paused under the whispering pine and looked back at the campus. Children were playing as their mothers watched them from behind younger siblings' strollers. After school seemed like such a relaxed time. I searched for the little boy who hugged me, but he vanished into the throng of happy children. There was something magical about that moment and many of the moments with the children.

As I stood pondering the magic, I gazed at Grandmother Oaktree standing peacefully by the creek. In a vision, I saw the ancient oak when she was young, with Ohlone children playing nearby. I knew the tree was at least three hundred years old. I had consulted with a tree expert some time ago. When she and I examined Grandmother Oaktree, she had verified the tree's age.

In the next moments, I peered hesitantly into the future. Would there still be children here laughing and running? What were we doing to preserve this beautiful earth? I looked up into the sturdy, full branches of the tree and listened to the wind whispering through her sharp, glossy leaves. My heart understood the wordless communication of the tree and the wind. There are mysteries and sacredness all around us. We suffer when we don't connect with that message and understand our place on this earth.

On a Monday in late March, we woke up to a seventy-degree day. Spring swung back and forth from cold, rainy days to hot, sunny afternoons that were almost too hot. My first graders were sleepy, it was the first day of Daylight Savings Time, and we were struggling from having awakened to darkness. We were working on reviewing the story diagram, retelling, and summarizing. I read a story about an elephant—the same one my sister gave me from the sanctuary a few years ago. Some of the children's work I sent on to the Elephant Sanctuary in Tennessee to thank them for the lovely story.

We made elephants and wrote stories under the pictures. They were beautiful, and I thanked my students for their excellent work.

"The elephants won't forget it either," Sarah said, "because they have good memories."

The second graders were excited this week. They shared with me stories of their "leprechaun traps." The next day was St. Patrick's Day. Their smart teachers had the children create inventive traps with tiny enticing (imitation, of course) gold coins to lure the little buggers inside. What a great idea!

St. Patrick's Day was Wednesday, and I brought my golden girl to school, wearing her (humiliating) "Kiss me, I'm Irish" headband. What a patient dog! The office staff and the students all lit up when they saw her, and she seemed to love the attention. I finally took off the headband as Lizzie looked up at me with a "Please, do I *have* to keep wearing this?" look.

Over and over, I heard children shouting to me, "I love Lizzie!" The day was partly cloudy but pleasant as we walked along with my honey-colored bundle of love. I collected each child from their classrooms, letting them have a turn at holding her leash. She was very calm and sweet to the children as they petted her and walked alongside her. I was so proud of my dog. We reviewed the lesson of wild/not wild, and I compared wild wolves with Lizzie. We howled together and then listened to Lizzie's heartbeat after they listened to their own hearts. What a great day!

Then, my first-grade children shared with me their leprechaun experiences.

One little boy, Thomas, was crying. "No leprechaun visited my house last night!" he cried.

The first-grade teachers apparently did something similar to the second-grade classes. When the children arrived on St. Patrick's Day, they found their classrooms a mess, with little jellybeans scattered all over, as if little green people came into the school the night before and left the mess. All the children helped clean up after the leprechauns.

Some of the first graders confided in me that "it is just pretending, but it is fun to play along. We think it is really our teacher who makes the mess!" After thinking about this, the somber child, Thomas, who bemoaned not having been visited by leprechauns, said, "But I *want* to believe it was the leprechauns! I thought it *was* them!" He became red-faced and near tears again.

"You can believe whatever you want, Thomas," I assured him.

It seemed too upsetting to him to say that the leprechauns weren't real, and Thomas continued to be distressed that they didn't visit his house.

"Perhaps the leprechauns only come to schools where the children set traps for them. Maybe they don't do home visits!" I suggested.

Thomas's face softened, and he smiled, satisfied with my explanation.

The next day, Thursday, I had to fast all day for a gallbladder test after school at four-thirty. A couple of weeks prior, right in the middle of an art lesson with my second graders, I felt a stabbing pain on my left side that did not subside. It was like no other pain I had ever experienced, so after two weeks of suffering, I called my doctor, and he ordered a test. I had a lot of problems with belching and eating fatty foods, but that could be from my previously diagnosed reflux problem. Regardless, the pain was most unusual for me.

I brought music, and we worked on Rothko-style watercolor paintings. We reviewed colors, looking at complements and warm/cool colors. I invited my students to relax and paint fields of color, no subject, but just to respond with feelings and basic shapes. One example was a fuzzy purple rectangle that was hung above another blurry box in yellow or orange. I invited them to play with the idea and to try several pieces. Preston really responded to this lesson and painted with great vigor.

By the last class, I was beginning to feel irritated and dizzy. The students seemed extra noisy that day, and the fact that it bothered me informed me that surely my hunger was starting to affect me. I couldn't wait for school to be over so I could walk home and rest before I headed to the hospital. I was also beginning to feel anxious because I was not sure how long the test would take. I assured myself it would probably only last an hour at the most. As I was thinking about these things, watching the clock tick away, Vicky, one of my fourth graders, came up to me.

"I look forward to the art class so much! I love art!" she said.

My fatigue was nearly drowning me, but Vicky's words were a lifeline. Another student remarked how relaxing this lesson was and how he loved the fact that I often brought music for them to listen to during the art class. *Yep, it was just me*, I told myself, drinking another slurp of water. The kids were doing fine. I was the one who had the problem for sure!

The gallbladder test was more involved than I imagined. The test took over two hours. I had to be very still in an MRI machine. I was famished and a bit nervous. They watched the bile flow from my gallbladder as they pumped dye into me through IVs. Fortunately, though, the results a few days later were a relief. The doctor said I could have passed a stone, but there were no signs of any now, and my gallbladder emptied just fine. The only problem they discovered was that I have a small polyp in my gallbladder that would need monitoring. As I left the hospital that day, I could have kissed the ground. I was grateful to be alive and well.

March came in like a lion with storms and ended like a lamb that year. The flowering trees in my backyard were gorgeous. They looked like a Japanese ink painting of cherry blossoms (though only one of them was a cherry tree).

I walked to school in the aura of all kinds of blossoms, from pink to popcorn-white along the sidewalk. In front of me, as I entered the schoolyard, was little Amy, one of my kinder students, walking hand-in-hand with her father.

As they arrived at the damp field, he scooped her into his arms and carried her on his shoulders as they crossed the field. The vision of this moment stayed tenderly in my heart. I watched them as they walked along, the sunlight in her dark hair as she rode like a princess across a green sea. I hoped Amy would always remember her father that way, too, in the days when she grew older and he was no longer there.

I thought back to when my father used to rock me to sleep at night and the wonderful feeling of being carried back to bed, my head resting on his shoulders. This only happened when he was wearing his artificial leg because when he used his crutches he couldn't carry me. The uneven steps he'd take as he walked were like a continuation of the rocking chair.

Those tender moments between my father and me still touch my heart to this day, as did the scene with Amy and her father that first day of spring.

After returning from a trip in the fall, I strapped a few of those á la cart tags you get from the airlines onto the art cart for fun. It didn't seem that anyone noticed them until finally, one day, Molly, one of my fourth-grade girls, came up to the cart and pulled at the bright green strap. She examined it with great curiosity.

"Did you really take the art cart on an airplane?" she asked.

I tried not to laugh as I saw she was serious.

"Well, I used the á la cart tags on my last plane trip and thought it would be funny to put them on the art cart," I explained.

Molly seemed relieved with my explanation.

"Well, it's just that you go all over with the cart, so I thought maybe you took it with you on a plane!" she answered.

"Well, I haven't taken it with me on a plane trip . . . yet!" I replied with a laugh.

Lesson: Anything is possible!

Hummingbird Courage

I always told my students to "Fear No Art." In fact, I had a button that said just that and wore it for many years before I lost it. "You're not a brain surgeon," I told them, "so mistakes are not only good, they can lead you to new horizons you never considered before." Mistakes are essential teachers, and if it hadn't been for some significant errors, I would never have created some of my best work.

Do we encourage children to make mistakes? Well, not outright, but do we teach them how to befriend their fears? Certainly not in these days of "teaching to the test." My husband experiences the results of indoctrination to sameness at the university level. Compared to when he first began teaching as a professor of music in 1986, students today don't appear to understand how to think outside the box (as much). Many of his composition students, who should be thinking creatively, just want to know the "right answers" and seem afraid to venture too far from safety. How sad.

Sometimes, as an art teacher, I felt pressured that my students' artwork needed to look perfect because I knew I would be displaying it in places where it would be admired. As an art teacher, I was aware of the role of PR in my job. I made sure my students' art was displayed for administrators, parents, and other teachers to see. The children created fantastic images that needed to be shared. But there was an inherent danger in this, too, as the tendency to hang more "ideal" pieces was tempting. Everyone's art can't always be displayed, and inevitably some students were more successful at demonstrating the concept or standards being taught for any given lesson. These were children for heaven's sake! How were they going to build confidence and self-esteem if only the "good" pieces got displayed?

I tried my best to be sure that everyone in the class had at least one piece up in the office or district building, taqueria or coffee shop sometime during the year. It was my intention for each child to feel pride and recognition for something they created in the art class. That was always my goal when I exhibited student art.

On a Friday in late March 2010, I switched with the PE teacher, Melissa, so she could have the day off. I was not thrilled to teach on a Friday, but I didn't mind doing my good friend and colleague a favor. All day, I kept thinking it was Thursday, and the children, my fourth and fifth graders, kept reminding me when I slipped up on the date. We arrived at the point where the students were cutting out their watercolor self-portraits and gluing them on a background color, adding some lines and patterns. This was in keeping with Picasso's style. The students signed their names on the artwork and composed their artist statements in their journals. Later, they would rewrite them to go on the back of their work.

I created a form that they would paste onto the back of their work, and one of the questions I asked them to consider was, "Who was the artist who inspired you?" Of course, for this lesson, it was obviously Pablo Picasso. However, throughout the day, I had several students ask me how to spell my name. At first, I didn't know why they were asking me this. It wasn't until the end of the day when I noticed their answers to the question of who inspired them: "Ms. Bickett and Pablo Picasso." Wow, I never would have thought! I was flattered and surprised.

Emphasizing that an artist should sign their work with a distinctive signature, I showed my students my unique style of signing my name. In one class, a student raised his hand.

"Ms. Bickett, are you a real artist? Do you have a certificate to show you are an artist?" he asked.

He wanted to know if, for someone to be called an artist, did they need a signed paper saying so? I smiled at him and thought for a moment, trying to think of the best way to answer his question.

"Well, Pablo Picasso once said, 'Every child is an artist. The problem is to remain an artist once we grow up,' so I guess I just didn't forget I was an artist, and that makes me still an artist." He grinned with approval at my reply, but I did add, "I do have a master's degree in art education that qualifies me to teach art, but no one has to have a certificate to *be* an artist."

The whole class seemed relieved with this notion.

"You are already artists, you always have been, and you always will be. I hope none of you ever forget that," I added.

I was pleased with the students as they proudly showed me their individual artist's signatures on their self-portraits. Very pleased.

During a fourth-grade class that Friday, Brianna approached me with a request to see the school counselor. We had talked during lunch as she confided in me about a problem she was having, and I recommended that she go talk with the counselor. However, the only time Brianna could do that had to be during art class, and I assured Brianna that would be fine. We agreed that she could start working on her piece in class and leave as soon as she was able. I would phone the counselor to see if she was available.

As Brianna was working in class, then, I searched for the phone to make the call. I couldn't seem to find it, and after searching around the teacher's desk, I was stumped. Where was the phone?

The regular teacher happened to be in the room working, so I asked out loud, "Does anyone know where the phone is?" I figured if none of the students knew where it was, which would be unlikely, then, at least, he could tell me. I didn't want to interrupt him during his prep work.

Mr. Tucker was hard at work in the back of the room when he heard me asking about the phone.

"It's over there under all that shit," he called out.

I stopped in my tracks and wondered if I had heard what I *thought* I heard (as I stifled a laugh). A student nearby looked up at me.

"*What* did he say?" the child asked.

Mr. Tucker was one of my favorite teachers. He was dynamic and very caring toward his students. He was not the kind of person to let something like that slip, and so I quickly replied to the student, "He said, 'It's over there under all that *stuff*!" The curious student looked a little confused but then smiled and said, "OK!"

I turned to hide my amusement at this atypical and obviously absent-minded response as I heard Mr. Tucker moaning behind me. Teachers are human, after all.

The following week, I joked with him about the slip, and he turned beet red with embarrassment. I assured him his secret was safe with me and that it didn't seem to bother the students very much. I doubted too many were listening. Thank goodness I had some music on! He seemed relieved though still uncomfortable. "I will make sure that phone is never under my clutter ever again though!" he said with conviction.

The last class this Friday afternoon was bonkers. The kids seemed totally crazy and ready to go home. A student named Lucy showed me a drawing of a horse she created at home, and she was obviously very proud of her work.

At the end of class, I asked her if she'd like to share what she made with the class, and so Lucy happily showed her classmates her horse drawings. As I was leaving class, Lucy offered me one of the pictures, "This one I made 'specially for you!" she said, beaming. It wasn't until I arrived at home that I noticed she wrote *Tennessee Walker* on the front and then my name on the back.

The funny thing was that my sister in Oregon had a Tennessee Walker named Fritz. Indeed, Lucy didn't know that. She was amazed when I told her this information the following week.

"I just knew you had to have that horse!" she told me.

It was one of those moments of serendipity because all day that Friday, I had my sister on my mind. It was a little thing and yet very precious to me. And I still have that drawing someplace among my other treasures that students gave me over the years.

Spring was such an abundant time to explore changes in nature, with so many blossoming trees and flowers springing up from the ripe earth. Over the years, I had brought students out to listen to the heartbeat of trees in the spring when the sap starts to pulsate and awaken. Sometimes we heard a faint echo, other times not. But that wasn't the point, anyway. The children experienced that a tree was a living being, vibrant, and responsive to the seasons like we are. I found that having them go through this process, whether we heard anything or not, brought a deeper connection and awareness to their precious lives.

Education can be harsh, with all the regimentation, the pressure to do well on tests, social dilemmas, and hectic schedules after school and at home. Quiet and reflective times being with nature and noticing the beautiful world outdoors seemed to help renew and refresh the children. There was no doubt in my mind it helped them perform better in their classrooms as well.

I was fortunate to have this time with my little ones, guiding them through various kinds of well-thought-out lessons related to the natural world.

One day, when I was out walking with my kinder kiddies, we passed by trees we'd been observing all year. In the fall, we'd marveled at the orange and red leaves as they descended and checked the sleeping buds during the nap of winter. We delighted to watch the bouquets of flowers bursting from the awakening buds. Dancing in the snowfall of white petals as they swirled and fell from the branches, we participated in one of life's great wonders.

There were lines of maple trees that we walked by every time I picked up the kinder kids, so it was easy to spend the year keeping track of all the comings and goings of the eloquent, three-fingered leaves. The previous week, we saw the buds bursting with new life. As a result, I was excited as I passed by the trees and saw the leaves had really grown huge in one week. I couldn't wait to show the children. What a surprise!

I gathered up my little chickens, and we set out on our "boat," with Sandra as the captain. "Take us out to sea!" I called as we neared the playground, where the trees were waiting for us. We often imagined the large blacktop area was the ocean. My explorers and I needed to cross it to get to our classroom. We saw all kinds of creatures—sharks, whales, sea birds, octopuses, and others. Anyway, I asked Sandra to pause by the trees before we moved on.

"Look! See the leaves! They are bigger than last week! No more buds or flowers!" I directed them. I waited for my students' usual squeals of delight and joy. Still, there was only silence as they all looked at me without their typical expressions.

"We know! We saw them this morning!" Sandra piped up.

And another student chimed in, "Yeah, we noticed them already!"

My balloon was deflated, and my bubble burst. Then I laughed and thought again. Perhaps I'd done my job well after all because my little students were noticing the trees without me!

Later that evening, Brian and I walked Lizzie through the schoolyard. It was about five-thirty, and there were still some children playing outside in the after-school care program. I needed to drop off some examples for my lesson the next day to Room 5. On the way out, we encountered two girls coming out of the bathroom. One of them I knew from my first-grade enrichment class. As Rebecca petted Lizzie, we noticed she wasn't wearing shoes, which was a little unusual for being at school.

"Where are your shoes?" Brian asked the child. Rebecca replied quickly and with gusto, "Ahhhh, shoes!" and she raised her feet into the air and waved off the silly idea of wearing shoes. We shrugged our shoulders and laughed with her, and then she skipped off to the room behind her friend.

My husband and I looked at each other with wide grins.

"Who needs shoes when feet will do?" we laughed.

Ah, to be a child and to be so carefree . . . at least shoe-free, anyway!

As we walked along the fence by the creek, we spotted a male Anna's hummingbird perched on the top bare branches of an old tree. I thought back to the many times my students and I had seen him there; it must be his favorite looking spot. The tiny bird's red, brilliant feathers glittered in the sunlight. He made his funny little sipping sounds, and we stopped to watch him. I thought of how, despite their small size, hummingbirds are very brave and have big hearts.

How do you hold a moment that feels like an eternity? Seconds, maybe minutes pass, who knows? It didn't matter, as it seemed the moment was stretched into one long, precious experience of time everlasting, of space and emptiness and fullness and wonder. And I hold that now, years later, deep in my heart and still see him there, as surely he will ever be, on the uppermost branch of the tree, waiting for absolutely nothing at all. Just being alive and taking it all in, everything.

Lesson: Imagination is the beginning of possibilities.

Life Happens

In April, I introduced a lesson about Mary Cassatt, an Impressionist painter from America who studied in France during the heyday of Impressionism. She had always been one of my favorite artists to introduce to younger children because of the gentle, loving images of women and children Cassatt created. The children conjured up numerous stories to go with some of her paintings when I introduced the lesson. With a poster of one of Cassatt's portraits at the front, the art cart was covered with student artwork and looked like a quilt of patterns, much like a Cassatt painting.

I adapted a lesson I taught in middle school the previous year, and it worked great with the second graders: we took turns drawing the back of the head of a partner. This lesson gave some essential proportion experience with head, neck, and shoulders without the complication of facial proportions.

I began to feel emotionally stretched to my limit, eager for the soon-to-arrive April break. The children were doing fine, and though they seemed to have more of a problem with this project than the children had last year, they were enjoying themselves. In my journal, when I was finally at home after school, I noted how much I was looking forward to getting away. The year so far had been most challenging.

The following week we painted our drawings of the back of the head. Bringing out the watercolor sets and all the vast array of supplies needed, I thought to myself, *This is crazy. I just don't have the energy for this lesson right now! I should have done something simpler this week!*

Happily, though, my self-talk was utterly untrue. As I watched the children work, I was filled with joy to see how joyful they were and how much they were engaged with the lesson. One child amused me as I observed him mixing all kinds of colors in his tray. He looked up at me and announced, "I was trying to mix colors to get white!" As he continued, I watched and said nothing. Suddenly, he beamed and said, "I thought I almost got it!"

The color he had in the tray and that he tested on the paper was quite far from white, and I hesitated to tell him you couldn't mix watercolors together to get white. I held off from trying to instruct him, and I was glad I did.

"If you add all the colors of the rainbow, you get white," he said.

I saw now what was going on in his bright little mind. Someone explained to him about color in light theory, and it was absolutely right.

I found it was time for me to step in a little.

"You are correct, Jerry! If you mix all the colors of light together, it does make white light. But, when you mix all the colors from the earth, called pigments, you get . . . what?" I asked.

Jerry looked down and saw the various versions of muddy browns he created instead of white and looked at me with pride.

"Brown! No, wait, mud! I made mud!"

Jerry proceeded to play with his "mud" for a time and then went back to painting his drawing of his partner's head. It was an encounter with pure discovery and joy.

I decided to stagger creek walks the two weeks before spring break, so I took my afternoon classes to the stream. We brought oil pastels with us and sat on the dirt path to draw the giant eucalyptus tree, with its graceful white branches dancing into the sky.

As I stood there watching them draw and chatter with ease, I realized I had been very harsh with myself. My inner critic berated me for not feeling well and pushed me to do better. Now, without effort, I was relaxed and fully present and at ease, too. Such was the gift of life, and it seems we have many chances to begin anew. I breathed deeply and sighed with relief. My lessons didn't have to be spectacular. There didn't have to be great themes. I could allow life to unfold, like the watercolor lesson. As I observed the students happily drawing that day, I watched them discover a hummingbird nest in the tree next to the eucalyptus. They were awestruck and elated to see the tiny nest being tended to by the parents. When given a chance, magic would reveal itself everywhere.

Every year, I pointed out to my kinder kids a spot under the eaves of a building where sparrows built nests and raised their chicks. In their classrooms, they were watching a peregrine falcon webcam that showed the progress of peregrine falcons downtown that were raising their family on the top of a high building. In addition to seeing the birds on camera, I liked the fact that we could also watch animals living their lives on campus. We talked about the similarities and differences between the two bird families as they reared their young.

The male sparrow, like the male peregrine, flew off to gather food for the newly hatched chicks. We observed this happening right before our eyes one day. The children were mesmerized and excited because they had just seen the male peregrine do the same thing in front of the camera! Making those connections and seeing how similar the two different kinds of birds were gave the children a rich experience that we continued to build on. As time went by, we noted more of the differences, too, but ultimately, we agreed that all creatures need food, shelter, and to some degree, parents who care for them.

My fourth graders visited the creek the week before break. It was a great day; I pointed out the valley oak versus the live oak trees along the trail. We came to the buckeye flowers where swallowtail butterflies danced above our heads. Quite serendipitously, the students found the same hummingbird nest the other children saw the previous week, something I didn't orchestrate. We watched the male sitting on a branch, eyeing us suspiciously while the female was sitting on her eggs. The students created many drawings of the scene.

What a great way to end the week, I told myself. As soon as I got home, I was already packing for a family trip to Maui. Brian and I had planned this trip with our son and his girlfriend. I was more than ready to take a break.

Although the relentless trade winds of the Hawaiian Islands didn't let up the entire time we were there, the change of scenery helped me to relax and breathe again. My dear friend lived (and still lives) on the Big Island, so I'd been back and forth between the mainland and Hawaii many times. A couple of years before this trip, Brian and I had once visited Maui, so we were excited to return. Also, another bonus of the vacation was the joyful announcement that my son's girlfriend was now his fiancée. This happy news gave me the energy to return to work. Without a doubt, I was still profoundly grieving Pat. Yet, I began to feel my footing again and was grateful to be surrounded by the love of my family.

I encountered some discouraging news upon returning to school. The new principal asked me to continue teaching kindergarten ELD and first-grade reading enrichment the next year without a contract. I would be paid hourly instead of receiving a salary. She beamed when she told me I would be doing twice the work for half the pay. I stared at her incredulously and told her I had to think about it. I did, for a few minutes, anyway. The decision was easy: No, thank you. I would teach art at Creek Side the following year, though I would miss my little ones in ELD and the reading-enrichment classes.

The news was a financial blow to my husband and me, but I felt I had to speak to integrity. I knew they were trying to save money, but Ms. Heart . . .

well, she always managed to find a way to make the extra ten percent happen for me. Most certainly, though, I did concede that things had changed. Surely, Mrs. Walton was doing what she felt was best for the school. I somberly realized I needed to find a way to make up for the loss of income in the coming year. Thank goodness I would be teaching at Montalvo Arts Center again that summer for a few weeks.

All year I had looked forward to a particular recycled art project with my fourth and fifth graders, and a modified recycling lesson with my second graders. It was great timing because Earth Day was occurring soon. The entire school was promoting the "Reduce, Reuse, and Recycle" theme. With great enthusiasm, I entered some fourth- and fifth-grade students' posters in a citywide art contest. I brought their creations to the mayor's office for consideration to be hung in local business windows downtown.

Trying to think of something intelligent and motivating, I designed and wore a plastic bag vest I made at home. I presented the lesson, and the kids loved it. We watched a few portions of a great DVD about recycled art from all over the world, and the students were ecstatic and ready to begin their projects. I brought painter's sticks, small cups from RAFT, and markers, and they created a toy where you had to swing three little beads tied to a string into the container. We had great fun with it as they decorated their creations with markers.

"Can we take these home today?" they asked.

"Yes!" I replied.

And then, the entire class applauded!

I was not expecting so many of my older students to have trouble tying the yarn but was happy to observe students helping other students to solve the problem. All the materials we used, even the yarn, were recycled or reused objects, except for the glue, of course. Also, the beads were from the teacher warehouse store. We had fun trying to swing the pellets into the cups. For weeks I saw students playing with our toys at recess and lunch.

As I was leaving that Thursday afternoon, a former student, who was now a seventh grader, stopped at the door to wave hello. I quickly remembered she loved to sing.

"Jeannie, do you still sing?" I asked her as she joined me behind the two cart managers headed toward Room 5. The art cart rumbled along like an old truck as we chatted, dodging exuberant students fleeing their classrooms.

Shrugging her shoulders in response to my question, Jeannie replied sadly, "No, not so much anymore."

"Do keep singing, no matter what. You have a lovely voice!" I assured her.

Jeannie told me that she and her brother had to move to live with her father. She looked very sad.

I hugged her, and then she slipped off a bracelet she was wearing and offered it to me. I looked at the words on it, and it read: "True Love."

"I will never forget this, Jeannie, and I will remember you," I told her. We went our separate ways, but I've always kept that bracelet. When I wear it, it reminds me to always act out of love. I think of the generous young woman who gave the bracelet to me, and I wonder if she ever started to sing again. I hope so.

When the fourth and fifth graders watched the recycling DVD, one thing we agreed on afterward was that all the artists in the presentation loved what they did.

"No matter what," I told them, "you are a success if you love what you do."

When I do something because I love it, I feel renewed and full of energy. I wondered if sometimes I didn't like my job, and that was why it was so tiring. But then, I realized it wasn't that I didn't love teaching. There were too many students to deal with, and I wanted to help them all. I wanted quality, and what we had was quantity, at least as art teachers. I wanted to make a difference and really leave my students with connections, and that was a daunting task when teaching three hundred students a week. Regardless, I did try.

Sometimes love isn't enough, and we need to love ourselves enough to know our limits and honor them. I sit here now and breathe deeply as I acknowledge this truth in myself. I loved teaching, but I didn't love the system. I couldn't love treating students like cattle being herded through the pastures toward a gate. Most teachers love their students (most of them . . .) and love their work despite the system. What a difference it would make to have smaller class sizes, more money for education, if we valued teachers more, and invested more in our children. How fitting that would be, indeed.

Lesson: Just do your best and let go.

Dinosaurs and Counting to One Hundred

On a warm spring day, I prepared two large sheets of craft paper with line drawings of a Stegosaurus and a Tyrannosaurus Rex. The language development children were not only learning about dinosaurs, but we were exploring meat-eaters versus plant-eaters. When the children arrived in the classroom, I read a story about both types of dinosaurs. They chattered with enthusiasm when they saw the two large drawings on the tables with all kinds of supplies available for them to use for decoration.

I stood back with great interest as I observed them adding colors, shapes, and textures to the inner space of each form. Even more intriguing were the stories they made up to go along with their experience. They were divided into two groups, and the first group, who were embellishing the T-Rex, imagined that the menacing carnivore ate a bunch of eggs. They drew eggs descending its throat to not one but two tummies! The children worked marvelously together, sharing and taking turns with the story details. Apparently, this particular T-Rex was an egg-lover and would gobble up eggs as it encountered them in nests.

Without much prompting from me, the children created terrific images and dialogue to go with their learning. I had no idea when I came up with this lesson just how magical it would be!

I wondered about the fascination young children have with dinosaurs. I suppose they must be similar to creatures like dragons and other mythical beings, sometimes terrible and sometimes kind. Dinosaurs were safe to explore because they no longer exist and therefore allow for all kinds of fun. If dinosaurs still existed today, I doubt we'd be quite so in love with them!

The students' vocabulary expanded during lessons like the ones about dinosaurs. I reminded myself that children were pretty smart as they learned new words such as "carnivore," "herbivore," and some of the longer dinosaur names. When you teach something children are interested in, and build on that prior knowledge, the lesson nearly teaches itself.

To help pay bills, I began to do private tutoring and art lessons in the afternoons after school. It was quite a treat to have one-on-one time with children. I had a few students who needed help with academics and a couple of small groups (no larger than three) of eager art students. On a Monday after school, one of my charges and I were walking home together. (In my fee, I included the service of walking to school to pick up the children, and the parents retrieved them at my house when we were done.) Richard was a very precocious second grader. Basically, my work with him was enrichment. I was also supposed to challenge him with special projects, as his mother felt he was bored in school.

My eager student begged me to take a long way home, and I acquiesced. On the narrow path before reaching the dirt road, Richard saw what he thought was a toy and pointed to it with excitement.

"Can I have that toy snake?" he asked.

I commended him for asking before reaching. You never know! When I stooped to pick up the toy, suddenly it moved! Very gently, I picked up the tiny ringneck snake, black with an orange band, and let Richard hold it. There was no need to worry about it being poisonous. After he pleaded to keep it longer, I decided we could take it, as I could use it with my kiddies the next day.

"Richard, by this time tomorrow, I will be back here to release the little guy, OK?" I wanted to be sure he understood the snake was a temporary guest.

The snake became the subject of a delightful story Richard wrote and illustrated.

The next day, my small charges were delighted with the tiny reptile as they took turns holding him. They asked a variety of questions, including, "What does he see with his eyes?" I was touched that they were gentle and tender with the snake. They drew inventive pictures of our guest and said goodbye to him as I tucked the little critter into a safe container for the journey back to his home.

As we were leaving the classroom, Sandra jumped up and proudly announced to me, "Ms. Bickett! I can count from one to one hundred!"

"OK! Let's hear it!" I challenged as I wondered if there was enough time for her to count that far before the recess bell rang.

"One to one hundred!" she said.

I waited and then asked, "Is that all there is?"

"Yep!" she responded with a huge smile.

Well, wasn't that easy?

Since it was Be Kind to Animals Week, the snake's visit was even more fortuitous. As we walked back to their classrooms, Sandra, the leader for the day, insisted we become a giant snake.

She continued with her counting: "Hey, Ms. Bickett, I can count to two hundred now!"

Her classmates yelled at her to proceed, so she said, "One hundred, two hundred! One hundred, two hundred!"

Turning to look at me, I smiled at her with a wink.

"You're really making progress!" I complimented her as she beamed and marched along.

We snaked our way back to their rooms just as the bell rang, and I heard the children boasting to their kinder classmates how they got to hold a snake.

"It saw us with its eyes!" I heard in the distance. "And its mouth was way too small to bite us!"

A while back, Lizzie and I had been guests to the Girl Scout group (that met in the ELD/enrichment room I used) one afternoon. Fortunately, I made copies of the booklet I had created about pet care featuring Lizzie and Zelda for each girl and handed them out, with signatures from both Lizzie and me on the first page.

The next day at school, one little girl, who was not a Girl Scout, slunk up to me with a frown. "I wish I had a book like the one you gave Alana [one of the Girl Scouts]," she whimpered.

The next day, I made sure she got a copy of the book, and she was very grateful. During a second-grade class, a few of the Girl Scouts came up to me and told me they had even created a play about Lizzie and Zelda! I was tickled that they would want to do that! How happy I was to learn from the scout leaders that the girls talked quite enthusiastically about the book for some time afterward.

Andy Warhol was my newly featured artist with my fourth and fifth graders. I saved my favorite lesson until after spring break because I was confident it would be fun for the students. During this time, they were required to take STAR (state-mandated academic testing) exams.

Preston, for the first time since last January, seemed to be very agitated in class and I did my best to calm him. Another boy caught on to Preston's antics and started to copy him. I noticed all my levels were talkative and feisty. I couldn't blame them; they had to sit quietly and bubble in all those answers to hundreds of questions nearly every day for a couple of hours. Little wonder everyone seemed a bit crazy!

Once the class was focused on their printmaking project, my parent volunteer and I kept the printing table going. Students took turns duplicating the images they had drawn from a sketch onto a piece of foam board. I felt the process was essential to understand and was happy that most of the students were thrilled with their prints. It was a lot of work, and I admit it was a challenge, but the day was over, and I gratefully headed home.

As I locked the door to Room 5, a kindergartener, Wally, came up to me with a card and a gift of hand lotion from his mother. The prior week had been Teacher Appreciation Week, and this was the one and only token of gratitude I had from my nearly three hundred students. I hugged Wally and thanked him warmly as he smiled and dashed back to his after-school care group. That hand lotion became an elixir of the gods to me. I used it like it was liquid gold. It was funny how one precious gift could make such a difference!

My second graders were now painting large Georgia O'Keeffe-style flowers. I was very grateful to my parent volunteers, who made a massive difference for the kids and me. Moms (and some dads) were there to help with creek walks and messy projects. I even had a few who came to class every week! We visited the garden and enjoyed the real blooms there. Later, O'Keeffe's flowers awed the children. The room was buzzing with laughter as the children painted their large flowers. One student, Suzie, who was dressed in a green flowered dress and a purple glass-beaded necklace, beamed when I complimented her gorgeous masterpiece.

"I want to be an art teacher like you when I grow up!" she told me.

Another girl behind her repeated the same sentiment, and suddenly, I heard a row of "yeah, just like you!" echoing around the room. I was pleased they wanted to be art teachers, and I hoped with all my heart there would be art classes for them to teach when they were ready.

We decorated the art cart with gorgeous, enlarged flowers of all colors, and it was fabulous. I was proud of how the art cart seemed magical . . . and that thought sifted down into the depths of my being until one day, after I retired, I would take the idea of a magic art cart, and—well, you'll have to read my trilogy to find out!

I did hear some good news, well, from not-so-good news. Unfortunately, the one-to-twenty ratio of teachers to students in kindergarten to third-grade classrooms was being increased to one to twenty-five the next year. Sadly, that meant a couple of teachers would have to be moved to other grade levels or even other schools. There would be some not-so-happy shuffling the next year. The good news? Because of the extra space the reductions would create, there would be at least one available room for art. I was to have a classroom the next year! I could hardly believe it as I pushed the art cart along, the sunny breeze teasing a few papers to the ground and a buzz of children dashing about at lunchtime. I was very excited at the prospect of a room of my own. As the art cart hobbled along gallantly, I sighed. Perhaps it would be the end of the magic art cart era!

Lesson: You never know!

Grace, Beauty, and New Old Shoes

For my students, I always wanted to be the kind of teacher *I'd* want to have, and the kind of teacher I'd want for my son to have as well. Most every day of my career I did my best to be authentic and to be there for my students.

The lesson of shoes came to mind, for in that spring of 2010, following my introduction of Andy Warhol and some experiences on printmaking, I decided, we must paint shoes. Warhol had several paintings/prints of shoes, all kinds of shoes, and I was inspired.

I asked my fourth- and fifth-grade students (what, was I crazy?) to bring in one old shoe, two if they could spare one for another student who showed up without a shoe. Pointing out how we take shoes for granted, we talked about how there were children right now, somewhere in the world, and even in our own communities, who did not have shoes to walk to school in.

"Let's celebrate shoes and what they do for us, letting Andy Warhol's images of shoes inspire us," I told my curious students. The note I sent home to parents explained the project, and somehow, with the help of extra shoes, we ended up with one shoe for each child to paint.

First, we created contour line drawings of the shoes, and they were exquisite! We looked at them with our *eyes*, and we saw them with our *minds*. I heard children saying, "Hey, I didn't know my shoe had this design!"

There were some very fancy drawings of the patterns on the bottom of shoes, which made great templates for prints or rubbings as well. Once this was done, the next week, I brought gallons of gesso. Gesso is a type of plaster of Paris or gypsum. Since my funds were spent by this time of year, I used my own money to purchase the supplies. We turned our cleaned-up shoes into bumpy canvases.

Of course, the dilemma was: Where do you keep the drying shoes? There was very little space in the regular rooms. Consequently, we did our best to dry them outside. I assigned a small crew of responsible students to gather up the shoes at the end of the day, bring them in with the newspaper pieces still under them to keep paint off surfaces, and leave them on their desks. By the next day, the shoes should be dry enough for the students to place under their desks until the following week. Whew, what a production! Bless the excellent teachers, too, for being so accommodating! I also had the fantastic help of parent volunteers. There was only one class I had to make it work in without any assistance. It was my last class of the day and the liveliest one.

Not surprisingly, my last class had a calamity of a lesson. I sent a couple of students at a time to gesso their shoes right outside the classroom. It was a warm day, and I could keep the door open to watch the students as well as rotate others to take turns gessoing. It was mayhem, and I was beginning to feel exhausted; the job was tremendous, one teacher to thirty-five students. The children outside came and went quickly, and I didn't get to check on them as much as I would have liked.

"Ms. Bickett?" a quiet girl, Melanie, nudged me as I was wiping paint off my face and trying to help her pick up her shoe with the newspaper to set it to dry outside.

"Yes?" I asked as I was watching a couple of other students finish up.

"Why does Billy get to paint the sidewalk?" she asked, gazing at the doorway.

I nearly dropped the shoe I was holding and spun around to look outside. There, a few students were standing and pointing at Billy, who was holding a paintbrush and, well, painting the sidewalk.

Setting the shoe down, I got to the doorway in a flash. I turned as Billy sat back against the wall and then noticed me.

"What are you doing? Why are you painting the sidewalk, Billy?" I was so aghast I didn't feel angry, just stunned and confused. "Did I send you out here to paint your shoes white or the sidewalk?"

Then, something astonishing happened.

Billy wasn't my brightest student, but he certainly understood directions. During the year, I had to keep him on a short leash, so to speak, from time to time, especially on creek walks where he could push boundaries. However, he was not a big problem, and Billy and I got along well. I was not completely surprised that it was Billy who was painting the sidewalk, but it did seem rather extreme even for him. I sincerely wanted to know what was going on in his curious mind.

Billy sat back, with not only his brush dripping with gesso, but paint all over his arm, and he looked at me with the most sincere and distraught expression.

"I don't know," he answered.

You know, it seemed he really didn't understand why he was painting the sidewalk.

"Well, Billy, you and I both know this is not OK. What are you going to do about this situation?" I asked.

"I guess I should clean it up," he said, standing up and looking at the whitewashed sidewalk, complete with some words he'd also written with paint.

There were some compassionate children in this class, as a few offered to help him. I sent one student to find the custodian and retrieved a pail while two classmates rushed into the room to find sponges. The students quickly set to work scrubbing and washing the sidewalk. In the warm afternoon sun, the paint had already begun to dry, and I worried it would be permanent.

"Just wait until Mr. Wells gets back!" one student said, shaking her head as she assisted Billy in his duty. Mr. Wells was their regular teacher on his prep break.

Billy, with the help of others, wiped up as much white paint as he could. When his teacher arrived, he looked stunned and told me he'd had problems with Billy a lot lately, so he, too, wasn't overly surprised this had happened. I watched the young man cleaning away, his face red, and it seemed he was holding back tears. I wondered about Billy, what his life must have been like, what his situation was like at home, and asked Mr. Wells not to be too hard on him. We spoke out of earshot of the children as we kept an eye on them, scrubbing away. Finally, it was time for my tired art cart and me to move on.

Before I left, I pulled Billy aside.

"Billy, I am sure you realize what you did was a mistake because the paint dries and is, as you can see, tough to clean up. I am sure you didn't realize what you were doing. I can see that."

He looked at me and nodded in agreement.

"I'm really sorry, Ms. Bickett. I just wasn't thinking," he answered.

"Billy," I responded, "this, I dearly hope, will be something you will never forget. What happens when we do something impulsively and don't think about the consequences? For example, your actions affect other people. The custodian now will have to come and use a strong solvent to get the rest of the paint off later today. This adds more work for him, and, as you noticed, other students, who by, the way, I hope you've thanked for helping you!"

Billy turned and thanked the art angels who chipped in to help clean, and they smiled back.

As I walked home that day, I yearned for those thunderclouds I saw on the horizon to burst loose. I thought of Billy and the expression of bafflement on his face. This was certainly not the first time I'd experienced a fourth- or fifth-grade boy's impulsivity in class. They did many things during the year that could get them hurt or in trouble. I realized it was the nature of their age and, to some degree, boundaries (or lack of) parents set at home, too. The consequences of actions need to be fair and transparent. Children sometimes push the limits because they *want* us to stop them or even just notice for that matter.

Spring arrived as we slid down to the last few weeks of school. My students, overall, seemed quite noisy, and I noticed a level of disrespect among some of my fourth and fifth graders. Walking on the footbridge over the creek, I paused to watch mallard ducks waddle along; a couple had made their nest somewhere nearby. I thought of Billy and how he may have just needed to express his feelings through paint. If I had had some large board for him to paint his heart away on, that would have been great. I reminded myself that next week they would get to decorate their shoes and that Billy would love that. He would have a chance to let loose, not on a school sidewalk, but on his own shoe.

As I looked at the enormous monolithic entities (the ball walls), I had an idea that would later prove to be excellent. In my first year at Creek Side, in addition to the funds for the mural we created at the front of the school, I had requested funds to paint murals on the ball walls. This ended up not being a practical plan, so I abandoned the notion. If we couldn't have permanent colors on the ball walls, why not let the children draw chalk images on them, images that would fade and be washed away? Temporary, lively art on the ball walls! *Billy would love that*, I assured myself.

I loved public art projects with kids and had done many over the years. At the first school where I taught in California, my special education students helped two artists paint a portrait of a giant eagle outside of the cafeteria. And at the middle school where I once taught, you can still see the massive mural at the entrance of the library where, again, students assisted a muralist in creating the landscape with eagles, again, the school mascot. Before that, when I taught high school art in Massachusetts, my art students painted murals all over the school! I'd like to think I've left trails of myself everywhere I've taught.

Alas, though, as I trudged homeward, I reminded myself I could only do so much. After all, I was only one person pushing a traveling art show around!

The next week, my older students happily painted their shoes while listening to music. We managed, with parent help (excepting the one class again), to pull it off, this time, without a glitch. Billy was happy with his wildly painted shoe and seemed to be doing just fine. I complimented him on his work, and he looked up at me. Our eyes met with a kind of understanding as I smiled at him. Words were not necessary at that moment.

Many students came up to me and asked, "Can I help you set up today?" or "Is there anything I can do for you, Ms. Bickett?" Despite the overall cacophony of behaviors and spring fever, I was reminded how my students were very kind human beings. My heart was touched deeply.

As I walked across the field pondering the budget cuts for the next year, I thought of the children getting excited about summer. I spied two little girls walking along, holding hands, their hair blowing in the sunlit breeze. Time suddenly stopped. I saw them. I saw them from my eyes to my mind and to my heart. At that moment, I was reminded of why I was here.

Lesson: We make a difference.

A Voice from the Past

That spring, another voice woke me from my dream of life. I was scheduled to give a presentation at a local art gallery where I had once shown my work. I was walking along the sidewalk downtown when I heard someone call out, "Ms. Bickett!" I turned to see a handsome young man smiling at me. Instantly I recognized him. Randall had been a student of mine ten years before my tenure at Creek Side. There was no surprise when he told me he was now an artist. Randall demonstrated evident talent when he was in my middle school language arts and social studies classes. I was very touched when he told me I was one of his security-password answers: I was still his favorite teacher!

We chatted as Randall accompanied me to the gallery. He stayed for my talk, and then as the guests gathered for wine and cheese afterward, Randall and I engaged in conversation again. He told me a sad story, one that reminded me we never know how our words or actions might affect a child.

Randall began his story.

"One day, when I was in elementary school, I was playing out in the playground and my friends, and I wandered close to where the principal was talking on his cell phone. He didn't see us, and we overheard everything he was saying. I heard him say, 'I hate these kids!' I always remembered that moment, and it hurt so much to listen to him say such a thing."

"You know, Randall," I told him, "I'm not going to defend such terrible words, but I will say, teachers, and even principals, are human. There have been days when I disliked how disrespectful some students were. But I've never hated my students. There is a big difference. I would like to think that he was having a bad day and really didn't mean he hated everyone."

I thought a moment longer, and Randall and I agreed that, perhaps, it was best to focus on what we love and to do our best to hate less. Since then, I've become acutely aware of when I use the word "hate." I don't use it nearly so much as I used to, and if I do, I often realize how horrible I feel afterward. Sometimes I do hate things, like pollution, willful ignorance, violence, racism, poverty, and injustice. But I think we overuse the word, and I can't help but think of how that sends negativity into the world. Hate is a poison, and I could see through Randall the effect of that hateful thought the principal had that day. Now, as an adult, perhaps he could use the hurt those words caused to bring more love into the world.

Lesson: Rise above it.

Stuck Smiling

As the year came to a close, a wonderful volunteer mom in a second-grade class wanted to take a photo of the art class for everyone. There was, of course, the usual, "Say cheese!" as we posed for a couple of shots. As the children were walking back to their seats, little Rusty came up to me slightly distressed and said, "Ms. Bickett, my smile is stuck!" He pointed to his face, and sure enough, stretched out was a long smile. "I can't stop smiling!" he said again.

I shrugged my shoulders and replied teasingly, "Oh, you'll be OK. I am sure you'll be frowning in no time!"

At that, he protested further, "Oh no, now you've gone and made me think of smiling again!"

Ah, such problems!

My darling kinder kiddies and I "ride on clouds," as Amy put it. She was the leader of our group one day as we went back and forth to classes. We each chose a cloud shape of dinosaurs, dragons, whatever we imagined. Amy decided the best way to get down from the clouds (as surely we needed to do when we "landed" at our classroom doors!) was to slide down a giant rainbow. And we did just that! I loved their imaginations and the enthusiasm they brought to the simplest things.

At lunch, I was startled when a fourth-grade student, Arleen, approached me.

"Are we having art this week?" she asked with wide eyes.

"Yes, of course!" I answered, a little perplexed why she would need this assurance.

"Oh good! I love art! I look forward to it!" she said with great relief.

"OK, see you tomorrow then," I said as she bounded off. Curious encounter indeed!

That weekend, I presented a lesson about birds at the local Youth Science Institute, a place I had taught many years ago. I had my crow puppet as I spoke about the variety of birds, how beaks reflect what birds eat, migration, and also instructions on how to draw a bird. I extolled the virtues of "bird brain" intelligence by demonstrating how crows use sticks as tools to get food. I took a crayon and put it on the table, saying that the crayon represented food my crow puppet would like to eat. But the "food" was out of the crow's reach. So, I had my crow find a stick nearby and use it to roll the crayon into its grasp.

Just as the crow was about to "eat" the crayon, a cute little red-haired girl sitting in front put her hands to her cheeks and gasped, "He's not really going to *eat* that, is he?"

Once again, I was taken by the imagination of the children and the totally unexpected! I smiled and winked at the girl.

"No, he is just demonstrating. He's going to pretend to eat the crayon but really spit it out," I answered. That seemed to satisfy the observant child.

That night, I accompanied my husband to a special award banquet in his honor. He was awarded a grant for composers from the Silicon Valley Arts Council, and I was very proud of Brian. As I sat and gazed at the art on the walls, a lithe dancer performed to an excerpt from Brian's composition. I was profoundly touched by the support they received. Not only did the Arts Council recognize them, but their family, friends, and teachers were vital because they encouraged them along the way. Right now, I realized I had composers, artists, dancers, and writers in all my classes at Creek Side. All they needed was to be seen and recognized and nourished.

When I was a child, I always felt lost in a blur. I would have loved dance classes or painting classes. Somehow, I was never good enough and never felt encouraged. Everyone else was better, prettier, smarter, and more talented than me. I was timid, and it wasn't until I was in sixth grade that a teacher, Mrs. Brooks, took particular interest in me. She told me that I didn't need to follow in my older siblings' footsteps and that I could be anything I wanted to be.

Throughout my teaching career, I believed if I made an effort, then like Mrs. Brooks (her real name), I could offer a child the same thoughtful words of hope and recognition. I found myself smiling at the memory as we applauded the artists being recognized that night. And I noticed the entire evening I'd been smiling. I guess my smile got stuck, too.

Lesson: Smile and make someone's day!

Retiring the (Magic) Art Cart...

The weather was too iffy for creek walks the previous week, so I did something I forbade myself to do. One day, I took five classes to the stream! It was a Thursday, and I woke up tired but determined to make the day my best no matter what. "Today," I told myself, "I will embrace magic and focus on the present and not worry about how tired I'll be at the end of the day." I planned to savor every moment with my lively fourth and fifth graders.

I laminated copies of hand-drawn field guides for my students to take with them to the creek to identify plants and trees. The concise guide showed the trees at the creek and their leaves, with classifications of shapes such as lobed, simple-toothed, or compound—and with corresponding scientific names. I was amazed by how well the children caught on. They really delighted in identifying the trees. There was a lot of teaching and re-teaching, and it was fun to see their minds working when I asked, "What kind of oak tree is this? A valley or live oak?" Some students even brought extra paper and pencils to draw and take notes. I was thrilled.

Swallowtail butterflies floated with us, as if curious about these happy, lively beings walking along the path. The buckeye trees were in full bloom, and we enjoyed smelling their fragrant blossoms. Walnuts, toyons, sycamores, and a bay laurel tree were all happily identified. We found our way to Hummingbird Hollow and sat in silence for a moment.

I spoke about loving the creek and taking care of the riparian environment.

"It's your creek, it is our creek, and it is the hummingbirds' creek, the swallowtail's creek, and the squirrel's creek," I said to them almost like a prayer. I was deeply gratified to see expressions of awe and joy on every student's face, in each class. I was reminded of how we started out the year talking about peace and how we could be peaceful inside. What a spiral to come back to that theme again at the end of the year.

A little bluebird flew by as the first class set out that morning. In another class, we were in the back of the school, identifying the redwood and mulberry trees when a tweeting phoebe demonstrated how to catch bugs. An Anna's hummingbird welcomed yet a third class into the creek as we opened the gate to enter the magical world beyond the school. All day, though, the Tiger Swallowtail butterflies danced along with us, leading the way, disappearing for a while, and then surprising us again. The children were enchanted!

Throughout the day, students made audible "ahhs" when we relaxed on the giant boulders of the Hummingbird Hollow.

"Hey, this is a beach!" a fourth-grade boy called out as he ran his fingers through the sand at the dry creek bottom. I marveled at seeing the older students touching the sand and enjoying the sensation of it running through their hands. Two girls had little tissue boxes that they used to scoop up and carry sand to take back to class.

One of the chaperones, a man in his forties, told us he played at this very spot in the creek when he was a child and that very little had changed. What a fantastic moment that was.

I shared with this group how an earlier class saw a peregrine falcon up in a tree before it flew off very fast into the sky. The children learned the names of the trees quickly, and I was impressed with their knowledge and enthusiasm.

I had a big surprise with one class that day. Half the students were on a field trip, so I ended up with fifteen students. They were all boys. Apparently, they hadn't earned the privilege of going on the excursion with the rest of the students. Honestly, it was a moment of Grace. I became distraught when only one parent showed up to chaperone, only to realize it was perfectly OK with the smaller group. These students, I noticed right away, were very active boys who could often be a challenge in class.

I was grateful that the creek walk gave me an excellent opening to get to know them better, and it was a precious opportunity. Billy, the boy who painted the sidewalk during the shoe lesson, came up to me and hugged me at the end of our walk. I was flabbergasted and almost cried. What a blessing to have had the small class to take to the creek. It made me think of how much better for the children and teachers smaller class sizes would be. We could genuinely reach children much more effectively with smaller class sizes. Our children deserve that, don't they?

As we walked back to the school at the end of the day, I was fulfilled and happy. My last class completed its turn, and everyone was jubilant. A fourth-grade girl skipped up to me and said as we made our way through the playing field back to the classroom, "Going to the creek is like going to a spa!"

She went on to tell me about a day at the spa with her mother. My heart swelled with joy. Other than a scraped knee in one earlier class, the day went very well. I felt protected by something mysterious and kind throughout the day. I did risk a lot by taking students to the creek: there were yellow jackets, bees, steep embankments, and other potentially harmful consequences. Yet, in all the years of taking children to the creek, I'd only had one yellow jacket sting and not even a handful of cuts and scrapes. We came back refreshed, and I agreed it did feel like a day at the spa!

The next Monday, my little kinder kiddies wanted to see a tree frog again. We went to the garden and found the container where the tree frog was the previous fall, and, sure enough, one lone tree frog sat on the tarp waiting for us. After taking turns holding the little guy, the children gently set him back onto the tarp, and we closed the lid.

"Just like magic!" Amy chirped as we turned to head back to class, and I couldn't agree more.

I took the first graders to the creek, and we sat in silence at Hummingbird Hollow. This was our first visit there, and after some quiet time, Alicia spoke up.

"I heard that same sound on a game I have on my computer!" she exclaimed.

"What sound?" I asked, perplexed.

"That sound we just heard—silence," she replied.

Another student, Alex, spoke up next.

"Yeah, and I practice being still because I play a Wii game, and I have to stand very still, or I lose points."

At first, I didn't know how to respond.

I felt sad they referenced silence in the woods with prior experiences being with machines. I sighed and smiled, realizing I needed to accept the reality of their lives and that perhaps I could help them find a balance between technology and nature.

"Well, that's great. You both know how to be still and understand silence. Isn't it nice to enjoy silence outdoors, too?" I asked.

They both agreed, and we walked merrily back to school as a swallowtail fluttered along, nearly touching the heads of the children as if it were counting us as we went on our way.

As I walked home from school, I felt the stirring of change come upon me again, gently but surely as the breeze that rattled the leaves above me. Perhaps I would have that elusive classroom next year. Maybe I would no longer be the traveling art teacher. I would have to become respectable and manage a classroom of my own. Good news, and yet . . .

Beyond that, I felt something more profound and farther off beyond the horizon. I had much more to discover about who I was and why I was here. There seemed to be something waiting to be seen. Each step I took, I felt I came closer and closer to the truth of who I was.

The next week would be the last week of my fourth year at Creek Side. I sensed a turn in the road ahead, and it was good.

When the last week of school arrived, it was full of tearful goodbyes. I was sad that I would not be teaching the English Language Development students or first-grade enrichment program again the next year. The farewells were especially poignant for me. I brought little flowers for all my younger kiddies and handed them out as we said goodbye.

My last Tuesday, we spent the day sketching seashells I had collected and brought in and later made photo prints of them outdoors. I showed the students a real pufferfish that a parent had given me years ago. (It was dead, frozen in time in the considerable alarm state it must have been in when killed.)

"I know you collect things, so I thought you'd like this," she had told me when she presented me with the fish. The children were warned not to touch the sharp spines as I showed this bizarre object to my classes.

I had a *déjà vu* moment when a little boy announced as he listened to a seashell, "It's not the sea you hear but the blood pounding from your heart that makes the sound." This comment was almost exactly like the one I heard a few years before from another fourth-grade student.

I smiled and asked him, "Well, can't it be both? Can't it be the sound of your blood and the sound of the sea?"

The sweet cards, drawings, and notes from my little second graders touched me. I wouldn't have them as students again that next year because I didn't teach third-grade art. All week we talked about what they would do over the summer vacation: trips, soccer games, reading . . . the one answer I would always treasure, though, came from little Kaila, one of my second graders: "I am just going to be thinking about you!"

I concluded my fourth year with my annual poem, reflecting what I experienced at my husband's award ceremony.

The Artists Among Us

All Great Artists
were once little children.
Wide-eyed and hopeful,
someone, somewhere, SAW them.
They were beheld, beloved, and embraced.

Pablo Picasso once said that
"We are all artists; it is just that
we grow up and forget."
But not all of us forget.

All Great Artists
come from our schools, our communities,
and right now, they are sitting in our classrooms.
Great Artists yearning to be SEEN,
longing for a word from us
that we know they are there.

Oh, and guess what? I was asked to pack up all my things and move again, this time . . . into my new classroom. It was a lot of extra work that last week of school, but did I mind? The boxes, along with the art cart, were moved to the new art room, where they would await my return in August for unpacking and organizing. As I dismantled my beloved art cart, turning it once again into a homely gray pushcart, all the magic seemed to drain away. I would surely find some use for it the next year, but it would never be the same.

Once again, the winds of change whispered from the boughs of trees. The giant pine nodded as I walked by, and I paused for a moment to consider the message from the thin needles as they brushed against the gorgeous summer sky. I had a brand-new curriculum to create for the next year. I couldn't believe I was already thinking of new art projects! I could start outlining, researching . . .

I smiled and listened to the trees swaying in the afternoon breeze as the long to-do list began to fill my head. I considered all that I needed to do by the end of summer. Then, in a flash, I dismissed all the chatter and turned toward home, leaving such notions in the dust.

Lesson: Time to move on.

Epilogue

The following year, and what was to become my last year of my tenure as a teacher, 2010-2011, I shared a classroom with the other art teacher. The magic art cart rested in the corner of the room. It still occasionally became a beast of burden when needed for outside art lessons. But it was never the same. Although I cherished finally having a classroom, I always treasured the challenges and rewards of offering *art á la cart* to the children of Creek Side School.

The magic art cart and the creek were the highlights of my tenure at Creek Side School. I found it difficult to let go because I felt what I did every day as a teacher made a difference in the world. One late afternoon in the autumn of 2011, after I retired, when Lizzie and I were strolling behind the school (I didn't always go that route because I felt I needed some distance from school at the time), we spied a group of children with an after-school program teacher. The students were so absorbed with notebooks and searching for something in the wild area behind the school with her they didn't notice us. I recognized the students right away, and I anticipated some sort of greeting, but not one child looked up. *Must be some lesson!* I thought to myself. The teacher looked up, and I smiled at her.

Let someone else do it now, I mused as we made our way down the street, walking on sidewalks shaded with trees shedding their leaves. I had invested a great deal of myself into my work, and now as a retired teacher, I needed to find ways to fill the void that being a teacher once filled.

Lesson: Let go so others can fill the space.

Note: I was gratified to be named KBAY Silicon Valley Education Association's March Teacher of the Month, 2011, honored for numerous grant projects written and received, and the creek program.

When I returned to Creek Side as an invited artist-in-residence as part of the Montalvo Arts Center's school program during 2013 and 2014, I was privileged to work with the second-grade teachers once again. It was fun to see my kinder students as second graders and, of course, many of the older students, who were once my art students. It was a brief return, however, as I decided in 2015 to pursue other interests. Indeed, it was time to continue reinventing my life as the writer I always wanted to become. The years at Creek Side School unknowingly became the seed of the Art á la Cart trilogy. I started writing in 2013. I created characters and stories about a wacky art teacher, Ms. Fitt, and her Magic Art Cart. Little wonder where my inspiration came from! Using my imagination and love of nature and art, bringing the Magic Art Cart to life was an act of joy and love. And that journey keeps unfolding.

I am a richer person for having been a teacher, and I have nothing but heartfelt gratitude to all my colleagues and students I've known along the way.

M. Bickett, 2022

Art Cart Photos

Classes took turns decorating the cart every month.

The art cart in the school garden with decorated paper feathers inspired by Tom the Turkey.

Valentine's Day art cart.

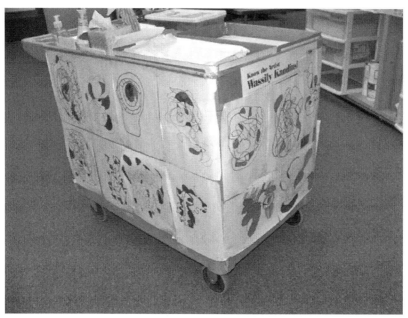

Kandinsky-inspired art cart art by a third-grade class.

All things green and wonderful March art.

Monthly themes inspired the art cart decorations.

The art cart parked in the shared classroom with supplies.

We Love the Creek

M. Bickett

At the creek:

The dry creek bed.

The author leads a group of third graders with a teacher and some parents on the creek trail.

Preschoolers touching Grandmother Oaktree.

Leaf print project in the dry creek bed with second-grade students.

Falcon at the creek watching us as we walked by.

Preschooler with magnifying lens examining a bug.

Fifth-grade students drawing and painting with the author at the creek.

Lizzie with the author at creek gate.

Diamond Winged Pony

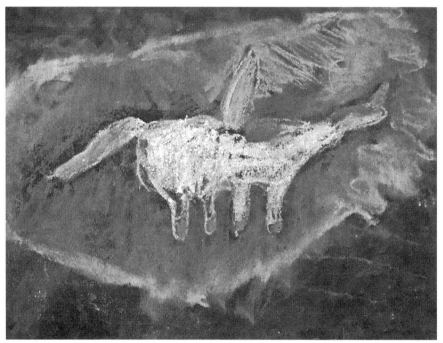

Student artwork of the Diamond Winged Pony. (Anonymous second-grade student)

Diamond Winged Pony

Marianne Bickett
arr. by Brian Belet

CHORUS 1

Danc-ers, oh Danc-ers   of the night— flight   Danc-ers, oh Danc-ers   of the   night flight

Give me my wish and a   wild po-ny fly - ing   Give me my wish and a   wild po-ny fly - ing

(To Verse 3 ...)

me   to the   moon!

Verse 3
A long time's passed and here I sit a-waiting
So far from my lost home
My love, he's gone and
I fear I'll never see him
And I'm here so all alone
Here so all alone

Verse 4
The years have gone and now I ask for leaving
I've packed my bags to go
No sign of him from way
Up in the heavens
And it's very cold up here
Very cold up here

CHORUS 2
Dancers, oh Dancers of the night flight
Dancers, oh Dancers of the night flight
Give me my wish and a wild pony flying
Give me my wish and a wild pony flying
Me from the moon!

Verse 5
I wander now from all the dark places
That I have traveled to
The sun looks bright
The horizon looms before me
And above me sails the moon
Above me sails the moon

CHORUS 3
Dancers, oh Dancers of the night flight
Dancers, oh Dancers of the night flight
Give me my wish and a wild pony flying
Give me my wish and a wild pony flying
Me to my home!

Diamond Winged Pony   3

CODA

Art Terms

Art Elements:

Line
Path of moving point through space

Shape/Form
Shape is two dimensional/Form is three dimensional
Basic shapes: circle, square, triangle
Basic forms: sphere, cube, pyramid

Color
Three primaries: blue, yellow, red
Three secondaries: purple, orange, green
Neutral: black, brown, white
Three properties: hue, value, intensity

Value
Lightness and darkness

Textures
Actual: tactile quality of object/Implied: visual representation

Pattern
Repeated motif or design

Space/Perspective
Organization of area/Representing volume or three-dimensional objects

Media: (plural) materials that are used to create art, such as (but not limited to) the following. Mixed-media art refers to art that uses more than one medium.

Medium (singular of media) used to make:
Drawing: dry tools such as pencil, charcoal, pen and ink
Painting: wet tools such as brushes, sponges. Used with water, oil, acrylic, or egg (tempera).

Printmaking: using etching (sharp incising tools), any process where images are incised or created on a hard surface (lithograph) from which multiple copies can be made. Other kinds of printmaking are screen-printing (usually on cloth), mono prints (one print, unique), texture prints (using textured surfaces such as corrugated cardboard, natural textures, etc.)

Sculpture: three-dimensional representation (viewed from at least three sides) using marble, wire, natural materials like rocks, twigs, etc., fabric, plaster, bronze, steel, concrete, etc.

Relief: combination of two-dimensional (flat) and three-dimensional (surface is raised, has enhanced texture)

Photography: cameras, dark rooms for developing film

Collage: cloth, paper, string, photos, pieces of paintings, etc. are combined to create a singular work of art.

Balance Systems:
Symmetry: approximately or exactly the same on both sides of a center line horizontally or vertically.

Radial: symmetry both horizontally and vertically, radiating from a center.

Asymmetrical: balance that does not use symmetry.

Art Periods/Styles:
This is a very general, shortened list to give the reader some background information. Please refer to appropriate art history books for more detailed and complete information. A brief list of a few of the period artists does not include all artists of that time.

Primitive: art using man-made tools and materials from nature, indigenous art, early history art, art that embodies primitive subjects or styles

Classical: Greek and Roman art

Medieval: 300–1400 AD in Europe, religious symbolism, abstracted; Donatello, Giotto

Renaissance: 1490s–1547 in Europe, naturalism, mix of secular and sacred art; Da Vinci, Rafael, Michelangelo

Mannerism: 1520–end of 16th century in Europe, elongation of the figure, less ideal; El Greco, Parmigianino, Tintoretto

Baroque: early 17th–late 18th centuries in Europe, realism, mix of secular and sacred, common scenes, real people; Siriani, Gentileschi, Rembrandt, Caravaggio

Rococo: about the same time as Baroque, lavish, ornate, fantasy, opulent; Goya, Gainsborough

Impressionism: 1860s, late 1800s in Europe, began in France, light affecting colors, pure use of colors; Cassatt, Monet, Degas

Post-impressionism: late 19th and early 20th centuries: led to expressionism via emphasis on expression of emotions through color, line, shapes; Van Gogh, Gaugin, Cezanne

Expressionism: Beginning of the 20th century, emphasis on expressive use of art media; Munch, Marc, Chagall

Abstract: early 20th century and on, art that changes reality, simplifies it, alters shapes and forms; Kandinsky, O'Keeffe, Matisse

Abstract Expressionism: combining the qualities of both styles; Pollack, Rothko, Kline

Non-objective art: term used to abstract/expressionistic art that does not literally represent any specific subject/object, removed from recognition other than basic art elements

There is a plethora of art periods and styles during the twentieth and twenty-first centuries. Please consult your art history resources for more information.

Favorite Art á la Cart Lesson Plans

Over many years of teaching, I have many favorite lessons. However, I needed to limit my choices, or I'd have an entire book of just lesson plans! Not a bad idea, but . . . I chose my top ten favorites plus my most treasured art lesson from the five years at Creek Side School.

You have my permission to copy these lesson plans and adapt/change as needed. Local, state, and national art standards have been omitted so that teachers, parents, and anyone else interested can match the concepts to the standards they need. Lessons are not in any particular order. Unfortunately, I did not keep copies of my lesson plans on my computer, so I am writing up very simple and easy steps from memory.

And always remember to allow students to help with distributing materials and clean up. It's an essential part of the art-making process! Always wrap up a lesson with student feedback, input, and evaluate how successful the lesson was in terms of your intentions. Allow serendipity to surprise you, though, as learning can take you to places you might never have envisioned! Be clear, but be open, too!

I created pre- and post-art concepts tests for all my grade levels, and I wish I'd kept copies of those after I retired. Besides deleting all my beautiful photographs of student artwork, I also felt I had to let go of all my paperwork. It helped me to move on.

Consider ways you can measure student learning with prior knowledge assessment and end-of-year evaluation. Doing this for art can be tricky; however, not impossible. When I gave the pre- and post-test, I divided a paper into four sections for my fifth graders. Then, I asked them to draw a cube in one, a face in another, a landscape, and then to demonstrate the idea of value. I repeated this at the end of the year, and it was very clear, as I was sure to teach those four concepts, what students learned. Lastly, always make meaningful connections to science, language, history, etc. as well as to music, dance, and theater.

Visit MarianneBickett.com for free downloads of more Nature Connections Activities.

Outline: *Art à la Cart* Lessons

1. **Blind Contour Partner and Self-Portraits** with charcoal and newsprint. Fourth through seventh grades. Picasso and others.

2. **Contour Line Drawings of Natural Objects:** animal skulls, seashells, leaves, or other inorganic objects such as tools, etc. with pencils and paper. Fourth through sixth grades. Various artists.

3. **Drawing Music** (Kandinsky/Schoenberg connection) with paper, Sharpies, crayons or watercolors, music. It can be adapted for all grade levels.

4. **Invisible Paintings** on an outdoor wall with buckets of water and large paintbrushes. K through third grades. Music and dance.

5. **Warhol's Shoes:** drawing, composition, (paper, pencils, markers, watercolors), and actual shoe painting (old shoes, gesso, tempera paints). Fifth through seventh grades. Theater.

6. **Field Guides** with papers, clipboards, pencils, color pencils. Fourth through seventh grades. Various field guide examples. Biology, ecology, earth science, waterways.

7. **Group 'Mural'** using small squares that are assembled into one giant piece with pre-cut square papers, pencils, crayons, oil pastels, watercolors, or mixed media. Third through seventh grades and older. Chuck Close examples.

8. **The Art Elephants** lesson with large papers, pencils, color pencils, or crayons can be adapted from K through seventh grades. Segue to drawing animals.

9. **O'Keeffe's Sunflowers** with paper, watercolors, and sunflowers. First through fourth grades.

10. **Self-Portraits in Various Styles:** da Vinci, Kahlo, Wood, Picasso, and Archembaldo, with Cassatt (back of the head partner). Papers, pencils, and multiple media, including collage. Fourth through seventh grades.

BONUS! My all-time favorite: Andy Goldsworthy's Outdoor Nature Sculptures

Blind Contour Partner and Self-Portraits
Fifth through Seventh Grades

- -

Concepts: Facial proportions, expression, familiarity with charcoal sticks for drawing (media exploration), eye-hand coordination, contour lines, confidence, fun (is there a standard for that?)

Materials: large newsprint papers, black charcoal sticks (not soft, medium to hard), masking tape, small non-breakable mirrors for each child/partner team, examples of Picasso contour line drawings, others made by the teacher or other artists.

Introduction/Directions: Show examples and demonstrate. Ask for a "victim" (haha) to come up and sit so you can go through the process:

1. Partner (in this case, your student volunteer) sits very still. In contrast, the teacher (later, the student partner) draws the subject without looking at his/her paper (in this case, the whiteboard). Introduce, if the students haven't used it before, the charcoal stick and explain it will make their hands black, but it is harmless and will wash off. Students can wear art smocks/aprons to protect clothing, but it will wash out.

2. Start at the top of the paper and look only at your subject, going back and forth from top to bottom as you outline his/her face, neck, and shoulders. Up to three peeks are allowed: pause and keep charcoal in place and quickly glance at the paper, then immediately back to subject and continue drawing.

3. Finish at the bottom of the paper. Look at your work and show your partner. This is where laughing is necessary!

4. Switch places: the subject becomes the person drawing.

Wrap Up: Ask students to write the name of the person who drew the image and the subject's name at the bottom of the paper with the date. The class can assemble to look at and discuss results. Doing this in different versions helps kids relax with art!

Either the same day or the following lesson:

Give students a mirror and ask them to consider facial proportions: Where do they notice their eyes fall? (Halfway down the face.) Where do their eyes sit, nose, mouth, etc.? Demonstrate by using the facial proportion grid of dividing the face into thirds (not half).

Students will then draw themselves using the same process as the blind contour without looking at their paper (three peeks). They can use this as a stepping-stone to creating a more detailed, finished self-portrait (realistic) later. Show examples of many artists' self-portraits (Rembrandt, da Vinci, Van Gogh, etc.)

Contour Line Drawings of Natural Objects
Fourth through Seventh Grades. Adapt as needed.

— —

Concepts: Contour line, organic versus inorganic (nature vs. human-made), size relationships, overlap, composition, negative-positive space, line value.

Materials: can start with newsprint and charcoal for practice then use at least 9 x 12 papers (white drawing) and pencils, seashells, animal skulls, leaves, sticks, acorns, etc.

Introduction/Directions: Allow students to touch and explore the objects. Demonstrate how to draw a contour line drawing and emphasize looking at the object, not the paper as much.

1. Students practice drawing an assortment of objects on the tables, sharing with team/groups.

2. Next, show examples of artwork where there are various objects, or the same object drawn over and over, arranged on the picture plane to fill the space excitingly.

3. If using the same object, vary the size of it, drawing it small, medium, and large in various places on the paper. Adapt to grade-level abilities.

4. Older students can allow objects to overlap and fill the space up. Emphasize composition (symmetrical/asymmetrical) and negative/positive space. How can we make the picture more interesting? How do the objects flow, leading the eye across the picture plane?

5. Emphasize this is a line drawing, but lines can be made light or dark to make it more interesting. Lines can have values. Adapt to older students.

Wrap Up: Students can discuss their drawings in small groups. Or display/go around the room to hold a class discussion about the lesson, any difficulties, questions, and demonstration that the concept(s) intended. This lesson obviously can be repeated in steps and can conclude in many ways. For example, you can have students draw the shapes of the objects and trace them onto colored (or black on white or white on black) papers. This exercise further enhances the lesson on composition and negative/positive space.

If you emphasized organic shapes, then another lesson can be using only inorganic shapes. The possibilities of connections and strands are endless!

Drawing Music

Kindergarten through Seventh Grade: this one is for all levels!

- -

Concepts: Rhythm, beat, timbre: connecting music and art elements, expressive line, feeling/emotions, line quality, and fun!

Materials: Large white drawing papers, black Sharpies (go over proper use with students), music—CD player or computer with the ability to play samples (classical such as Beethoven, Mozart, or more modern such as Debussy work well. You can choose a few different compositions to vary the response of the students. Younger children respond better to classical music.) Colored pencils or crayons may be used after the initial music response to fill in shapes created by the lines.

Introductions/Directions: Typically, I have the younger students stand up and move to music first but encourage all grades to make some physical response to music. Ask how the music makes them feel. It's best to have them close their eyes to do this.

Introduce Wassily Kandinsky and Arnold Schoenberg (artist and composer), who worked together and blurred the elements of music and art in their creations. Show examples.

1. Demonstrate on the whiteboard (or white paper with Sharpie) how to move your hand across the paper in response to the music. Be careful that this is not interpreted as a "right or wrong" response. You can show students the actual sound waves of flowing lines, the sawtooth wave, or a flat line in response to sounds. Play music while you demonstrate and close your eyes.

2. When materials are all distributed, turn off the lights if possible and ask students to be ready with a Sharpie at the top of the paper with their eyes closed. When the music begins, they may start moving their hand/Sharpie any way in response to the music.

3. After a reasonable length of time (it doesn't take long before the paper is filled with lines!), stop the music, and have students stop drawing and open their eyes.

4. Showing the students pictures of Kandinsky's work, students can fill in the spaces created by lines (not all of them) with color.

Wrap Up: Have students share their experiences and results. Can they see areas of their work where the music got loud or soft? Fast or slow?

Invisible Paintings (outdoors)
Kindergarten through Third Grade

- -

Concepts: Manipulation of large brushes, brush strokes, imagination, fun, large-scale art, group cooperation
(This is a lesson I feature in the back of the third book of my Art á la Cart trilogy of the Magic Art Cart, *The Present: Kala's Song*.)

Materials: Large paintbrushes (the larger the better, such as easy-to-handle house-painting brushes, cheap, of course), buckets of water, a warm, sunny day, towels, and an empty wall outdoors.

Introduction/Directions: Having extra help for this lesson is essential. Let parents know you have this outdoor art lesson ahead of time and recruit volunteers to assist you. Go over the rules carefully: no painting classmates, paint only the wall, no running, use your imagination, have fun.

1. Give each child a large paintbrush.

2. Have four children share a bucket, so you'll need at least five or six buckets of water ahead of time. This activity is where your parent volunteers come in big time!

3. They can wear art smocks/aprons if available.

4. Demonstrate how to paint with water on the wall. Oohs and ahhhs happen when the children see the lines slowly disappearing!

5. Show how the brush can make thick and thin lines, short and long lines, and other textures.

6. Enjoy the fun!

Wrap Up: This is a short lesson, as it doesn't take long before children are ready for too much mischief. Have everyone put their brushes in containers, and children can help dump water on plants nearby. Parents can clean up while you stand back and admire your fantastic mural before it vanishes!

Ask the children what they enjoyed the most and talk about how the art didn't last. Was it still fun?

Warhol's Shoes (a lesson in many parts)
Fourth through Seventh Grades

- -

Concepts: Contour line, colors, shapes, textures, composition, repetition, variation, 2-D vs. 3-D (two dimensional versus three dimensional), sculpture. Plan a "shoe theater" presentation whereby the shoes are used as puppets and interact with each other. See below. Ask parents to volunteer for the second part of this lesson if you choose to do it because it will be messy!

Materials for the first half of this lesson: drawing papers, shoes to draw (students can use their own), pencils, color pencils or watercolors, pen and ink, tempera paints, etc. This first step can take at least two days to complete.

Materials for the second half of this lesson: Students bring in one old shoe, usually tennis shoes, to gesso. After the gesso has dried, students will need tempera paints to paint the shoes. This part will take at least two days to complete.

Introduction/Directions: You don't have to do both of these lessons; you can do one of the two. It's a seamless development to go from the drawings to the actual shoe, but it is a lot of work. Start with Andy Warhol's shoe print to show repetition that isn't exactly alike. Point out the variations of the different shoes, but what they have in common is that they are all shoes.

1. Students will draw, using pencils, Sharpies, or ink, their shoes in a divided paper (into fourths at least), showing different views of their shoes.

2. Students can, if time, add color to their drawings.

3. Each student brings in an old shoe (a pair is OK in case some students cannot find a shoe to bring) and gessoes it. Use newspaper under the shoes (do not gesso the bottom!). Set to dry.

4. Students then paint, with tempera paints, their white shoes, using expressive colors. Set to dry.

5. To further this lesson, have the students work in teams of four. Each student gives his/her shoe a name and personality. Students write a script and have the shoes as puppets to act out a scene. Provide scenes for each group. Suggesting ideas saves time. For example: act out a way to help someone in need, have a shoe get lost and found again, have a shoe speak a different language and how do you communicate, etc. Have fun with this! It's a hoot! I wasn't able to do this at Creek Side but previously with older students.

Wrap Up: Display the artwork, both the drawings and the actual shoes. Discuss the process and concepts. Ask if the students view their shoes any differently now. Remember to point out that anything can become art! When I did this lesson, we even ended up discussing how some people don't have shoes. I taught this at the very end of the school year, but if it had been sooner, I would have initiated a shoe drive for the homeless or shelters!

Field Guides
Fifth through Seventh Grades

Concepts: Illustration of plants or birds, descriptive writing, observation, organization, bookmaking, drawing from nature, plant or bird identification, species exploration—science connection, riparian environment, human impact on nature, etc.

Materials: Outdoor area accessible from/at school where there are trees or the school garden (at Creek Side, we adopted the nearby creek), clipboards and pencils to begin with, then color pencils if needed, drawing papers, books about plants/birds, examples of field guides, science vocabulary suited to grade level, access to library/computers for research.

Introduction/Directions: Find a place on/near campus where you take your students regularly and where they are familiar with the surroundings. If you plan to go off-campus, you'll need the principal's and parents' permission. Identify (students could share books) trees, birds, etc., using field guides. Begin creating a site-specific field guide. You can assign groups to do the plants and others the birds and other wildlife such as squirrels, etc.

1. Once these assignments have been made and students are ready, spend a couple of days outside, allowing students to draw. If they are creating a tree field guide, they can sketch the entire tree, then add leaf rubbings or drawings with specific leaves for identification.

2. The drawings should be on the size paper the students are planning to make their field guide. For example, will it be an 8 ½ x 11-inch field guide or half the size? They need to have that all figured out because their illustrations will go into their booklet.

3. Once the drawings are completed, provide opportunities either at the library or at computers for students to research their plants/animals, looking for scientific names, descriptions, etc.

4. Students then write information about each object in their booklet.

5. Embellish with color if time permits.

Wrap Up: Students can share their field guides with another class. Take a younger group out to the area and have older students pair with more inexperienced children and teach them about the plants and animals at their school. Display the field guides at your district office or someplace in a visible area. Invite parents to attend a field guide day where the students teach their parents about the local fauna and flora. Students can go on to write an essay about one of their discoveries.

Group 'Mural'
Third through Seventh Grades and older

- -

Concepts: This lesson teaches about interdependency, teamwork, cooperation, and public art/murals. Students also learn about math, ratios, and part-whole concepts as well as the art elements. Students can begin to value each person's contribution.

Materials: First, have a theme. What are students studying in their regular classrooms? A unit on the ocean? Earth science? Communicate with teachers to find your focus. I chose the opportunity to enter art in a local marine center art contest, so over the years, my theme was marine mammals. Find a photograph of a theme subject/object and divide it evenly using a grid. Sometimes you have to cut off part of the picture and create squares of drawing/painting papers, one for each child that corresponds to the grid you made on the photograph. Number the photos on the back and put the corresponding number on the back of the square drawing paper you'll give students. This activity takes a lot of prep. That's why I'm putting it in the materials section. Choose your media: pencils, crayons, colored pencils, oil pastels, watercolor, or tempera paints.

Introduction/Directions: Make connections to prior knowledge and current exploration in their classrooms. Explain how you are going to make a smaller picture into a larger one, using a grid where you measured on the small paper. Explain how you used the process of ratios to enlarge precisely, for example, two times the size. Show the students the math; it's exciting. Older students can explore ratios further.

1. Have the grid pieces of the photograph/picture cut up, tape onto a piece of paper with the number (that's also on the back of the image and the back of the student's drawing square). Hand out to each student. Sometimes there are extras. Those can be done by students who finish first.

2. Demonstrate how to start at the top and, drawing lightly, divide their square piece into fourths (use rulers), and just copy what they see in corresponding sections of their photograph. This experience is fun because, often, students can't identify what they are drawing, so they have to go on faith and see the big picture! Pretty metaphorical!

3. Once their contour lines of the image are complete, students can begin filling in with values, colors, textures, etc. using the medium of choice.

4. The great fun is assembling all the pieces! Have a large portion of craft paper, any color (black is dramatic), where you tape/glue the individual pieces on a wall in the classroom or on a large table for everyone to see.

Wrap Up: Celebrate! Stand back and compare the small image with the large. Students love seeing how their small piece connected with others and made this massive mural—display at the district office or front office or wherever possible.

The Art Elephants
Kindergarten through Seventh Grade

- -

Concepts: According to each grade-level standard, the art elements are presented on the Art Elephant. Choose appropriate ones: line, shape, form, value, texture, color, and perspective. This activity helps teach the art elements; save for future reference in portfolios or folders.

Materials: Drawing paper, pencils, crayons, color pencils, pen and ink (for older students), pictures of elephants, and examples of the art elements—posters, images from books, photographs, real illustrations, etc.

Introduction/Directions: Review the art elements for each particular grade level. Show pictures of elephants and tell them you are teaching them a way to help remember the art elements. They are going to draw an elephant (younger students, basic shapes such as one circle for the head, oval for the body, rectangles for legs, triangles for ears, etc.) and demonstrate the elements on the elephant.

1. For line, have the students write "line" near the line drawing of the elephant.

2. For shape, label "shape" by the ears and head, etc.

3. For form, older students can shade and create value to show the illusion of three-dimensional art. Write "form" and "value."

4. For texture, ask the students to show what the elephant's skin would look like through repeating lines creating a pattern. It can be crisscrossing to show etched-like rough texture or repeating stippling/dots, etc. Write "texture."

5. For color, have the students color the elephant and write "color."

6. For perspective, older students, you can have them draw a tree behind the elephant to demonstrate near/far, size relationship, atmospheric perspective (light/dark). The tree would be lighter, smaller, and a little more upon the paper (special relationship). For perspective, you can have older students draw the elephant in an environment where there is a road behind it that goes to a vanishing point. Write "perspective."

Wrap Up: Tell your students that every art lesson you'll be using the art elements. They can use their Art Elephant to help them remember what art element they are using. See the Elephant Sanctuary website in the **Resources** section that follows the lesson plans.

You can use this lesson to segue to drawing animals, using any of the techniques and elements illustrated.

O'Keeffe's Sunflowers
First through Fourth Grades

- -

Concepts: Observation, color wheel, color relationships, textures, size, picture plane, color and emotions, radial balance, cool and warm colors.

Materials: Large watercolor papers, watercolors, pencils, clipboards, photos of sunflowers, or, better yet, the real thing in your school garden. Examples of Georgia O'Keeffe's sunflower paintings.

Introduction/Directions: Visit the school garden in the fall when sunflowers might be blooming. Perhaps that previous spring, you've managed to be sure there are sunflowers planted someplace in the schoolyard for this lesson! Show examples of Georgia O'Keefe's sunflowers and her love of nature. Engage the children in a discussion about the flower's shape and colors, how they look like a shining sun. Observe sunflowers moving their heads to follow the sun! Notice the birds enjoying the sunflower seeds in the center and the pattern the seeds make.

1. Once the students are wholly enthused about sunflowers, bring them to the garden or distribute photos of the flowers for them to practice drawing.

2. Instruct the students to transfer their practice drawing to the larger watercolor paper to be painted next. Emphasize these are giant sunflowers, and the flower is the leading and only subject in the foreground, against the blue sky in the background. Notice all the warm colors that contrast with the serene atmosphere. Notice the circular design is in the center of the paper (radial balance, but younger children don't need to go into it as much).

3. Demonstrate the use and techniques of watercolor painting. Instruct that they will paint the background blue sky. First, let it dry, then add the flowers the next time.

4. Once the flowers are painted, students can write a poem about their flowers. Mount on large construction paper to frame the artwork.

Wrap Up: Engage the students in sharing their paintings and poems. Display in the classroom or elsewhere. Perhaps in the spring, some of the seeds from the flowers can be used to plant the next year's crop!

Self-Portraits in Various Styles
Fourth through Seventh Grades and older

– –

Concepts: Facial proportions of front and side of the head and back of the head. Also, expressions, mood, colors, textures, values, shapes. Besides, students explore some perspective elements. They will experience art styles such as realism, surrealism, expressionism, abstract expressionism, and abstraction.
I found doing a few self-portraits every year was very beneficial to the students to explore who they were in the world and how to express themselves.

Materials: I am going to list a few self-portrait lessons, and you can use any media you choose. Mixed media works well for most of these, such as collage. Papers, pencils, scissors, glue, construction papers, magazine pictures (filtered by you, of course), etc.

Introduction/Directions: For all of these, emphasize that a self-portrait expresses who you are, inside and out. Some, realistic like Kahlo (though surreal) and Wood, show a face as it would appear but with or without expression. Others, such as Picasso and Archembaldo, use basic proportions. Still, the work is more of representation rather than the actual image of the person—another kind of truth. I'll explain Cassatt separately in *Back of the Head* lesson.

1.   The da Vinci, Kahlo, or Wood styles show many examples of how the
     artists represented people. What kind of expressions are there? What
     explains the person in the background and foreground? Students can
     create a drawing of themselves, after practicing facial proportions, with
     something(s) in the picture that gives clues about what they like and who
     they are.

2.   For the Picasso or Archembaldo portraits, go through the steps of ab-
     straction to show how the artist arrived at the final image. Abstraction
     is merely changing or simplifying something real. In this portrait, I
     encouraged students to break up space in the background for Picasso. For
     Archembaldo, I left it one solid color because there is so much going on as
     the fruits and vegetables form facial features.

3.   One strand is also to do a self-portrait from the profile view using collage.
     The children fill the inner space with all kinds of images of things that
     represent them and what they like. I used black construction paper, oil

pastels, old maps, and magazine images along with words for this project. You can go over how the facial proportions from the side are different from the front.

4. For the Mary Cassatt *Back of the Head* lesson, I need to credit Ms. Neiderhaus from the middle school where I taught because this was her idea. It's a great way to introduce drawing the head, neck, and shoulders in proportion by having students sit behind each other in a giant circle and . . .

5. Outline the back of the head with hair and whatever clothing (collar, shirt top) they are wearing. They draw and then later paint with watercolors. This experience is an excellent second- through sixth-grade lesson! It's not technically a self-portrait; instead, it is a portrait of the back of a classmate's head! I wrote this lesson, which was featured in the *School Arts* magazine, several years ago (see **Resources** section).

Wrap Up: Put up artwork and share. Students can write about themselves as part of their self-portraits or write about the person they drew. Consider different styles and how they each represent things and people from different viewpoints with different emphasis. Display wherever possible!

Andy Goldsworthy's Outdoor Nature Sculptures: My Very Favorite!
Fourth Grade through High School

- -

Concepts: Temporary art, art process over permanence, natural materials vs. human-made. Balance systems of radial, symmetrical, asymmetrical use of space. Students will explore textures, colors, form—sculpture, three-dimensional, ecological balance, and respect for nature and fun!

This lesson is my all-time favorite experience because of the students' joy and excitement!

Materials: Find someplace outdoors on the school grounds where sticks, rocks, leaves, etc. may be easily collected either by students during the lesson or ahead of time placed by teacher/parent volunteers. Make sure you've chosen a place free of yellow-jacket nests, broken glass, or other harmful trash. Make sure you've selected a site free of poison oak or poison ivy or other potentially hazardous plants. It can be done in the school garden with prior preparations.

Other materials: Andy Goldsworthy's DVD: *Rivers and Tides*, digital camera, printer, construction papers (black or various colors), color pencils, pencils, and writing papers.

Introduction/Directions: This lesson may take a few weeks to complete. It can be done in stages.

1. First, show part or most of the DVD *Rivers and Tides*. Seeing the artist at work motivates and inspires the students! Explain they'll be working in pairs or teams of four, and they will work together to create their temporary outdoor sculpture. Go over balance systems: radial, symmetrical, or asymmetrical.

2. Review group/team cooperation. Older students can create a proposal/plan of what they'd like to create ahead of time using the materials list you provide. Otherwise, I allowed serendipity to prevail, and students, on the day of the adventure, worked together to collect sticks, rocks, leaves, etc. that interested them.

3. Monitor the activity carefully. When all teams/groups have completed their work, go around and take a photo of each sculpture. Be sure to have a list of the names that go with each sculpture.

4. Students can walk around to view others' work before class is over. Discuss which balance system was used.

5. Next class, hand out photographs of their sculpture to each child. Provide color pencils for them to color them as they wish. Provide paper and pencils so they can write a poem or short essay about their sculpture. Mount on construction paper. Discuss how the sculptures have slowly deteriorated over time by weather and wind, people destroying them, or animals disturbing them.

Wrap Up: Students can share their work, read their poems/essays. Display in the front office, library, district office, etc.

Examples of student-created outdoor temporary sculptures (fourth/fifth grades). Location: behind the school in the wild area.

Arts in Your Classroom

During my tenure at Creek Side Elementary School, on three separate occasions, I was a presenter at the annual *Arts in Your Classroom (AIYC)* teacher workshops at the Montalvo Arts Center, Saratoga, CA.

My first workshop, in 2008, was with Chris Carson-Seals (then Bullock). We presented teachers with the *Rock Art Program* we were developing for the Santa Clara County Park Program at Chic-tac-tac Adams Park. We engaged teachers in creating pictographs (painting on sandstone rocks) and petroglyphs (both foam board prints and incising in stones and clay).

The second time I was a presenter, in 2011, I shared with teachers the program sponsored by the Santa Clara Water District. We created *Water Cycle Totem Poles* out of cardboard.

That afternoon, I taught the following lesson (click on the link or find it at the address below online) in connecting art and nature:

https://www.scribd.com/document/51510214/Capturing-Nature
-Navajo-Travel-Blanket-Marianne-Bickett

The third workshop I taught while I was an artist-in-residence at Creek Side School through the Montalvo Art Center Residency in 2014. My husband, composer Brian Belét, and I co-taught concepts relating to art and music. We engaged teachers in some basic rhythm and movement exercises that included the *Drawing Music* lesson featured in the *Art á la Cart* Lesson Plans.

Resources

Websites:

Visit www.MarianneBickett.com for more Art Connections, recommended Art Materials (natural paints, etc), and more Resources.

Below, I am offering national and local resources as examples of what you might find in your specific city or region. I include places that I referenced in this book.

National Arts Education Association:
https://www.arteducators.org
https://www.arts.gov/grants/apply-grant/.../state-and-national-standards-arts-education

Davis Publications (Art Education curriculum and teaching art books):
https://www.davisart.com
Davis Publications also publishes *School Arts Magazine*

The Elephant Sanctuary:
https://www.elephants.com
Contact the Elephant Sanctuary for educational materials.

Defenders of Wildlife:
https://defenders.org
Contact for ways you can get your students involved in learning about wildlife, local habitats, and conservation measures in your area.

Kokua Hawaii Foundation:
https://kokuahawaiifoundation.org
This is a dynamic education/outreach organization that also is active in local environmental issues, recycling, river and beach cleanups, etc. Check your area for similar foundations.

Black Hills Wild Horse Sanctuary
https://www.wildmustangs.com
Visit or write to this mustang rescue sanctuary to learn about ways you can make a difference.

Save Our Shores Organization:
https://saveourshores.org
Explore opportunities to volunteer and get involved and teach students about how
our actions affect our environment, especially our water and our oceans.

Santa Clara Water District Education Program:
www.valleywater.org
Check with your local Water District for ecology and water-wise programs as well
as creek adoption potential in your area.

Youth Science Institute (Silicon Valley):
www.ysi-ca.org
Look for local science foundations in your area for field trips and school
presentations as well as classes and workshops for students and teachers.

Silicon Valley Education Foundation:
https://www.svefoundation.org
Look for local education foundations that provide grants and support for arts and
environmental programs in your area.

San Jose Museum of Art:
https://sjmusart.org
Look for local art museums that bring arts into your classroom and/or provide art
programs on site.

Santa Clara County Parks:
https://www.sccgov.org/sites/parks
Look for school programs and field trips that relate local art and history as well as
environmental education programs in your area.

Silicon Valley Arts Council:
https://www.artscouncil.org
In most cities, local arts councils provide grants for art programs and may also
have artists-in-residence programs.

Montalvo Arts Center:
https://www.montalvoarts.org
In addition to local arts councils, there may be venues in your area where art
programs are offered that also offer teacher in-services and workshops, artist
residencies, and classes for students.

Environmental Volunteers Organization of Silicon Valley
https://www.evols.org
Provides on-site, in-classroom, and field trips for schools in the Bay Area.

Books:

Visit Davis Publications website listed on previous page for a wealth of books for
students and teachers.

Art Book for Children, New York, Phaidon Press, 2006.

Paul Klee, *Painting Music,* Munich, Prestel Verlog Press, 1997.

Andy Warhol, *Paintings for Children, Adventures in Art* series, Munich, Prestel Press,
2004.

Joyce Raimundo, *Picture This! Impressionism*, New York, Crown Publishing, 2004.

MaryAnn Kohl and Kim Solga, *Discovering Great Artists*, Washington, Bright Ring
Publishing, 1996.

Rachel Rodriguez, *Through Georgia's Eyes*, New York, Henry Holt & Co., 2006.

The Blue Rider, Munich, Prestel Press, 2004.

Amy Novesky, *Me, Frida*, New York, Abrams Publishing, 2015.

DVD:

Andy Goldsworthy, *Rivers and Tides*, Mediopolis Films, Art and Design, 2004 New
Video Group.

School Arts Magazine Articles by Marianne Bickett:

November 2009: page 28, *Chicken Art* (Based on live animals as inspiration).

February 2011: page 36, *Art Rocks with Rock Art!* With online Make a Mark* with
foam prints (Mentioned in the book as a lesson with Park Interpreter).

March 2011: page 34, *Portraits from Another View* (This is the Mary Cassatt *Back
of the Head* Lesson aforementioned in the body of the book and Art á la Cart
Lesson Plans).

March 2015: page 16, *Art Cart Tales*, Managing the Art Room (Guidelines for
Traveling Art Teachers!).

March 2016: page 42, *Acting as an Artist, Bringing famous artists to life* (Sharing my
experiences as appearing as famous artists).

In the mid-1990s I had a *Clip Art* contribution about creating a spherical ceramic-tile
project with elementary school students where students created the clay used
directly from the earth.

*You can view the foam board Rock Art lesson at the site below:

https://www.davisart.com/Promotions/SchoolArts/PDF/2_11-elementary-studio-art-
lesson-plan-making-a-mark.pdf

Newspaper Article by Marianne Bickett:

Combining arts education with STEM bolsters learning, San Jose Mercury News, Friday,
July 4, 2014. Making the case for STEAM.

Acknowledgments

First and foremost, I am deeply grateful to my beloved and steadfast husband, Brian Belét for his loving support during my long teaching career and for his expert editing skills and wise advice in the creation of this book. Thank you, Brian. You are ever my hero.

Next, I thank my son, Jacques, who put up with his mom being a teacher all those years. It wasn't easy sharing your mother with hundreds of other children! You are an amazing human being.

Heartfelt gratitude goes to all the dedicated parents of Creek Side School who volunteered over the years. There is a long list. However, one parent, in particular, stands out to whom I am deeply grateful. Jill Steinacker, you are one fantastic mom and human being; thank you for going above and beyond for your remarkable children, Kala and West, and for all of the students.

I am very grateful to my faithful initial readers: Rose Shank, Rayna Currier, Nancy Meyer, Colleen Campbell, Joan Veteran, and Carol Greene for your very helpful insights. And to my sisters, Jane Bicquette, Penny Fuller, Kathy Nucifora, and Betsy Baartman for your years of loving support in all my projects.

Great thanks to Magdalena Montagne for your initial editing. It got me to where I needed to be for the next great step.

Thank you so very much to Lawrence Knorr, Marianne Babcock, Teresa Woodcock, Jennifer Cappello, Crystal Devine, Joe Walters, and Christina Fenwick at Sunbury Press. I am deeply grateful for your expertise and patience! You have been a wonderful team to work with, I am honored for this book to be a part of the Sunbury family.

There are many people I owe my gratitude to, and I hope I am not remiss in forgetting specific names because this was a long journey of nearly ten years in the making.

I have heartfelt gratitude to the teachers, the principals, and the students at Creek Side Elementary School for going along with my wild ideas and honoring me with the privilege of being an art cart teacher.

About the Author

(Photo by Kerry McFarland of Earthdarling Portraits.)

Marianne enjoys retirement and loves writing fiction and non-fiction, poetry, artmaking, yoga, music, traveling, hiking, and gardening. She cherishes time with her husband, Brian, and their son, Jacques, his wife, Irish, and grandsons Jaxon and Jacen. Marianne also enjoys helping her sister, Jane Bicquette, on her "Begin Again Ranch" with two adorable ponies and one big Paint horse. The author divides her time between Oregon and Hawaii.

Marianne continues to support environmental causes and the welfare of animals. Visit her at her website and sign up for her quarterly newsletter at: MarianneBickett.com

Follow her on Instagram: @MarianneBickett

Made in the USA
Middletown, DE
22 February 2022

61658666R00154